ISLAMOPHOBIA AND RACISM IN

Islamophobia and Racism in America

Erik Love

NEW YORK UNIVERSITY PRESS
New York

NEW YORK UNIVERSITY PRESS
New York
www.nyupress.org

References to Internet websites (URLs) were accurate at the time of writing. Neither the author nor New York University Press is responsible for URLs that may have expired or changed since the manuscript was prepared.

ISBN: 978-1-4798-0492-4 (hardback)
ISBN: 978-1-4798-3807-3 (paperback)

For Library of Congress Cataloging-in-Publication data, please contact the Library of Congress.

New York University Press books are printed on acid-free paper, and their binding materials are chosen for strength and durability. We strive to use environmentally responsible suppliers and materials to the greatest extent possible in publishing our books.

Manufactured in the United States of America

10 9 8 7 6 5 4 3 2 1

Also available as an ebook

For Aurora,

looking toward a bright future

CONTENTS

LIST OF FIGURES AND TABLES

LIST OF ACRONYMS AND ABBREVIATIONS

AAI: Arab American Institute
AAUG: Association of Arab American University Graduates
ACCESS: Arab Community Center for Economic and Social Services
ACLU: American Civil Liberties Union
ADC: American-Arab Anti-Discrimination Committee
CAIR: Council on American-Islamic Relations
DHS: Department of Homeland Security
DOJ: Department of Justice
EEOC: Equal Employment Opportunity Commission
FBI: Federal Bureau of Investigation
ICE: Immigration and Customs Enforcement
ICIRR: Illinois Coalition for Immigrant and Refugee Rights
INS: Immigration and Naturalization Service
ISNA: Islamic Society of North America
JACL: Japanese American Citizens League
LCCR: Leadership Council on Civil Rights
MALDEF: Mexican American Legal Defense and Education Fund
MPAC: Muslim Public Affairs Council
MSA: Muslim Students Association
NAAA: National Association for Arab Americans
NNAAC: National Network for Arab American Communities
NSEERS: National Security Entry-Exit Registration System
RWG: Rights Working Group
SAALT: South Asian Americans Leading Together
SALDEF: Sikh American Legal Defense and Education Fund
SMART: Sikh Mediawatch and Resource Taskforce

ACKNOWLEDGMENTS

Over the many years that I spent researching and writing this book, I was fortunate enough to receive extraordinary support from many institutions, colleagues, and friends. Any success that this project may enjoy is shared with everyone who contributed to it, and all the shortcomings in this work are entirely my responsibility. Completing this book has been the most rewarding professional experience of my life, and it would not have been possible even to begin without the generosity and patience of the sixty-two advocates who, despite the tremendous demands on their time, agreed to meet with me for lengthy interviews. Without exception, these dedicated, impassioned civil rights advocates trusted in me and engaged in sometimes-challenging conversations. My greatest hope is that they find what I've written here somehow useful.

The roots of this project extend back to the year 2000, when I traveled on a study abroad program to Jerusalem under the direction of my mentor and dear friend, Len Berkey. I met Len a few years earlier in his Introduction to Sociology course, where he encouraged me to study race and ethnicity. He eventually recruited me to join the Great Lakes Jerusalem Program, an innovative and unique course of study in Israel/Palestine developed by the late Tony Bing. During my time in the Holy Land, I realized that, despite seriously studying race for years, I had never encountered any scholarly work specifically written about Arab Americans or Muslim Americans. This struck me as odd, because of course these communities have long dealt with bigotry and discrimination. Upon my return to the US in December 2000, I resolved to learn more. On Len's advice, I started reading the work of scholars like Michael Suleiman, Suad Joseph, and Yvonne Yazbeck Haddad. This only whet my desire to better understand the way that race and racism affect these communities, and that is what led me to pursue graduate study in sociology a few years later. Thank you, Len.

At the University of California, Santa Barbara (UCSB), I had the good fortune to have Howard Winant, a scholar who needs no introduction, as my mentor. He graciously took me under his wing, and over many hours of discussion and debate, the ideas that form the foundation of this manuscript began to emerge. Howie was patient and kind, and he was a dedicated advisor who always went out of his way to make sure I was making the most of every opportunity. His leadership is the only reason this project got off the ground and stayed in the air for more than a decade. Thank you, Howie.

I am also deeply indebted to many other professors at UCSB who advised me and guided the development of this research. In particular, I want to thank Lisa Hajjar, John Mohr, Kathleen Moore, and G. Reginald Daniel for their thoughtful guidance and advice over many years.

Thanks to everyone at New York University Press, most especially to Ilene Kalish for her patience and trust in this project. Special thanks also to Caelyn Cobb for her dedication and expertise, Jodi Narde for her careful and thoughtful attention to detail, and to Dorothea Halliday for bringing it all together.

I must also thank the institutions that gave financial support to this research. This project would not have been possible without the support of a grant from the National Science Foundation. I also thank the Richard Flacks Fund for the Study of Democratic Possibilities, the UCSB Graduate Division and Sociology Department, the University of California Center for New Racial Studies, and the Dickinson College Research and Development Committee for their generous support. Thanks also to the Institute for Social Policy and Understanding for allowing me to serve as a fellow. Of course, my analysis and opinions as expressed herein do not reflect in any way upon these institutions.

I'm deeply grateful to Jessica Cobb for her careful review and extensive help with developing this manuscript. For lending their special research talents, for giving thoughtful feedback on drafts, and for their transcendent and insightful advice, I want to extend very special thanks to these great friends and superb scholars: Shawn Bender, Neda Maghbouleh, Bob Ngo, Amy Steinbugler, and Ed Webb. I also thank several anonymous reviewers for their helpful comments. For research assistance, I thank Savannah-Grace Leeman.

Special thanks to Medhi Bozorgmehr and Anny Bakalian, the co-founders of the City University of New York's Middle East and Middle Eastern American Center—a unique and important institution. They extended me gracious invitations to speak and participate in various colloquia, and Mehdi took a keen interest in my work very early on. He has been overflowing with support and guidance for many years, and I am deeply grateful.

At UCSB, I was privileged to take part in a vibrant community of scholars. So many friends and colleagues touched my life and contributed to this project, and I want to thank them all. In particular, I thank Carlos Alamo-Pastrana, Reza Aslan, Nura Azzam, Yousef Baker, Hillary Blackerby, Krista Bywater, Clayton Childress, Magda Campo, Joseph Conti, Brianne Dávila, Francesca Degiuli, Maryam Griffin, Melissa Guzman, Katrina Kimport, Daraka Larimore-Hall, Lisa Leitz, Patrick Lopez-Aguado, Devin Molina, Moira O'Neil, Rachel Parker, Greg Prieto, Dwight Reynolds, Elena Richardson, Jennifer Rogers, César Rodríguez, Christine Shearer, Jessica Taft, Emily Tumpson Molina, James Walsh, and Kevin Whitehead.

At Dickinson College, I have joined an excellent community of scholars and teachers, and I am extremely grateful to the support and friendship of my colleagues in the Sociology Department and the Middle East Studies Program. In particular, I want to thank David Commins, Vickie Kuhn, Susan Rose, Dan Schubert, and Ted Pulcini. Many other friends and colleagues in and around Carlisle, Pennsylvania, have been supportive of my work in so many ways, and in particular I want to thank Suman Ambwani, Jennifer Bryson, Derek Mancini-Lander, Harry Pohlman, Eric Schaefer, and Jennifer Schaefer. Thanks also to the many excellent students who have challenged and inspired me, and who have contributed their passion and their ideas to the study of race and civil rights.

During the final stages of writing this book, I was fortunate enough to join the Sociology Department at Temple University as a visiting scholar. Thanks to everyone at Temple who extended a warm welcome, and to those who attended the colloquium where we discussed my work, I extend a special thank you. Extra special thanks to Kimberly Goyette and Sherri Grasmuck.

While I was in Detroit for some of my earliest research interviews, the staff at the Arab American National Museum in Dearborn, Michigan, provided me with a base of support and allowed me to work as a volunteer docent. They re-introduced me to my hometown and helped in many other ways to jump-start this research. Thanks to everyone there.

In Washington, DC, where I did the bulk of my research, I relied on a network of dear friends and allies. I am particularly indebted to Nancy Astifo, Jeff Boyd, Reema Dodin, Brigitte Dubois, Yousra Fazili, Arlene Fetizanan, Alison Hathaway, Rahul Mittal, and Anjali Thakur-Mittal. The staff at all of the organizations where I spent time were extremely helpful, and I want to thank everyone who worked with me, offered me tea, and laughed at my jokes. In fact, I even thank those who did not laugh at my jokes.

I also want to thank colleagues at various conferences and workshops where I received valuable feedback on some of the thoughts that made their way into this volume. I want to thank the late Michael Suleiman for somehow finding my work and inviting me to join a conference he organized in Kansas—one of the greatest honors of my life. I also thank Amaney Jamal and Sally Howell for inviting me to participate in their innovative workshop. At these and other meetings, I learned from some of the most influential and brilliant scholars working in this area, including Hisham Aidi, Richard Alba, Kristine Ajrouch, Mucahit Bilici, Louise Cainkar, Edward Curtis IV, Carol Haddad, Nancy Foner, Sarah Gualtieri, Juliane Hammer, Deepa Iyer, Annie Lai, Karen Leonard, Amir Marvasti, Karyn D. McKinney, Debra Minkoff, Ann Morning, Nadine Naber, Dina Okamoto, Jen'nan Ghazal Read, Helen Samhan, Andrew Shryock, and John Tehranian.

Many friends and fellow travelers have contributed to this project, especially Trevor Aaronson, Noorjahan Akbar, Wajahat Ali, Hani Bawardi, Khaled Beydoun, Jennifer Carlson, Randa Kayyali, Sonal Nalkur, Saher Selod, R. Tyson Smith, Rita Stephan, and Stephen Steinberg. And for his wisdom, encouragement, and feedback on early drafts, I extend a special thanks to my brother from another mother, my oldest and most cherished friend, Ian Douglass.

Finally, I thank my family. My parents, Robert and Sue, have given everything they have to their children. They are my heroes. My sisters, Katie and Melissa, and my sister-in-law, Erin, have always been there for me, even as they pursue their dreams and achieve many remarkable accomplishments. I am so proud of them. I hope to live up to their example in all that I do.

And to Helene, my awe-inspiring partner for more than ten years, I love you. Not only did you guide and support my work, and read through even my worst drafts, you also took care of me. You have given me more than you'll ever know. Words will never fully express my gratitude, so I will simply say thank you.

1

The Racial Dilemma

Cameron Mohammed was shot in the face because he "looked Muslim."

On January 3, 2013, Mohammed and his girlfriend were walking to their car in a Wal-Mart parking lot near Tampa, Florida. A man suddenly approached, shouting, "Are you Middle Eastern?" Mohammed, who was raised in Florida and born in Trinidad, simply said no. "Are you Muslim?" Mohammed is Catholic, so again, he said no. The stranger scowled, "Nigger with a white girl." Suddenly, he pulled out a gas-powered pellet gun and fired at Mohammed's head, at point-blank range. A hailstorm of pellets lacerated Mohammed's face and neck. The shooter, a White man named Daniel Quinnell, fled the scene before police arrived. Fortunately, Mohammed recovered, but he needed surgery to remove some of the pellets. A few days after the shooting, Quinnell was captured by police. When an officer informed him that Mohammed was not Muslim, he did not seem to care. "They're all the same," he reportedly said.[1]

This hate crime is an example of "Islamophobia," even though Cameron Mohammed is not Muslim, because the attack was motivated by a desire to harm a Muslim or someone from the Middle East. This shooting bears disturbing similarities to the brutal murder of Balbir Singh Sodhi, a Sikh American who was shot and killed on September 15, 2001. The shooter in that case, also a White man, intended to avenge the 9/11 attacks by, in his words, "shooting some towel-heads."[2] Dozens of violent attacks like these have been reported in recent years. Sikh Americans have been frequently targeted. Like Cameron Mohammed and Balbir Singh Sodhi, everyone hurt or killed in these attacks were vulnerable to Islamophobia because they "look Muslim"—*because of race.*

"Looking Muslim": The Middle Eastern American Racial Category

It should go without saying that the world's 1.6 billion Muslims span the full range of human appearance. There is no way to *actually* "look Muslim." Nevertheless, race operates at the very core of Islamophobia.

The racial lens through which Americans see the world distorts and conceals the obvious truth that it is basically impossible to accurately determine someone's religion based solely on their physical appearance. That racial lens is why it is possible to "look Muslim" in America. In other words, there are a set of physical traits and characteristics that can mark someone as "Muslim," regardless of their actual religion, ethnicity, or nationality. Race is the only way to explain how this is so.

The process by which Islamophobia came to affect anyone who "looks Muslim" is an all-too-familiar process, one that has constantly roiled American life: the social construction of racial categories. Race is what links aspects of physical appearance (facial features, skin tone, attire, hair texture, etc.) to an ascribed social identity such as White, Black, or Asian. In America, as a fact of life, everyone gets ascribed with a racial identity. In today's America, "Muslim" or "Middle Eastern" is one of the most commonly ascribed racial categories. Most of the time, getting racially ascribed with this identity is quick and easy. But the violence in some Islamophobic hate crimes serves as a reminder that racial identification is not benign.

Quinnell, the shooter in the Wal-Mart parking lot in Florida, saw Cameron Mohammed's physical features and then placed a racial identity upon him: "Muslim." At that point, Quinnell had done nothing out of the ordinary; looking at someone and assigning a racial identity based on physical appearance is unavoidable, nearly automatic in America. Racial identity is always there, in every social interaction. Usually it remains in the background—silently understood by everyone. Sometimes, however, race enters the foreground, like when someone makes race the topic of conversation. Sadly, on that January evening, Quinnell's brazen questioning—"Are you Middle Eastern?"—and the shocking violence that followed it made the usually invisible and automatic process of racial identification all too visible. Race made Cameron Mohammed vulnerable to Islamophobia, as it has so many others.

In the United States, anyone who racially "looks Muslim" is similarly vulnerable to Islamophobia. Many South Asian Americans are Muslim, but many others are Hindu, Sikh, Christian, Buddhist, or have no religion at all. Whatever their ethnic, religious, and cultural heritage, South Asian Americans often get caught up in Islamophobia because of race. Similarly, many Arab Americans are Christian, Jewish, or agnostic, but race exposes them to Islamophobia all the same. Because of race, these communities and many others have been pulled into the swath of Islamophobic discrimination, social exclusion, and violence that has marred American life for decades.

Even as non-Muslims have been directly affected by Islamophobia, there is, of course, no doubt that Muslim Americans and American Islamic institutions have been severely affected by Islamophobia. Slanderous rhetoric about Islamic faith has dramatically increased in intensity in recent years, as politicians and pundits frequently proffer uninformed opinions about Islam and Muslims.[3] Along with the renewed trend in anti-Muslim rhetoric, denial of fundamental civil liberties such as basic religious freedom has been a growing problem across the United States. Mosques have been vandalized and faced protests against their very existence. Moreover, Muslim Americans have suffered the second-largest number of reported hate crimes over the past few years, second only to Jewish Americans, according to official Federal Bureau of Investigation (FBI) hate crimes statistics.[4]

Somehow, Islamophobia remained largely under the radar until the 2000s. Despite decades of widespread, extremely damaging effects, Islamophobia did not attract a great deal of attention in America until recently. No doubt the new attention is mainly due to the unprecedented scale of the terrorist attacks of September 11, 2001 (or, 9/11), which led to an extraordinary surge in Islamophobic hate crimes and discrimination. This led many analysts and scholars to conclude that a "new" wave of specifically anti-Muslim sentiment had appeared in the United States. A great many books and articles have described the challenges facing Muslim American communities and the specifically anti-Muslim components of "post-9/11" Islamophobia. But limiting the discussion of Islamophobia to the "post-9/11" era obscures the long history of racial discrimination affecting Arabs, Muslims, Sikhs, South Asians, and others in the United States. In fact, discrimination that would today be called "post-9/11" Islamophobia has thrived in one form or another in the United States since at least the seventeenth century. Understanding the problems posed by Islamophobia requires not only looking farther back in time than just 2001, but it also means expanding the understanding of Islamophobia beyond religious and ethnic frameworks. Race must be part of the analysis.

This is because American Islamophobia developed in very much the same ways as all American social structures that involve race. As a form of racism, Islamophobia is built into American institutions. White supremacy and Islamophobia stem from the same root, and they are both burrowed into the foundations of American institutions. Therefore, any effective understanding of Islamophobia must take into account the full scope of American race and racism.

This presents a tremendous challenge, to contextualize Islamophobia as part of a newly salient manifestation of a centuries-long process that classifies people from North Africa and Southwest Asia (i.e., the Middle East) as *racially* distinct. Explicating this process requires elaborating the co-constituted nature of Islamophobia and the very concept of race itself. Each of these dynamic, overdetermined concepts—race and Islamophobia—is too complex to encapsulate fully in any one study. Despite the challenges and necessary shortcomings of any attempt like this one, there are significant analytic advantages that can only be brought by the endeavor to understand the co-constituted nature of American racism and Islamophobia.

Placing Islamophobia into the well-worn context of American racism makes it less anomalous and less mysterious. Racism has always been present in the United States, so it should not surprise us that Islamophobia has roots that extend far deeper in history than 2001. This approach also seeks to apply the tools developed for understanding racial discrimination to the analysis of Islamophobia. Drawing the connections between race and Islamophobia provides, among other insights, the only plausible explanation for why Christians, Sikhs, Hindus, and people of all faiths are vulnerable to Islamophobia. Moreover, shining a light on the intrinsically dehumanizing elements of racism enables an understanding of connections between hate crimes and discriminatory "counterterrorism" policies, both domestically in the United States and globally on the so-called battlefields of the "War on Terror." All of these flow directly from the same source: Islamophobic racism. Seeing the links between them requires an understanding of how racism is embedded into American social institutions.

The Race with No Name

To illustrate the difficult task of untangling the complex web that connects race and Islamophobia, consider that there is no name for the socially constructed racial category that has been used to collectively ascribe Arab, Muslim, Sikh, and South Asian Americans. This category is called by many names: "Muslim," or "Middle Eastern," or sometimes it is rendered with an acronym like "MENA" (Middle Eastern and North African). Even when there is acknowledgment that there is, in fact, a racial category here, it has been nearly impossible to find a generally accepted term for it, yet all the while it finds constant expression through everyday encounters and in strucutral Islamophobic discrimination.

Currently, the most common colloquialism for this racial category is probably "Muslim," but over the years, the most popular term for this racial category has varied quite a bit. Thirty years ago, the term "Arab" referred to people from a broadly conceived Middle East, while at that time "Muslim" had a close association with Black American communities. That these terms have shifted is not at all unusual. The popular names for racial categories change all the time. White people were more likely to be called "Caucasian" in the recent past, and that bizarre term still lives on today. Similarly, a Black American person would have been called "a Negro" sixty years ago, but today that term is generally considered archaic at best (and more than a little offensive). Moreover, the exact physical attributes associated with any racial category have never been static, much less obvious. The contours of racial categories are always contested and changing. Nevertheless, there is no doubt that the racial categories exist. Elasticity—in terminology and otherwise—is an intrinsic part of the constant social reproduction of racial categories in the United States.

Today, based solely on his appearance, Cameron Mohammed might often get called "Muslim" or "Middle Eastern" by many of the people he meets. A century ago, however, in the early 1900s, someone looking like him would most likely have been called "Syrian." That was the most common collective term for people from North Africa and Southwest Asia at that time. In the decades since then, as the terminology shifted, the contours of the "Syrian" (or Arab, Middle Eastern, etc.) racial classification—the physical features thought to be associated with it—underwent changes as well. The embodied, corporeal characteristics associated with this category, such as facial features, skin tone, hair color and texture, and so on, have never been consistent or definitive. Despite these variations, there can be no doubt that a socially constructed racial category exists, and has existed for a long time. There has been an undeniable consistency in the application of this racial category to people who have heritage in the vast geographic region stretching from India and Pakistan to Algeria and Morocco, from North Africa to Southwest and South Asia. Today that huge region is often referred to simply as "the Middle East."

There are profound implications to recognizing that a single racial identity spans across Arabs, Muslims, Sikhs, and South Asians in America. Consider that when most Americans today use the term "Muslim" in conversation, they are probably not really talking about Muslims. Instead, they are calling up this longstanding racial category, one that haphazardly includes hundreds of ethnic groups containing both Muslims and non-Muslims. Because this particular racial term, "Muslim," also happens to connote a religion, it has the unfortunate confounding effect of ascribing both a religious and a racial identity to a seemingly indiscriminate collection of communities.

This is the awesome power, the terrible magic, and the ignoble wonder of race: to ignore diversity, to reject indigenous identity, and to promulgate its own version of history all at the same time. Muslim Americans—people who follow the religion of Islam—represent a tremendous diversity of communities. That vibrant diversity is simply ignored by the racialization process. What's worse, this process also distorts the histories, identities, and cultures of all the myriad people and communities of non-Muslims swept into the racial category. The mishmash that is race in America violates all of these communities, Arabs, Muslims, Sikhs, and South Asians especially. Apart from denying the heritage of so many people, numerous malicious stereotypes are closely associated with the socially constructed "Muslim" racial category. Most notably there is the bigoted assumption that "Muslims" are somehow predisposed to become "radicalized" terrorists.

The racist and demonstrably false stereotype about terrorism and "Muslims" is so pervasive that openly asserting it has become a perfectly acceptable, mainstream opinion in the United States. Such opinions find expression in nearly any discussion about terrorism, whether it takes place on the floor of the United States Senate, on nationally broadcast news programs, or around the family dinner table. This stereotype is so deeply ingrained that only acts of violence committed by "Muslims" are immediately and unquestioningly labeled as "terrorist attacks." In today's political climate, it is seen as a mark of seriousness, of "telling it like it is," to assert impudently that "Muslims" are uniquely dangerous and predisposed to commit terrorism. Anything less than that is maligned as wishy-washy "political correctness."

Remember, because of race, nearly all references to "Muslims" in discussions like these actually point to the racial category—the racial category that includes Arabs, Muslims, Sikhs, and South Asians. Bigoted statements like "Most terrorists are Muslim," or "Islamic culture encourages terrorism" (as though there is only a single "Islamic culture") are therefore necessarily racial statements that reinforce the perception that anyone who "looks Muslim" may be dangerous. When public officials like Senator Ted Cruz and Congressman Peter King propose policies to increase surveillance of "Muslims," they not only place Muslim Americans in harm's way, they also endanger Arab, Sikh, and South Asian Americans as well, because of race.

Defining the Middle Eastern Racial Category

Using the colloquial term "Muslim" to refer to the racial category is confusing, to say the least. Again, actual Muslim communities are extremely diverse and cannot be described as a singular, homogenous group. Therefore, the term "Muslim" will not suffice for an in-depth analysis in large part because it is not precise enough. At the same time, listing Arab, Muslim, Sikh, and South Asian Americans when referring to the racial category is cumbersome and still inaccurate, because communities and individuals beyond those described even by that long list are swept into the racial category. Moreover, there is no other racial identity category commonly referred to by listing some of the various ethnic, religious, and panethnic groups swept under the umbrella of racial ascription. In short, the lack of a name for the racial category is a big problem.

Advocates have long struggled with this situation. Finding a widely agreed-upon identity term is often a crucial part of building an effective advocacy effort. For much of the latter half of the 1900s, the term "Arab American" was the preferred term for many advocates. It became a politically powerful identity category due to the successful organizing of advocates beginning in the mid-1900s. By the turn of the twenty-first century, however, "Arab American" had been largely (but not completely) replaced in mainstream discussions by the term "Muslim American."

Since 2010, there have been several attempts by advocates to come up with a new, succinct collective term for the racial category, one that avoids singling out just one group like "Arab" or "Muslim." Some have tried using the acronym AMEMSA (Arabs, Middle Easterners, Muslims, and South Asians). Others have promulgated a different acronym, SWANA (Southwest Asians and North Africans). Both of these have a certain pronounceable quality to them. Each provides a way to describe the various groups with ties to the vast geographical space across North Africa and Southwest Asia, and SWANA does do without using the controversial term "Middle Eastern." These are noble efforts, but no other racial category is referred to with an acronym. In any event, neither acronym has yet taken hold, and the term "Muslim" remains the most prevalent one in common parlance in the mid-2010s. There are simply no good alternatives to "Muslim." Every alternative has significant drawbacks.

Despite the problems with it, I will use the term "Middle Eastern." Throughout this book, I refer to the Middle Eastern racial category. I use "Middle Eastern American" when describing the American communities ascribed with this identity.[5] This term has the advantage of fitting in with similar racial terms. Compare "Middle Eastern American" with "Asian American," which also denotes a racial category by making reference to a vast geographic region with unclear boundaries. No firm definition exists for determining who qualifies as an Asian American, yet saying "Asian American" today conjures up a clear racial image in the minds of Americans. I contend that saying "Middle Eastern American" evokes a racial image in exactly the same way, despite the lack of an accepted definition for "Middle Eastern."

Like all racial categories, the exact borders of the Middle Eastern category will always be contested, and they will always be in flux. The process of racialization that created this category is ongoing, and it is messy. Nevertheless, this racial category exists, and it has real meaning. Powerful forces have embedded it deeply into fundamental social structures. There is also some evidence that increasing numbers of individuals are using the term "Middle Eastern" to self-identify.[6] Informally, I have noticed the term "Middle Eastern" used more frequently to describe people (and not just restaurants) over the past decade.

Still, using the term "Middle Eastern" in this way poses many problems. For one thing, the term "Middle East" has its origins in brutal colonialism, which is why many people actively avoid using it. Military officers in the British Empire are thought to have invented the term to refer to a huge expanse of geography stretching from the Indian subcontinent to northern Africa.[7] Perpetuating the use of "Middle Eastern" might very well serve to legitimate colonialism, in effect denying agency and a more meaningful social identity to the formerly colonized communities from this region. Almost anyone from the region would hesitate before identifying themselves as Middle Eastern people (although some living there do use that term). Perhaps most importantly, saying "Middle Eastern" to refer to a group of people is extremely imprecise at best and offensive at worst. It is arguably even more confusing or offensive to say that a Sikh man "looks Middle Eastern" than it is to note that Sikhs are "mistaken for Muslim." Is the Punjab region of India, the origin of Sikhism, in the Middle East? What about Pakistan? Is Turkey in the Middle East, or Europe, or both? How can a single category encompass Sikhs alongside Copts, Berbers, Kurds, Turks, and Chaldeans? Even more problematic is how Middle Eastern racial identity does not at all correlate with Muslim religious identity. Many Muslim Americans do not identify in any way as Middle Eastern, and many Middle Eastern Americans do not identify as Muslim. Many Muslim Americans are Black, and many others are White, Asian, and Latin@. Therefore, the term "Middle Eastern" just cannot be equivalent to the term "Muslim."

Despite these problems, using the term "Middle Eastern" to refer to the ascribed identity category involved in Islamophobia is the least bad option. After all, Middle Eastern is already used as a shorthand—albeit a crude one—for the ethnic, religious, cultural, and national groups in North Africa and Southwest Asia. No term is perfect, but "Middle Eastern" will work well enough for my purposes.

To sum up, I join with a growing group of scholars who find that a Middle Eastern racial identity category exists in American culture.[8] Like other socially constructed racial categories, it is unstable even as it firmly connects stereotypes and prejudices with physical appearances. It coexists with many overlapping social identities. As a result, perceptions of the Middle Eastern category depend on social context. Someone who "looks Middle Eastern" in one neighborhood might, for example, "look Latin@" in a different neighborhood. These contradictions and discontinuities do not nullify the existence of the racialized Middle Eastern category. On the contrary, these sorts of inconsistencies and illogical tensions always exist in the social construction of racial identity categories. These categories are necessarily arbitrary, volatile, and often bitterly contested by those they purport to describe. Yet racial identity categories are nonetheless quite real, and they retain a great deal of social power. Particularly in the area of counterterrorism policy, due to the racist stereotype that Middle Easterners are predisposed to commit acts of terrorism, there is a great deal of race-based discrimination built upon this racial category.

Islamophobia and Structural Racism

It goes without saying that the government should make every responsible effort to prevent terrorist attacks. The people working on the front lines of counterterrorism have committed themselves to saving lives, and they face a difficult and often thankless task. Unfortunately, many of the architects of American counterterrorism strategies have created deeply flawed and often bigoted programs. The federal government's counterterrorism programs have been ostensibly designed to catch terrorists without regard to race, religion, or ethnicity. In practice, however, many of these programs have been used almost exclusively to target Middle Eastern Americans.[9] These programs have expanded in recent years to include the power to detain suspects of terrorism nearly indefinitely, even without trial; the use of torture during interrogations of suspected terrorists; the use of secret evidence in deportation hearings; the ability to designate organizations as "sponsors of terrorism"; the deployment of unmanned aerial vehicles to kill terrorist suspects without a trial; and the surreptitious surveillance of restaurants, cafes, entire neighborhoods, and even places of worship where terrorist plots are thought to be in development. Almost every one of these programs and policies has been disproportionately used against Middle Eastern Americans.

Because of race, when counterterrorism programs disproportionately affect Muslim American communities, they also have a direct impact on the broader communities of Middle Eastern Americans. Discriminatory counterterrorism programs therefore both draw from and contribute to the bigoted stereotype that Middle Eastern Americans are inherently dangerous and more likely to become terrorists.

Such an obviously bigoted belief should be recognized as false on its face, but this stereotype has motivated a gigantic amount of law enforcement, military, and intelligence resources over the past several decades. To be clear, there is no evidence to support the conclusion that Middle Easterners or Muslims are uniquely predisposed to violent extremism.[10] In fact, between 2001 and 2011, "radicalized" White Americans—most often from the right-wing fringe—were deadlier than Muslim terrorists in the United States.[11] Policymakers, intelligence agencies, and law enforcement willfully ignored this evidence in crafting their responses to terrorism. There seems to be a persistent, bigoted belief among counterterrorism officials that something about Muslim or Arab culture contributes to terrorist impulses, that Middle Eastern Americans are prone to "self-radicalize" into "lone wolves," or to strike from shadowy "sleeper cells." No amount of evidence to prove that these fears are unfounded has stopped the freight train of counterterrorism resources directed at Middle Eastern American communities. Indeed, one Arab American advocate who met regularly with officials from the Department of Homeland Security flatly told me that "the White boys in charge are convinced it's Islam"—that Islam is the root cause of terrorism.[12] On this basis, officials in federal agencies have created and expanded programs that target Middle Eastern Americans for extra scrutiny in counterterrorism efforts.

One such program is the FBI's counterterrorism surveillance and "sting operation" program. In an effort to find and preempt terrorists before they have a chance to strike, the FBI has employed a network of tens of thousands of undercover informants.[13] Since 2003, these informants have produced over 200 terrorism-related criminal prosecutions.[14] Nearly every single one of the cases generated by this "sting operation" program has ensnared Muslim Americans, sending dozens to prison as convicted terrorists on "illusory" charges, according to Human Rights Watch. Critics of the program have shown that the FBI is creating the very enemy it hunts: "Middle Eastern terrorists."

In many of these cases, the FBI informants provide everything the supposed terrorist needs: money, weapons, and perhaps even the concept for the deadly attack. Critics observe a clear pattern. First, the FBI recruits a confidential informant—often someone who is in trouble on some unrelated criminal charges or immigration violations—and in exchange for participating they offer cash incentives, leniency in sentencing, or some other reward. Then, the confidential informant is sent "undercover" to observe people or a place—often a mosque, Middle Eastern restaurant, or another place where Muslims are known to congregate—and the informant is instructed to look for signs of trouble. Knowing or believing that the rewards from the FBI are based on producing results, the informant soon "discovers" a terrorism plot brewing. Frequently, the "dangerous radical" is a petty crook eager to score some quick money, someone with an intellectual disability, or an impressionable, troubled youngster eager to prove their mettle. The FBI, according to critics, preys on these vulnerable members of the Muslim American community, because they are easier targets.[15] Many of the people targeted by the FBI would receive counseling, referral to social services, or perhaps court-ordered psychiatric evaluation if the context were something other than "counterterrorism."

To establish the deadly intent of the "terrorist," the FBI informant surreptitiously records conversations over a period of weeks, months, or in some cases, years. Then, after the "radical Jihadist" finally commits to carrying out an attack, just in the nick of time, FBI agents swoop in and make a dramatic arrest. Juries have unfailingly convicted people caught by this program, frequently on charges of conspiring to provide material support to terrorist organizations (even when the "terrorist organization" was really just the FBI in disguise and there was no actual contact with known terrorists). These charges typically carry twenty-year federal prison sentences, or even longer imprisonment terms. To be sure, the juries in these cases are often faced with someone who tried to commit mass murder—so the lengthy sentences are not necessarily unjust. Still, investigative journalist Trevor Aaronson's analysis found that this has happened so often over the course of this fifteen-year-old program that "the FBI is responsible for more terrorism plots in the United States than any other organization."[16] Human Rights Watch called the FBI program that produces these terrorism cases "abusive" and recommended "robust oversight" of the program.[17]

It is obvious that this FBI "counterterrorism" program is targeted at Muslims. But targeting Muslims, a religious group, is not, strictly speaking, racist. Nevertheless, the effect of this FBI program is racist, because of the way the program is justified, the methods by which it is sustained, and how the FBI presents its work to the public.

Eager to show its prowess in disrupting terrorist plots, the FBI almost always holds a dramatic press conference to discuss the arrest of the "radicalized terrorists" who came so close to causing massive harm. Photos of the accused terrorists are splashed on TV screens and in news reports, where the press almost always uncritically reports on the horrific terrorist attack that the FBI "thwarted." The media reports focus on the awful damage that the fake terrorist attack would have caused, but the reports frequently fail to point out that the FBI controlled the fake attack from start to finish, and no one was ever actually in danger. Meanwhile, the visual images of the alleged terrorists—nearly always young, Middle Eastern men—reinforce the pre-existing racial stereotypes around Middle Eastern Americans and their propensity to commit terrorist acts.

In essence, what we have is an FBI program that is both motivated by and contributes to a racial stereotype. The reason that confidential informants so often target Muslim Americans is due to the stereotype that Middle Eastern Americans are the likeliest source of terrorism. As each of the hundreds of "sting operations" develops, they accordingly reproduce this stereotype, literally by reproducing "Middle Eastern terrorists." The images of the young, Middle Eastern men caught up in this FBI program appear repeatedly in the media, making it seem as though the FBI is barely containing the "Middle Eastern terrorism" problem. This vicious circle repeated again and again, with another "sting operation" case on average once every two months between 2009 and 2013.[18] Despite renewed criticism after the FBI failed to prevent several attacks, and after agents shot and killed a "suspected terrorist," FBI officials revealed in a 2016 interview with the *New York Times* that they not only plan to continue using these "sting operations," but they have expanded their use in a purported effort to stop the so-called Islamic State, or ISIS.[19]

Because there is already a racial identity in place that makes it possible to "look Muslim," Muslim American communities are not the only ones affected by this FBI program. Everyone who fits into the Middle Eastern racial category—especially Arab, Muslim, Sikh, and South Asian Americans—are affected by the stereotypes that this program perpetuates. In addition to the fundamental civil liberties implications of the FBI's "sting operation" program, the racist stereotype bolstered by this program leads directly to hate crimes, like the attacks on Cameron Mohammed and Balbir Singh Sodhi.

This is one prominent example of how the bigoted idea that "Muslims are predisposed to terrorism" has led to the institutionalization of racism affecting Middle Eastern Americans. This stereotype justifies many discriminatory programs and policies, including torture, mass surveillance, and indefinite detention. In response to critiques of these programs, the policymakers and project managers responsible assert that such policies are only intended to harm "terrorists," or "bad guys." These are euphemisms that rely on the Middle Eastern racial category. There is usually no need to say explicitly that only Middle Eastern Americans and other communities of color will be affected, and "regular Americans" (read: White Americans) have no need to fear torture, surveillance, or indefinite detention. This racial meaning is encoded in ways that enable the seemingly non-racial justification of these so-called counterterrorism policies. In turn, these programs and policies serve to reify the Middle Eastern racial category. Race and Islamophobia are thereby intrinsically linked in a vicious cycle.

Coming to Terms with Race

The sudden salience of the Middle Eastern racial category in recent years should not come as a surprise to anyone who understands the history of race in America. Throughout American history, in addition to the emergence of new racial categories, those that already exist have frequently undergone major shifts. The intrinsic fluidity of racial categories means that someone perceived as Asian today may one day find a different racial identity placed upon her. Physically apparent differences between groups of human bodies have always existed, but the criteria for placing those people into various different racial categories is based entirely upon the social and historical context in a given place. The process of racial formation drives these changes, sometimes gradually, and sometimes quite rapidly.[20]

The upshot to all of this is that race has always been central in American life. Ignoring race in the understanding of Islamophobia, or asserting that religion or some other factor is more important than race, are similar to assertions that race can be reduced to class. These assertions are naïve at best. Race must be understood *as race*.

The beginning of that understanding comes through the foundational realization that race is a social construction that plays a powerful part in shaping nearly every aspect of American life. Even though biologists have confirmed again and again that there is only one human race, social scientists have conclusively shown again and again that race still *matters*. Given the centrality of race in American life, just about everyone in the United States has at least a passing familiarity with what race means and the fact that it has social power. Most Americans would, if asked, rattle off a list of racial identities that they personally recognize. Just because "everyone knows" about race does not mean that it is trivial to describe how race actually works, though. Scratching the surface of race exposes massive cracks in its facade. For starters, any effort to provide a taxonomy of all currently existing racial categories is doomed to fail. Racial categories undergo constant change, and they are never fixed. Such a list will always fail to account for huge numbers of groups that do not easily fit into any single category. Still, despite these contradictions, David Hollinger suggests the existence of a relatively stable "ethno-racial pentagon" in the contemporary United States.[21] This is a sort of "top five" list of racial identity categories that have dominated mainstream American culture over the past few decades.

Specifically, Hollinger names five socially constructed racial categories as dominant in American culture: Native American, Asian, Black,

Hispanic/Latin@, and White. Of course, "dominance" does not mean that these categories face no challenges. For example, an individual who self-identifies as Latin@ may be perceived by others as Black, or Native American, or White. Furthermore, multiracial identity, either as a distinct category or as a specific combination of two or more racial categories, has always posed a significant challenge to the "pentagon." Another challenge comes from changing demographics. As the relative size of various groups and subgroups change, classifications sometimes change with them.

Despite the contradictions and inconsistencies in the "ethno-racial pentagon," it is undeniable that most Americans today classify themselves and each other according to this "top five" list of racial categories. The absurdity of this racial reality is profound. Nearly every single individual in America is placed into one of these five imperfect and often offensive categories in every social encounter that they have. Even worse, social programs and policies based upon this racial classification produce a tremendous amount of social power. Membership in these racial categories is correlated with unequal access to health care, education, wealth, political opportunity, and more.

Where do Middle Eastern Americans fit on the "ethno-racial pentagon"? Some would say that a "Middle Eastern" category should just join the rest to create a "top six" list of generally accepted categories. They might point to all the ways this has already become an accepted social identity. Americans enjoy Middle Eastern cuisine, listen to Middle Eastern music, and enroll in Middle East Studies academic programs. There is no question that "Middle Eastern" is already a recognized, actively used social category. But many others would insist the contrary: that there is no Middle Eastern racial category at all, nascent or otherwise. After all, the Middle East is not a racially distinct place. There is no actual culture or ethnicity that can properly be called "Middle Eastern." The Middle East, an enormous geographic expanse, contains people from a huge diversity of groups—ethnic, racial, religious, and cultural. On this view, there is no good reason to single out race as the main factor at work by speaking of Middle Eastern Americans as a racial group. The often-heated debate over whether there is a racial category that includes "Muslims and those mistaken for Muslims" signifies that, at least at the moment, there is no room on the "top five" list for the Middle

Eastern racial category. It is too controversial, and it is not universally recognized.

The lack of a recognized racial identity for Middle Eastern Americans contributes to a great deal of confusion for individuals, advocates, policymakers, journalists, and scholars. It is a tremendous challenge to speak accurately about the racial dynamics at play in Islamophobia without a clear recognition of the racial category that sweeps so much diversity into a single undifferentiated group. The lack of an accepted identity category makes the conversation about the co-constituted nature of race and Islamophobia even more difficult.

To illustrate how difficult this is, allow me to share one personal anecdote. For the past several years, I have asked undergraduate students in some of my courses to write an essay on this issue. I pose a question about whether there is a clearly defined racial category for Middle Eastern Americans. They compose this essay after spending two months studying sociological theories about race alongside the histories of Arab, Muslim, Sikh, and South Asian American communities. I have been surprised to find that, year after year, the class divides almost exactly in half on this question.

As this racial confusion continues, the discussion of American Islamophobia has been dominated by studies with religion as the focus. Most of the scholarly analyses of Islamophobia and the coverage in the popular press over the past decade have centered on Islam and Muslims, and few of these have considered race in their analyses. There is a lot of value, of course, in looking at Muslim American experiences with Islamophobia since 9/11. The problem is that the racial nature of Islamophobia has been obscured because of analyses that rarely go beyond that framework.

There is no single explanation for why race has been largely absent from discussions of Islamophobia, but part of the reason stems from problems with the word itself—"Islamophobia." This term is not very helpful, but it is unavoidably popular. Its suffix, -phobia, denotes irrational fear. Irrational fear often motivates Islamophobia, but history, social patterns, and cultural developments, at least as much as irrational fear, also drive Islamophobia. At the same time, the *Islam-* in *Islamophobia* implies that it is something that *only* involves Islam, the religion, and Muslims. This stands to reason, because, of course, Muslims have had to bear the brunt of Islamophobic prejudice and discrimination since 9/11. Still, Islamophobia constantly affects many communities, not just Muslim communities.

Moreover, Islamophobia is a complex phenomenon that involves a wide range of social issues. Religion, gender, class, sexuality—all these and more play crucial roles in the reproduction of Islamophobia. Race is not the only contributing factor. Any given Islamophobic hate crime or policy will have elements of most, if not all, of these factors. This means that it easy to look at any given manifestation of Islamophobia without noticing the race and racism embedded within it.

This presents a major challenge, because there is a general tendency in America to deny the existence of racism whenever possible, even if racism is as plain as day. Many (if not most) Americans believe that the last vestiges of racism are slowly but surely fading away, even as evidence mounts of persistent racial discrimination. The obvious racial segregation of American cities and schools is often explained not by referring to racism, but by looking at any other possible explanation: economic inequality, "choice" of where to live, and differences in "culture." When White police officers shoot unarmed Black people, for example, many explanations are proffered, and the claim that racism has something to do with it is debated and sometimes even decried as radical and "divisive." Likewise, proponents of increased racial profiling and immigration restrictions insist that racism plays no part in their proposals. Commentator Bill O'Reilly, for example, flatly proclaimed that "it is not racist to support a wall on the border or stringent vetting of Muslims entering the USA from terrorist precincts."[22] Similarly, supporters argued there was nothing even remotely racist about a policy in Arizona that would have required police to determine the immigration status of anyone they stopped if they had a "reasonable suspicion" that they might be an undocumented immigrant.[23]

Examples like these underscore the reality that many Americans do not accept the premise that racism presents a serious problem today. If there is any believable way to show that race is not the only factor at work in a social issue, then you can expect many Americans to jump to the conclusion that race cannot be a cause of the problem. Americans, generally, prefer to think of the United States as a society that is moving away from a racist past, not as a society still riven by racism.

These complications partly explain why many scholars studying Islamophobia often simplify their analyses by describing religious discrimination and ignoring or minimizing the role of race. In a survey of the scholarly literature, Nasar Meer found a "virtual absence of an established literature on race and racism in the discussion of Islamophobia."[24] Rather than go into the complex racial implications of Islamophobia, most scholars examine Muslims in isolation, neglecting the many non-Muslim communities directly affected by Islamophobia because of race.[25] Many treatments oversimplify Islamophobia in other ways, as well, mainly by referring to the phenomenon as a "new" form of discrimination that emerged in the "post-9/11" world. In this context, Islamophobia is presented as time-limited "backlash" after terrorist attacks, rather than as a longstanding, centuries-old social issue. The inability to see the racial origins of discrimination against Middle Eastern Americans leads to difficulty in showing how Islamophobic policies and programs have an impact on everyone in that racial category.

Anti-Racism and Confronting Islamophobia

The good news is that most Americans genuinely want to live in a society free of racism. Legal and social protections against hate crimes and discrimination create a clear distinction between the America of today—the so-called post–civil rights era—and the long era of unchecked racist violence that came to an end in the mid-1900s. The civil rights movement transformed America, and by the end of the 1960s, racial discrimination and outright racial bigotry became legally and socially unacceptable.

Racism nevertheless persists. The civil rights movement accomplished a great deal, but there is no question that work remains to be done. In the decades since the height of the movement in the 1960s, community advocates have continued to uncover hidden racial disparities, confront bigotry, and demand an end to discriminatory policies and practices. Advocacy organizations emerged as the vehicle for this work, organizations defined primarily by racial identity.[26] Hundreds of organizations advocating on behalf of Asian, Black, Latin@, and Native Americans have stood up for improved civil rights, part of the "advocacy explosion" in the post–civil rights era.[27]

While in theory any individual can stand up for their rights, in practice, professional civil rights advocates do most of the day-to-day work of enforcing civil rights protections. Advocates working in these organizations call out racial discrimination affecting their communities. They reach out to the authorities, and they can rightfully expect swift action. In some cases, advocates compel change by filing a lawsuit to win a court-ordered remedy. They appeal to policymakers in legislatures and in corporate boardrooms. They also take their case directly to the public. To advance their cause, civil rights advocates organize rallies, boycotts, and sit-ins, they take part in community forums, and they engage in other forms of protest. Generally speaking, many of the grievances of civil rights advocates get addressed in some way in today's United States, more often than not through existing anti-discrimination programs and policies. Because racism is so abhorrent, when community leaders call out racial discrimination, they have a powerful moral claim. That alone is sometimes enough to bring about an attempt at resolution.

This system of civil rights protection, whereby civil rights advocates file grievances and bring about relief, has operated, more or less, since the 1960s. There have been ebbs and flows in the ability of advocates to win major reforms. Many would argue that since 1980, there has been a gradual fraying of civil rights protections, and this is why so much discrimination and inequality remains intractable some fifty years after the passage of the Civil Rights Act of 1964. Nevertheless, it remains true that blatant racism is still generally not accepted in today's United States. Unless that racism is Islamophobic.

The Durability of Islamophobic Racism

Given the aversion to racism in American public life, it is remarkable that Islamophobia has risen to become so mainstream in recent years. Islamophobia, frankly, is a popular form of racism. Prominent, national leaders—even candidates for President of the United States—frequently make patently bigoted, Islamophobic statements, and they seem to suffer few significant consequences.

The 2016 presidential campaign produced some of the most egregious examples of Islamophobic political rhetoric in recent memory. Businessman and television personality Donald J. Trump led the quest to deliver the most far-reaching counterterrorism policy statement of the campaign season by demanding a "total and complete shutdown of Muslims entering the United States until our country's representatives can figure out what is going on."[28] This proposal attracted the support of a majority of Americans polled in March 2016, with a striking 81% of Republicans in favor.[29] Meanwhile, Senator Ted Cruz attempted to match his opponent for the Republican nomination with a proposal to "empower law enforcement to patrol and secure Muslim neighborhoods before they become radicalized."[30] Cruz, apparently unaware that the FBI and several local law enforcement agencies had already implemented some version of this bigoted idea, managed to convince some 45% of Americans to agree with his proposal, including 74% of Republicans.[31]

The rhetoric of Trump, Cruz, and other nationally prominent politicians should not be surprising. By now, the inclusion of patently Islamophobic statements is a well-worn tradition at all levels of American politics. For example, in 2005, then-Congressman (and later Senator) Mark Kirk of Illinois stated that he is "OK with discrimination against young Arab males from terrorist-producing states. I'm not threatened by people from China. . . . I just know where the threat is from."[32] Congressman Peter King of New York, a member of the House Homeland Security Committee, agreed that "the threat of al-Qaeda recruiting individuals from within the American-Muslim community is real."[33] Along similar lines, South Carolina State Senator Jake Knotts once described Governor Nikki Haley as a "f—ing raghead" who would bring foreign influence into the state because of her Sikh ancestry. Knotts later apologized, and claimed he was only joking.[34]

Leading political commentators frequently echo Islamophobic slurs made by public officials. Popular FOX News television host Brian Kilmeade explained to his audience that "not all Muslims are terrorists, but all terrorists are Muslims."[35] After he apologized, he nevertheless continued repeatedly to call for discrimination against Muslims. Among other ideas, Kilmeade proposed expanding the use of "racial profiling" in terrorism investigations and suggested "bugging Mosques" to find hidden terrorists.[36] There are many more examples like this—again, not from the fringes of American politics but from well-respected elected officials and from commentators with prominent national platforms. One study found that speaking out about the "Muslim threat" can even

be profitable due to the generous support of a $40-million industry pro-
viding grants and good-paying jobs to self-declared experts willing to
promote Islamophobia.[37] In a society where racism is considered abhorrent, it is quite unusual for openly bigoted statements like these to remain socially acceptable and even promoted by well-known foundations
and wealthy individuals.

Part of the explanation for how Islamophobia became mainstream
in American politics is the common insistence that it is not racist to
express concerns about Muslims and Islam. Consider the controversy
in 2014 when Oklahoma State Representative John Bennett commented
to his supporters that Muslims are "a cancer in our nation that needs
to be cut out."[38] He defended himself by asserting that Islam is not a
racial group, which means that he cannot be called racist for speaking
out against Muslims.

> They said, "Oh, Rep. Bennett, that guy on TV, he's a bigot and a racist.
> He's an Islamophobe." Well, if I'm an Islamophobe for speaking the truth
> about Islam, then you're absolutely right. But I find it hard to believe.
> How can I be racist against Muslim or Islam when the ethnicity is actually
> Arab? This is kind of confusing.[39]

The bizarre reference to an Arab ethnicity was Bennett's attempt to assert
that Islam is not a racial category, meaning that his critical statements
by definition could not be racist. Bennett's maneuver here is typical in
the post–civil rights era. Americans will generally accept any excuse to
avoid seeing racism. By narrowing the definitions of race and racism, it
becomes possible to tolerate even blatant bigotry.

The takeaway from all of this is that the slipperiness with which racism has been redefined not only enables Islamophobia to pass as legitimate discourse, but it also helps Americans avoid talking about racism,
even when it is patently obvious. This tendency to reject the conclusion that racism is operative in Islamophobia presents a profound dilemma for Middle Eastern American advocates working to confront
Islamophobia.

Confronting the Racial Dilemma

Strategically, does it benefit civil rights advocates to call out Islamophobia as racism? Or would it be wiser if they avoided the controversial issue of race? For example, they might instead describe Islamophobia as an infringement upon religious freedom, or a violation of human rights, or find some other way to discuss Islamophobia without bringing up race explicitly. By steering clear of the rhetoric of racism when describing Islamophobia, advocates can sidestep the thorny terrain that always surrounds the topic of race.

On the other hand, using the language of race to link their efforts against Islamophobia to venerated, longstanding civil rights campaigns against racism might provide Middle Eastern American advocates with a powerful moral authority. Calling out Islamophobia as racism might also bring additional support from a broader community of racially marginalized communities. The racial dilemma for these advocates is the choice of how to frame their efforts—whether they choose to represent themselves as marginalized communities of color struggling against racism, or position their communities as mainstream, regular Americans who just want to be treated equally.

Aside from the strategic concerns for Middle Eastern American advocates, this dilemma represents a crucial turning point in the tortured American history with race. If one of the most pervasive and damaging forms of racism—Islamophobia—is not challenged *as* racism by advocates, what does that mean for civil rights in America?

In an interview with me, a leader at the Council on American-Islamic Relations (CAIR), one of the largest advocacy organizations confronting Islamophobia, explained why he did not believe racism is a central issue for Muslim Americans.[40]

It [racism] does appear, but that's not the main thing. I'll tell you why. Most of the time our criticism of laws or proposed laws is based on criticism of the merits of the law itself. We usually oppose the substance of the law, the premise of such laws. . . . [If] you're assuming that Muslim countries are producing bad guys more than other countries, that's not true. Now, dealing with the racist aspect of it is one of the factors, one of the elements. But the real element is the premise, the dangerous aspect of starting to separate Americans by ethnic groups and religious groups and so on. . . . When you get stopped by a police officer, and he asks you, 'Which mosque do you go to?', you usually are initially stopped because you were darker [in skin tone] than some other person. So there is an element [of racism] there but it is not the main driving force.[41]

Even as he describes a situation where physical appearance—"darker" skin tone—leads directly to discrimination by law enforcement, this Muslim American advocate simultaneously asserts that racism is not a "main driving force" in Islamophobic discrimination. Rather than describe the problem as racism, he instead stresses the ideal that all Americans deserve equal treatment regardless of their religious or ethnic identity. Furthermore, in his view it is counterproductive, or even "dangerous," to speak in terms of racial identities. For him, to "separate Americans" would only serve to perpetuate more discrimination, so it is better to assert a common American identity. This framing allows him to sidestep the issue of race while still advocating against Islamophobic discrimination.

Many Arab, Muslim, Sikh, and South Asian American advocates routinely use language like this. This is how they navigate away from the sensitive issue of race. One of the goals of this approach is gaining mainstream approval. On this view, bringing up race or accusing someone of being "a racist" will make advocates appear too radical, or too unreasonable, and it could potentially result in many Americans tuning out the message instead. The advocacy strategy of avoiding race therefore requires carefully tuned messaging that will not offend the sensibilities of an American public divided on race and concerned about terrorism.

One of the most common ways advocates avoid talking about race is by describing Islamophobia as religious persecution. Religious communities enjoy a great deal of respect and legitimacy in the United States, and standing up for religious freedom is almost never controversial (unlike standing up for racial justice). By highlighting religious identity—Muslim, Sikh, Hindu—advocates can make the unimpeachable claim that their community should not be treated any differently than Christians or Jews. This approach also has the perceived advantage of avoiding associations with stigmatized, racially defined groups like Blacks and

Latin@s. With this strategy, many advocates champion religious freedom without making broader calls for racial justice.

To further develop this strategy, several Middle Eastern American advocacy organizations worked with Hattaway Communications, a high-profile Washington, DC, public relations firm in 2012. Grants from generous donors, including the Open Society Foundation and Kellogg Foundation, enabled Hattaway to conduct a national survey with 1,200 respondents, interviews with "a wide variety of advocates and policymakers," and "focus group discussions across the country." The resulting "message manual" recommended specific phrases for use in public statements by advocates to "address fear" and "promote fairness." The manual warns:

> Messages aimed at addressing fear fall flat if they suggest that preserving important values, such as civil liberties, should take precedence over keeping America safe. Instead, we must deliver messages that: 1) offer an approach to terrorism that doesn't unfairly target American Muslims, [and] 2) show that American Muslims—like other Americans—help to address terrorism.

Notably, the words "race" and "racism" do not appear anywhere in the message manual. Instead, the manual recommends focusing on messages that emphasize national unity and religious freedom. The authors note that statements around "religious freedom" are "highly effective" in promoting "tolerance."[42]

By using poll-tested, carefully crafted messages like these, which stay away from controversial statements about race, many advocates believe they can position themselves firmly in the center of American political discourse. The vocabulary used to accomplish this can be such a stretch that it might be humorous, if the issues were not so serious. Advocates describing hate crimes when Sikhs or Hindus are attacked frequently use the laborious construction "Muslims and those mistaken for Muslims." Used in this way, "mistaken identity" becomes a euphemism to avoid explicitly mentioning race and racism.

This race-neutral advocacy strategy has been effective at winning some significant reforms. One victory, in 2010, saw the Transportation Security Administration (TSA) dismantle a program that required extra scrutiny of airline passengers traveling through a short list of "high-risk" countries, which apart from Cuba were all Muslim-majority countries. TSA hastily announced that they would pull aside all passengers traveling from these countries after an al-Qaeda-affiliated militant attempted to detonate a bomb in his underwear on a jetliner flying over Detroit on December 25, 2009. Because all of the Muslim-majority countries on the TSA list were in Africa and Asia, the advocates could have chosen to use a familiar term to describe the problem with this program: "racial profiling." Instead, they avoided the term "racial" when describing the discrimination. Advocates from CAIR and several other advocacy organizations issued a statement that the TSA program was based on "religious and ethnic profiling."[43] In response to the petitions for change from CAIR and other organizations, the TSA ended the discriminatory program less than five months after introducing it.[44]

Because of successes like this one, using language that avoids race might indeed be the most effective strategy for advocates confronting Islamophobia. However, there are potential advantages in an explicitly race-conscious approach to civil rights advocacy, as well—one that embraces calls for racial justice.

A race-conscious strategy would seek to co-opt racial identity for leverage as it ignores and obscures ethnic, religious, and cultural diversity. Islamophobia unavoidably pushes Arab, Muslim, Sikh, and South Asian American communities into an undifferentiated Middle Eastern racial category. Recognizing that collective racial identity could open various avenues for coalition building and dynamic advocacy strategies. For one, the collective Middle Eastern identity could become the basis for a coalition spanning a wider range of community organizations. Rather than only working separately as advocates for dozens of groups defined by nationality, religion, or panethnicity (Lebanese, Sikh, South Asian, etc.), a Middle Eastern American coalition could bring together all of these communities. This would enable a pooling of resources and an efficient division of labor among diverse allies. Moreover, by positioning Middle Eastern Americans alongside other racially marked communities of color, this strategy would promote even larger advocacy coalitions with Asian, Black, Latin@, and Native Americans. Finally, recognizing the role of race would allow for the use of the powerful moral language of civil rights: characterizing Islamophobia as not just objectionable or offensive but specifically *racist*.

Some anti-Islamophobia advocates have adopted a race-conscious strategy. A prominent example is the Arab American Association of New York, under the direction of Linda Sarsour. Speaking in terms of "multiracial coalitions," Sarsour led several efforts in the 2010s to coordinate with Arab, Muslim, Sikh, and South Asian American organizations, and to expand these coalitions by joining with other communities of color. For example, in 2014, Sarsour traveled to Ferguson, Missouri, joining Black Lives Matter protests against police brutality after a young Black man, Michael Brown, was shot to death by a White police officer. Sarsour organized a "Muslims for Ferguson" campaign, and she explained her strategy in an interview with *Colorlines* magazine:

> We were thinking about what our role is as Arab Americans and Muslims, as the children of immigrants or immigrants ourselves. What is our role in the larger conversation about race and racism in the US?[45]

Sarsour's framing of the issue deals directly with race and racism. Unlike advocates who avoid race, here Sarsour does not seek to gain popular acceptance by obscuring the role of racism. She positions herself as a civil rights protester demanding reforms with the moral language of the racial justice movement. In another 2014 campaign, Sarsour explicitly linked racial profiling of Blacks and Latin@s in police stop-and-frisk policies with the need for New York City public schools to recognize Muslim holidays. Both of these issues discriminated against communities of color, in her view. This perspective motivated a multiracial coalition of organizations to pressure the city government to change policies on both of these issues simultaneously. The coalition won significant reforms: major changes to the stop-and-frisk policies of the New York Police Department (NYPD) and the addition of two Muslim holidays to the public school calendar.

The differences between the CAIR leader's strategy and Sarsour's approach—one "colorblind," and the other outspoken about race—clearly illustrate the strategic dilemma that race presents for Arab, Muslim, Sikh, and South Asian American advocates. Both approaches have merits and drawbacks. And each approach carries wider implications for the construction of race, writ large, in the United States.

Civil rights advocates have always played a pivotal role in the development of American racial thinking. The actions and statements of civil rights campaigners have historically had tremendous power to shape and even to transform the social construction of race in America. By challenging discrimination and enabling anti-discrimination policies and programs that can lift up subjugated communities, civil rights campaigns in the twentieth century achieved nothing less than a major reconstruction of American politics and culture. Now and in the decades ahead, Middle Eastern American civil rights advocates have a crucial role to play in determining how the nation deals with race and racism. In this book, I explore the strategic choices and challenges that lie between both the race-conscious and the race-neutral strategies as they are described by American advocates working to confront "Islamophobia."

Research Methods

To learn more about how Middle Eastern American civil rights advocates have crafted strategies to deal with the racial dilemma, I spoke with dozens of Arab, Muslim, Sikh, and South Asian American advocates. Alongside these interviews, I conducted a contextual analysis of documents such as pamphlets, conference programs, newsletters, and websites published by several of the largest Arab, Muslim, Sikh, and South Asian American advocacy organizations. I also built a database with information about hundreds of advocacy organizations in these communities across the United States, with data from 1980 and 2004.

Most of this research was conducted between 2005 and 2014. I made several research trips to Detroit, Los Angeles, and Washington, DC, to meet in person with advocates and to get copies of documents produced by several leading advocacy organizations active in these locations. I also spoke by telephone with activists in New York City, Chicago, Minneapolis, and a few smaller cities as well. Throughout the time that I gathered these data, I continually developed and added information to my database describing the wider Middle Eastern American advocacy field. I describe each of the three components of my research below, and additional details about my methodological choices appear in the methodological appendix.[46]

Interviews

I sought out current and former board members, executives, staffers, volunteers, and members from several prominent advocacy organizations for in-depth, qualitative interviews. I found these advocates by calling, writing, or visiting the offices of the advocacy organizations. After each meeting, I asked for the contact information of anyone else with whom I might speak, and through this "snowballing" technique, I quickly reached several dozen potential interview subjects. I did not limit interviews by institutional affiliation, but I instead took the approach of speaking to anyone working in this field in almost any capacity, from new volunteers to longtime board members. I ended up meeting advocates working at more than twenty advocacy organizations, and I was also able to speak with a few government officials working at agencies that interface with advocacy organizations, such as the Department of Justice and the Department of Homeland Security. In all, I conducted seventy interviews with sixty-two advocates and officials (this includes eight follow-up interviews).

Each interview was, of course, customized for the person I spoke with, and I asked different questions based on what I already knew about the advocate and her or his organization. Generally, each interview covered organizational history, the differences and similarities among various organizations in the field, the advocate's opinions on important organizational decisions, strategies, and tactics, and the goals and dilemmas facing the organization and the field. All interviews included a discussion of coalition building, and most of those conversations included detailed discussions about the role of race and racism in anti-Islamophobia advocacy work.

I promised to keep each respondent's identity confidential. This enabled everyone I interviewed to offer their thoughts and opinions freely, without worrying about damaging their reputations among their colleagues or in their communities. All names and other information that would personally identify the source for my interview quotes have been altered or omitted, except in rare cases where I have been given explicit permission to identify a source for a quote.

The data generated from these interviews allowed for a close analysis of organizational strategic decisions and the relationships among organizations covered in the study. Overall, the interview data provided a vivid picture of the field of anti-Islamophobia advocacy at the national level, from the late 1970s through the early 2010s.

Content Analysis

I conducted an analysis of documents produced between 1980 and 2014 by ten national-level advocacy organizations. The documents include websites, press releases, and pamphlets produced for the general public, newsletters directed toward organizational members and subscribers, and internal memoranda, conference agendas, research impressions, and other assorted materials. The documents contain a wealth of information about these organizations: details on prioritized issues and concerns, events and campaigns, services offered, promotions and public relations, lobbying and other governmental relations, fundraising efforts, membership drives, opinion articles, electoral voting guides and endorsements, and media talking points.

The analysis allowed for additional information on how strategic decisions were made, which issues were (and were not) considered important by leadership at the organizations, how and when coalitions and jointly coordinated campaigns were undertaken between different organizations, and it allowed for a general examination of the efforts (or lack thereof) at coalition building with other advocacy organizations.

Database

The third and final component of the study involved building a custom database with information about hundreds of Arab, Muslim, Sikh, and South Asian American advocacy organizations. The design and idea for this database were adapted from a method originally developed by Debra Minkoff.[47] Data for this project were primarily obtained from the *Encyclopedia of Associations*, a directory produced annually since the 1960s by Gale Research. The *Encyclopedia* catalogs information in an effort to describe every voluntary association in the United States, including large corporations, political action committees, and civil rights advocacy organizations. The research staff at Gale seek out new organizations for inclusion by Internet, from references in newspapers and periodicals, and by referral. The *Encyclopedia* includes a wide range of basic information on each organization, including the year that the organization was established, its membership size, geographic location, a narrative description of its goals and activities, and its relationships to other organizations in the same field.

I coded two separate editions of the *Encyclopedia*, the 1980 edition and the 2004 edition. This allowed me to observe changes between these years. I augmented the 2004 data with more recent information (typically 2010 or newer) from the Guidestar database on funding levels and budgets for many of the organizations listed in the *Encyclopedia*.[48]

The *Encyclopedia* does not contain information about every Middle Eastern American civil rights advocacy organization. In particular, newer, smaller, or short-lived organizations were unlikely to be included in the database. Even with this selection bias, the sample obtained for this study is significant and includes a large proportion of the organizations working in this arena.

Limitations

While my methods have produced an extensive amount of data on the field of Middle Eastern American advocacy, my study has several major shortcomings. Perhaps most notably, my discussion of Black Muslim organizations is extremely limited. It goes without saying that there is a deep tradition of civil rights advocacy among Muslim Americans in Black communities. In any discussion of race and Islam, the histories of Black Islamic movements are crucial. The constellation of racial contradictions in motion when discussing American Muslims—many of whom are Black—are examined by scholars like Sherman A. Jackson and Aminah McCloud.[49] In order to do justice to the deep history of civil rights work in these communities of Muslim Americans, I would have to write a different book. I touch on these dynamics in several places in the book, but in an unavoidably insufficient way.

In addition, my analysis focuses on the racial issues at work in Islamophobia, and intersectional issues get insufficient attention in my analysis. Gender, sexuality, class, and other axes of difference all operate simultaneously with race. I chose to focus almost exclusively on race because, in my view, it is the axis of inequality that is the most contentious and the most relevant when discussing strategic concerns for anti-Islamophobia advocates. This is especially true when finding ways to develop coalitions among Arab, Muslim, Sikh, and South Asian American organizations. I discuss some of the gendered and classed aspects of Islamophobia, but my attention to sexuality is wholly inadequate. Again, by focusing my critique on race, my intention is to highlight the intersectional nature of Islamophobia and other forms of discrimination, but no single study could possibly do justice to all of the elements of intersectionality involved in Islamophobia.

Another important limitation in my study comes because of my focus on large advocacy organizations with a national scope. While I argue that this level of analysis is important, I recognize the weaknesses in this approach. In fact, early in the development of my research, I planned to focus on local-level advocacy organizations to avoid the weaknesses associated with "top down" research. I began this project by meeting advocates working in the Detroit area. While there, I came to realize that the local chapters of prominent anti-Islamophobia organizations relied a great deal on the guidance and support of their national headquarters. Furthermore, to describe the historical co-constitution of race and Islamophobia, I quickly realized that I would need to focus on the national level. Race takes on different contours in each local context, but much of the strategic advocacy decisions on dealing with race take place in the national headquarters of advocacy organizations. Many of the advocates I interviewed described how the advocacy field in Detroit differed from that found in Chicago, or New York. Others noted that the Washington, DC, headquarters of organizations like ADC and CAIR, while important in many ways, were not representative of some of the work done in local field offices. I make reference to some of these variations, but it is not possible to describe all of these nuances in a single study. There is a pressing need for more studies, like Nadine Naber's in San Francisco and Louise Cainkar's in Chicago, that describe local advocacy fields in rich ethnographic detail.[50]

Finally, I want to emphasize that my study is in no way an attempt to instruct advocates on their best course of action. I understand that in my role as a scholar I might provide some new context, and I attempt to find new perspectives on old problems. Many advocates described to me how the nature of their work leaves very little time for reflecting on history.

I was surprised that several of the advocates I met asked me about history of their own organizations, because they honestly believed that I would know more than they would. One fact that was clear from early in my work is that there are extraordinary demands on the time of civil rights advocates. It is more than a full-time job just keeping up with the day-to-day cacophony of Islamophobic statements from public leaders, and all too frequent calls for help from people facing discrimination. My greatest hope for this book is that some advocates might find some value in my attempt to get "above the fray" to offer a unique vantage point on the issues that they deal with every day. I cannot give a comprehensive history of each organization I studied, but I intend to show how race intersects with the strategic decisions that many anti-Islamophobia advocates make. Perhaps in some small way this analysis can contribute to a discussion among scholars and advocates on the issues of race and Islamophobia and how they can best be confronted.

How This Book Is Organized

Chapter 2 begins by going into further detail on sociological theories of race to show that it is a paradox. Racial identity is both obvious and invisible, and it is both a cause and an effect of Islamophobia. To get to the bottom of this paradox, I use racial formation theory to lead a deeper dive into the relationship between race and civil rights advocacy. This puts into sharp relief the racial dilemma that has frustrated Middle Eastern American advocates for decades: Should advocates describe Islamophobia as racism?

Then, in chapter 3, I present the parallel histories of American racism and Islamophobia in culture, politics, and policy. I begin with the construction of "the Orient" in Western scholarship and discourse. This shows the thread that connects racist stereotypes about Middle Easterners through the early 1900s melodramas around Middle Eastern piracy, the nefarious, cartoonish "oil sheiks" of the mid-1900s, and the menacing specter of "Islamic terrorism" in the 2000s. I juxtapose these stereotypes with a history of racial discrimination in general, explaining how the parallel development of racial ideology and Islamophobia had a profound impact on Middle Eastern American communities throughout the 1900s. I then discuss how present-day policies and practices discriminate against Middle Eastern Americans in an ostensible effort to prevent terrorist attacks. I review the problems of racial profiling, political exclusion, and immigration policies that all serve to reinforce the bigoted stereotype that casts Middle Easterners as "dangerous."

I then turn to focus squarely on the advocates working to confront Islamophobia. Chapter 4 describes the history and trajectory of six of the most important organizations in the Middle Eastern American advocacy field. By reviewing key moments in the development of these organizations, I show how the racial dilemma has presented a challenge for Middle Eastern American advocates, even from the earliest days of their work in the 1900s. Then, in chapter 5, I describe how Middle Eastern American advocates have crafted varying strategies in an effort to solve the racial dilemma. I find that for a short time in the 1970s and 1980s, some Middle Eastern American advocates used race-conscious strategies, and sought to build durable, transformational coalitions with Black civil rights organizations. By the time 9/11 presented a new crisis, though, advocacy strategies had shifted toward a colorblind approach that eschewed the language of racism. The largest Middle Eastern American advocacy organizations did little coalition work in the early 2000s, even as the federal government led efforts to encourage race-based coalitions among Arab, Muslim, Sikh, and South Asian American organizations.

Finally, in chapter 6, I conclude by looking toward the future of American civil rights in general, given the persistence of Islamophobia and the seemingly intractable racial dilemma that has confounded Middle Eastern American advocates. I argue that the lack of durable coalitions among Arab, Muslim, Sikh, and South Asian American organizations is mainly because of the success of the conservative reaction to the civil rights movements of the 1960s. I close the book by asking whether American civil rights advocates in the years ahead will have to develop new, race-conscious strategies as America becomes a so-called majority-minority nation by the mid-2000s. There can be little doubt that the way that Middle Eastern American advocates have navigated the rapidly shifting terrain of civil rights advocacy over the past forty years will prove to be one of the most crucial case studies illustrating how the United States responds to racism in the post–civil rights era.

2

The Racial Paradox

Racial identity is a paradox. It is deeply private and personal, yet also public and political. It exists outside of individuals, but individuals reproduce it all the time. Like most fundamental social constructions, race is both cause and effect. It seems that everyone is always aware of race, even if no one says anything about it.

Perhaps one the cruelest ironies of race comes when choosing which box to select on the multiple-choice checklist of racial identities that appears so often on bureaucratic forms. Usually the "top five" racial identity categories appear: Asian, Black, Latin@, Native American, and White. In surveys ranging from the decennial US Census to opinion surveys, workplace diversity forms, and political polls, race is almost always treated as a simple independent variable. There is just a list of racial categories for each person to choose from, and that is that. Of course, racial identity is never that simple. An immediate complication arises upon realizing that the distribution of social resources depends upon racial identity in many ways, so the stakes are high for which boxes appear on these bureaucratic checklists.

Activist students at the University of California understood this, and they won recognition at their school for a new racial category for students of Southwest Asian and North African descent in 2013. Sahra Mirbabaee, a student activist at UC Berkeley, reflected on her experiences with racial identity and the official university forms that asked her to check "White" as her identity.

> I have to put myself in a category where I don't fit in. . . . Even for an Iranian, I have dark skin, so I don't think it's correct for myself to be in the category of White, because it doesn't represent how I'm perceived by society.[1]

Mirbabaee's frustration illustrates the paradox of race. Like so many other Middle Eastern Americans, she found herself constantly ascribed with a racial identity, yet at the same time few were willing to recognize how deeply race affected her life. She found that society placed her into a non-White box, but then she was instructed to check that White box anyway. Hence the paradox of race: Which comes first, ascription or assertion? Does a racial identity exist when society "perceives" it, or when the individuals and communities it marks demand recognition?

When discussing racial difference, many teachers and parents repeat the line, *race is a social construction*, almost like a mantra. It is easy to repeat this line, but it leaves a more difficult question: Just how does race get constructed? Do racial identity categories spring into existence simply because most people believe they exist? Or do the people ascribed a racial identity need to accept it? Put another way, if most Middle Eastern Americans do not call themselves "Middle Eastern," does that mean there is no Middle Eastern racial category? Conversely, if most Americans recognize a Middle Eastern racial identity, does that mean one exists, no matter what the people ascribed with that identity have to say about it? The frustrations that Middle Eastern Americans face when dealing with this impossible racial paradox put these questions into sharp relief.

Given the inherent absurdities with racial classification, Sahra Mirbabaee's experience at the University of California has been shared by countless Middle Eastern Americans for decades. Imagine the similar frustration faced by someone originally from, for instance, Pakistan, when presented with a race question on surveys or on official forms. Which of the five boxes should she choose? Perhaps "Asian" is the best answer? Pakistan is in Asia, after all. Whatever the checklist says, many Americans with heritage in Iran, Pakistan, and many other places find themselves unavoidably ascribed with a Middle Eastern racial identity. In other words, many people would probably offer up some variation of "Middle Eastern" if pressed to describe the racial identity of, for instance, an Iranian friend. Yet most documents and surveys simply do not have a Middle Eastern box to check. Part of the problem comes because most such documents use the same racial and ethnic classifications as those adopted by the US Census Bureau.

The Census defines Whiteness as inclusive of many Middle Eastern Americans, including Iranian Americans. It places Afghan, Indian, Pakistani, and other communities from the eastern edge of the Middle East region into the Asian American racial category.[2] This does not match up with the current, popularly understood boundaries between racial groups.

The lack of a clearly recognized racial identity for Middle Eastern Americans creates challenges not only for individuals as they attempt to check the "right" box. This situation also hinders the compilation of accurate demographic statistics, and it curtails accurate descriptions of the challenges facing these communities. This makes it difficult to describe Islamophobic discrimination as a racial phenomenon that affects everyone ascribed as Middle Eastern, regardless of religious and ethnic background. The language and the data simply are not there to develop an accurate, comprehensive, and effective analysis of any issue affecting Middle Eastern American communities. This is yet another aspect of the racial paradox: the racial roots of Islamophobia are there but unrecognized, and they cannot be adequately described. The frustration felt by individuals like Sahra Mirbabaee may not get fully relieved by the addition of some new checkboxes on surveys. But understanding the collective difficulties faced by Middle Eastern American communities nonetheless requires recognition of a Middle Eastern racial category. Again, the racial paradox stands in the way.

In order to break down this racial paradox that surrounds Islamophobia, we have to surround it. It is first necessary to conduct a brief survey of several centuries' worth of history, during which time various events and processes contributed to the ongoing social construction of the Middle Eastern racial category. To begin this brief but hopefully illuminating journey, I travel all the way back to before the Christian Crusades in the Middle Ages, which eventually gave way to an era of colonialism that saw most of the Middle East placed under oppressive European rule for many decades. Successful twentieth-century efforts at decolonization and independence were more or less directly followed by the current era of American-led interventions, including multiple wars and invasions. Throughout all of this varied and uneven history, a remarkably consistent thread extends, enabling a broad dehumanization and racialization of the many peoples living in the Middle East.

My brief and necessarily incomplete examination of this vast history sets the stage for a discussion of how migration from the Middle East to America further solidified the racial category that would blur distinctions between the diverse communities from North Africa, Southwest

Asia, and South Asia as they settled in the United States. In the second part of this chapter, I describe how explicitly racist immigration policies in the US affected people coming from Lebanon, India, Iran—indeed, the entire Middle East. This linked immigration history unsurprisingly created a range of shared experiences for many people in these communities, experiences that continue right up into the present day.

After tracing the outlines of these processes, I describe the contemporary demographics of various Middle Eastern American communities. Further demonstration of the processes by which the Middle Eastern racial category has been constructed comes from examining the similar trajectories of the Asian American, Latin@, and Native American histories. The final part of this chapter considers the ways that advocates from those communities have strategized around racial formation, and how they co-opted their ascribed racial identities in advocacy work. This will prove instrumental later on, when discussing how the racial paradox complicates the ongoing racial dilemma confronting Middle Eastern American civil rights advocates.

Defining the Middle East: From European Crusades to American Adventures

The Crusades are an arbitrary place to start unraveling the twisted roots that sprouted the Middle Eastern racial category, but in any event, there is a great deal of history that will unavoidably get omitted when trying to summarize thousands of years of history with a few simple generalizations. One common misconception caused by compressing all this history into a short space is the idea that since the beginning of time, all of the various European and Middle Eastern powers were constantly at war. This myth often supports popular culture representations of an endless "Islam versus the Christian West" trope.[3] In fact, despite the intermittent violence generated by the Crusades and other conflicts, not all contact between European and Middle Eastern empires resulted in bloodshed. Prosperous trade relationships, effervescent cultural exchanges, and long-term eras of peace were interspersed with periods of conflict and war. There is no stable, ancient, and immutable basis for conflict here. Across the ages, sacred, religious motivations for conquest mixed with more profane, sociopolitical factors as well. The political map constantly shifted as populations migrated, and various empires rose and fell. These were often, but not always, violent transitions.

The stage for the various interspersed eras of conflict was set in motion in ancient times, literally millennia before the present-day geographical boundaries of Europe and the Middle East were in place. During the Classical period, ancient terms like "Mauri" were ascribed onto various North African communities as a way to distinguish them from the Greeks and the Romans. Much later, the "Moors" (the English language derivative of "Mauri," referring to North Africans of mainly Arab and Berber descent) ruled the Iberian Peninsula during the era of the Umayyad Caliphate in the eighth century of the Common Era. The expansion of Umayyad forces further north across the Pyrenees was stopped by the Franks at the Battle of Tours in 732, an event later valorized by Renaissance-era European historians as a triumphant moment when the "Moors" were kept away from the so-called heart of Europe.[4] Today, the term "Moor" and its relatives survive in several languages as derogatory terms for Middle Easterners.

Centuries after the breakup of the Umayyad Caliphate in the mid-800s, the Crusades began. They were a set of military campaigns by various European powers that took place between the eleventh and fifteenth centuries.[5] The stated goal in each of the Crusades, which were officially declared by several Catholic Popes, was to take away Jerusalem and the Holy Land from various Asian and African powers. The wars involved dozens of combatants, various political entities across many different European kingdoms, and numerous emirates—the Fatimid and Abbasid Caliphates, empires such as the Byzantine, and dynasties including the Ayyubid, Hafsid, and Mamluk.

As the various Crusades came and went, clear social distinctions emerged—not racial in today's terms, but social distinctions nonetheless—that served to categorize people in Southwest Asia and North Africa as distinct from Europeans. Spinoffs of the socially constructed categories from the Crusades that split Europeans and Middle Easterners, which developed out of the primordial "Christian" and "Moor" categories, are still with us today.[6]

By the time the Crusades started, European combatants sought to conquer territory held by people they came to collectively refer to as "Saracens." This was a popular term that was used to lump together people who lived in the deserts around the Arabian Peninsula. Even in the twelfth century, biological differences in skin color were sometimes considered socially relevant. In *The Song of Roland*, for example, an epic written around 1100, the Saracens are described as having exotic black skin.[7] The term Saracen gradually faded out of use, but it was replaced with different catchall terms for people from Southwest Asia and North Africa. This process repeated, with new collective identity terms rising and falling through the centuries. At any given point, terms like "Arab," "Moor," "Muhammedan," "Muslim," "Oriental," and "Turk" would be popular in various parts of Europe to collectively describe people from various parts of the Middle East—including South Asia. Religious markers mixed with geographic, ethnic, and wholly made-up identity terms. The most elemental foundations of the present-day race concept are based in part on these social distinctions between largely Christian Europeans and the various religious and ethnic groups in Africa and Asia.

In his groundbreaking study, *Orientalism*, Edward Said describes how European scholars and political leaders picked up the threads left by the Crusaders to develop knowledge about "Orientals."[8] These scholars thereby constructed the image of "the Orient" while working in European institutions, beginning in the 1700s and continuing into the twentieth century. Said critiques this promulgation of European conceptions of a vast region never precisely defined but generally confined to the Arab-majority regions of North Africa and the Muslim-majority countries of Southwest Asia—today's Middle East. Stereotypes of Orientals as "backward," foolhardy, hedonistic, sexually insatiable, and immature were seen throughout European art, literature, and scholarly publications from the 1700s straight through to the 1900s. Said argued that these stereotypes informed projects like Napoleon's 1798 conquest of Egypt and Syria, the construction of the Suez Canal in the 1860s, and the colonization of much of Africa and Southwest Asia by European powers in the nineteenth and twentieth centuries. He describes how Orientalism remained intact as it spread from Western Europe to the United States, noting that leading American scholarship in the 1900s mostly just repeated the faulty tropes developed by Europeans.

Beginning as early as the initial European settlement of the New World, Americans basically adopted the European conception of the Orient, and Said charged the American government with engaging in neo-colonialist "adventures" in the region that were informed by the old Orientalist stereotypes and misconceptions. Holly Edwards extended Said's analysis by looking closely at Orientalism as expressed in American art and literature between 1870 and 1930.[9] She found that after the Civil War, a new fear of American national weakness centered on a "Barbary captive" narrative. These stories enthralled American audiences with tales of brave seamen taken prisoner by sinister pirates operating off the North African coast. The pirates were consistently depicted in ways that closely resemble twentieth and twenty-first century stereotypes of "radicalized" Middle Easterners: turbans, flowing robes, scowling faces, swarthy brown skin, and so on. Edwards showed how these stereotypical images influenced contemporary American culture, from novels to advertising campaigns and eventually the Hollywood film industry. Douglas Little provides a succinct summary of what today would be called Islamophobia in American popular culture from the 1700s through the 1900s: "Muslims, Jews, and most other peoples of the Middle East were 'Orientalized' and depicted as backward, decadent, and untrustworthy."[10]

Over time, the term "Oriental" in the American context came to be more closely associated with Eastern Asia, although like all collective identity terms its boundaries were always imprecise. Various other umbrella terms like "Syrian" and "Arabian" became popular in America for describing people from the Middle East. Stereotypes of Arabs as oversexed, greedy, misogynistic, and dangerous began to reach the mainstream by the 1940s and 1950s. All the while, the term "Arab" was used to denote not only people who self-identified as Arab, but it also was used to ascribe Persians, Sephardic Jews, South Asians, Sikhs, and others who were perceived as belonging to the Arab category due to their physical appearance.[11]

Recurrent violence in the Middle East and several terrorist attacks perpetrated by extremist militants from the 1960s through the 2000s were reflected in repetitive Hollywood depictions of Arabs as violent and bloodthirsty. The taken-for-granted stereotype repeated again and again in American popular culture was that Arabs were predisposed to turn to violence. Villains in films and television shows were virtually the only representations of Arabs ever seen in American television and cinema: suicide bombings, terrorism, and anti-American sentiment became all but synonymous with the term "Arab." Rarely did American art include humanized depictions of "regular" Arabs—in his landmark study, Jack G. Shaheen found only few examples across decades of Hollywood productions.[12]

From "Saracen" to "Muslim," from Orientalism to Islamophobia, the racial formation of the Middle Eastern racial category developed amid the construction of fundamental American racial logics from the colonial period through to the 1900s. These are the very same racial understandings that promulgated the "one-drop rule"—that any African ancestry demanded Black as the primary identity—which denied the vast ethnic and cultural diversity among Black Americans. The same racial processes reduced countless cultures and nations down to "Indian," which helped to justify the brutal ethnic cleansing of Native Americans. The very same racist logic underpinned the Asian Exclusion Acts that affected Chinese, Korean, Japanese, and dozens of other communities—it was because of race that these endlessly diverse communities were viewed by most Americans as one and the same.

On precisely the same line, the racial formation of the Middle Eastern racial identity collapses the myriad ethnic and religious groups among Arab, Muslim, Sikh, and South Asian Americans. Afghan, Armenian, Berber, Chaldean, Druze, Egyptian, Lebanese, Moroccan, Persian, Palestinian, Punjabi, Sikh, Turk, Turkmen, Yemeni—all these groups and many more are denied their self-identity and reduced to a single racial category in contemporary American discourse.[13]

After the rise of al-Qaeda in the 1990s, the collective term "Arab" began to fall away in favor of "Middle Eastern" and "Muslim." In the years following the 9/11 attacks, "Muslim" won out and replaced "Arab" as the most prominent umbrella term used in the United States. Those who were once described in media and other popular narratives as "Arab terrorists" now became "Muslim terrorists." What was once called "anti-Arab racism" was recast as Islamophobia. Muslim Americans, communities at one time perceived as predominantly Black and African American, became more closely associated instead with the Middle Eastern racial category. Anti-Muslim rhetoric, discrimination, and hate crimes expanded rapidly.

There was a great deal of political expedience to the rearticulation of the catchall identity term to "Muslim." The shifting terms, all used to refer to similar racial formations, followed shifts in the political land-scape. Western geopolitical interests expanded in the late 1900s and early 2000s from beyond Arab territories toward the broader Muslim world. As Edward Said observed, the application of stereotypical char-acteristics to describe "Orientals" has always been part and parcel of political projects that culminated with colonialism and occupation. Describing "Arab oil" and "Arab terrorism" was politically powerful in the 1950s through 1970s. This coincided with Western efforts to install pro-Western leaders in mainly Arab countries (and also in Iran). By the end of the 1990s, "Muslim" became more politically beneficial as the United States and other Western nations sought to expand their direct influence (and military presence) to include non-Arab places in Central and South Asia, especially Afghanistan, Pakistan, and Turkey. Hence, "Islamic terrorism" and "Muslim extremists" came to dominate the po-litical discourse, and conveniently "Muslim" is today the most common term to mean "person from the Middle East."

In short, the deepest roots of the Middle Eastern racial category that enables these collective terms to collapse divisions between Arabs, Mus-lims, Sikhs, and South Asians began to take shape many centuries ago, even before the Crusades. The reproduction of clear social distinctions between modern Europe and what today is called the Middle East began as far back in the 1100s, and it continued as an unmistakably racial for-mation in the sixteenth through twenty-first centuries. This process was dynamic, contested, and uneven as it constantly proceeded while the United States developed immigration policies and attempted to deal with increasing numbers of migrants arriving from the Middle East.

Linked Histories: Arab, Muslim, Sikh, and South Asian Americans

Immigration policy in the United States considered people from north-ern Africa and from western and southern Asia as a single group for more than one hundred and sixty years. Although people from the Mid-dle East first appeared in the Americas as part of the transatlantic slave trade in the fifteenth century, historians agree that people from these regions did not willingly migrate in significant numbers until the end of the nineteenth century.[14] Middle Eastern immigration to the United

States took place despite explicitly racist policies in the United States meant to curtail the migration of anyone who was not from Western Europe.[15]

In addition to inhospitable immigration policies, around the turn of the twentieth century, non-Whites in the United States were subject to unchecked violence and state-sanctioned racial discrimination. Middle Easterners were no exception, even as their Whiteness remained a hotly debated question both in literal courtrooms and in the court of public opinion.[16] Kathleen Moore describes the struggles of Middle Eastern immigrants to define their identities and gain basic civil rights during the late 1800s and early 1900s.[17] The 1790 Naturalization Act, which remained in effect until the 1950s, specified that only White people and certain Native Americans could become naturalized citizens of the United States. (After the Civil War, some former slaves also gained some benefits of citizenship.) The explicit goal of immigration policies at the time was to keep out groups thought to be racially undesirable, while making it relatively easy for mostly White Europeans—especially from northern and western Europe—to enter the United States.

Efforts to block migrants from places outside Western Europe expanded throughout the 1800s and 1900s. Policymakers created "barred zones" in the Immigration Act of 1917, specifically prohibiting "immigrants from India, Siam, Arabia, Indo-China, the Malay Peninsula, Afghanistan, New Guinea, Borneo, Java, Ceylon, Sumatra, Celebes, and parts of Russian Turkestan and Siberia."[18] With this act, the government effectively grouped together people from western, central, and southern Asia as non-White and excluded their immigration on that racist basis.

Until at least the end of World War II, the overriding presumption in American popular thought and scholarship was that all White immigrants would assimilate into the "melting pot" of mainstream, White American culture. By contrast, non-White immigrants were believed incapable of assimilation and thus incapable of living as "real" "Americans. Laws designed to enforce this idea meant that the only way for immigrants to gain access to United States citizenship was to prove their "Whiteness."[19] To do so, they went to court.

Case histories show that legal appeals by Middle Eastern Americans to establish Whiteness and thereby gain citizenship through the provisions of the 1790 Naturalization Act produced contradictory results.

Some judges denied Whiteness to persons of Middle Eastern origin while other judges granted Whiteness and its corresponding rights.[20] This piecemeal approach to defining racial status under the immigration system led to myriad conflicting court opinions regarding whether particular ethnic groups counted as White.

For "Syrians"—the term popular in the early twentieth century to describe immigrants from present-day Syria, Lebanon, Jordan, Israel and Palestine, Iraq, and the Arabian Peninsula—multiple conflicting court cases unfolded in the early 1900s.[21] Ian Haney López details how some courts denied White status to "Syrians" and blocked their citizenship, while others did exactly the opposite. One of the best-known cases, that of George Najour, resulted in the first official declaration of Whiteness from a federal court to a "Syrian," in 1909.[22] The judge decided that Najour was White in appearance and that a "scientific" study confirmed that Syrians were "part of the Caucasian or White race."[23] Very quickly after this ruling, other "Syrians" petitioned for Whiteness in other courtrooms across the country. Three of these petitions were accepted and four rejected.[24] In 1942, Ahmed Hassan applied for citizenship as an "Arabian," looking to set a new precedent on Whiteness by avoiding the term "Syrian." The Michigan court that heard his case ruled that "Arabians" are not White and could not become naturalized citizens.[25] Then, just two years later in 1944, a court in Massachusetts ruled that a man named Mohriez was, in fact, White and that "Arabians" like him actually were eligible for naturalized citizenship.[26]

In many ways, South Asians (or "Hindus" in the vernacular of the time) had an even more difficult time accessing the benefits of Whiteness than "Syrians." Moore analyzes the largely identical struggles faced by South Asian communities and "Syrians," finding "ample" evidence of intentional official exclusion of these groups from American social and political life. Indeed, the Attorney General of the United States personally declared in 1907 that South Asians were ineligible for citizenship. But in 1908, the US District Court in New Orleans disagreed, saying that South Asians had the same "racial origin" as Whites.[27]

In 1923, this issue finally reached the Supreme Court. In perhaps the most famous petition for Whiteness, Bhagat Singh Thind relied on the *Najour* precedent to argue he was "scientifically" Caucasian.[28] Rejecting his argument, the Supreme Court quoted the "barred zone" clause of the 1917 Immigration Act to say that "reasonable" people all agreed that Whites and South Asians were racially distinct. The Supreme Court held that no Asians could obtain citizenship in the United States. This resulted in the revocation of citizenship certificates granted prior to the *Thind* case—including certificates granted to South Asians, Syrians, Afghans, Arabs, and Persians.[29] The *Thind* decision was overturned more than a decade later in 1936, but its sweeping effects evidence the linked history of shared exclusion faced by migrants from regions collectively defined as the "Greater Middle East" today, regions that include much of western and southern Asia. According to the legally enforced racial order of the nineteenth and twentieth centuries, Arabs, Muslims, Sikhs, and South Asians were "Syrians" and "Hindus," and they were all excluded from Whiteness. Whether from India, Pakistan, Lebanon, or Algeria, these racist policies affected all of these migrants in similar ways.

Meanwhile, outside the courtroom, early in the twentieth century, individuals from these communities faced widespread discrimination, including blatant voter intimidation, and violent hate crimes. Moore quotes Philip Hitti's discussion of a 1920 political campaign in Alabama. In this election, one candidate described himself as "the White man's candidate."[30] The candidate's campaign advertisement gives a remarkable window into the prevailing racial attitudes of the time, and it drew a line between Whites and "Syrians."

> They have disqualified the Negro, an American citizen, from voting in the White primary. . . . The Greek and Syrian should also be disqualified. I DON'T WANT THEIR VOTE. If I can't be elected by the White men, I don't want the office.[31]

This suggests that, in the popular conception of the early 1900s, "Syrians" did not qualify as White. It was not only legal and "scientific" opinion that Middle Eastern Americans were not White—this was the common understanding as well.

A terrible example of this common understanding getting reinforced by violence against South Asians came in Bellingham, Washington, in 1907. As it was in the South, the West Coast had also attracted a large number of laborers from the Middle East despite racist immigration controls. Various anti-immigration hate groups (and specifically anti-Japanese and anti-Chinese) operated with impunity all along the West Coast. These organizations brought together a huge riot on September 4, 1907, where some five hundred Whites forcibly rounded up nearly two hundred South Asian workers, imprisoning them in the basement of the Bellingham City Hall. In the process, the mob went on "indiscriminately beating people, overpowering a few police officers, and pulling men out of their workplaces and homes." The goal of this organized act of racist exclusion was to spread unchecked fear, and it was successful enough to cause "the entire South Asian population" to leave Bellingham in less than two weeks.[32]

A 1929 lynching of a Syrian man in Florida provides even further dramatic evidence of the racial ideology that constructed Middle Eastern Americans as not only non-White but also racially inferior to Whites. Sarah Gualtieri describes the scene of the lynching:

> "Mob in Florida Lynches White Man; Wife Slain" announced the bold-type headline of the *New York Evening World* newspaper on 17 May 1929. . . . The accompanying article describes briefly the circumstances surrounding the killing of "N.G. Romey, White, a grocer," by a mob after a dispute with the local Chief of Police. Other reports in the English and Arabic-language press revealed that the dead man was Nicholas Romey who, with his wife Fannie and their children, was a member of one of two Syrian families living in Lake City, Florida. . . . But what did it mean that Romey, an immigrant from Southwest Asia, was lynched as a "White man?" Was this simply the *New York Evening World*'s way of distinguishing him from the scores of Black men who were more typically the victims of "Judge Lynch"? Or, was there something more complicated about Romey's racial status that rendered the designation White as much a problem as a description?[33]

Gualtieri goes on to describe how the lynching of Romey in this era, when mob violence to enforce racial borders was commonplace, demonstrates the persistent racial ideology that created a non-White category for Middle Eastern Americans throughout the twentieth century. Indeed, the newspaper's account of a "White lynching" underscores how even as the Middle Eastern racial category made the Romey family vulnerable to racist violence, the paradoxical lack of a clear recognition of that racism made it difficult to describe.

The Romey family's horrible ordeal also serves to illustrate that many who successfully maneuvered through the racially charged immigration process and managed to become naturalized citizens did not find adequate protection from racial discrimination merely through gaining citizenship. Immigrant communities faced all kinds of discrimination, much of it rooted in jingoism, as the United States engaged in World War I and World War II.

Only fifteen years after Romey was lynched in Florida, President Franklin Delano Roosevelt ordered the beginning of what became a definitive event in racist federal policymaking after 1900: the mass internment of Japanese and Japanese Americans. Anti-Japanese sentiment was widespread in the 1930s and 1940s, especially in Hawaii and along the West Coast where sizable Japanese American communities lived. After the Japanese attack on Pearl Harbor in 1941, Roosevelt enacted a policy meant to allay widespread fears that hidden Japanese spies living in the United States might threaten the homeland. Mere hours after the Pearl Harbor attack, Japanese American leaders were captured and detained. A few months later, on February 19, 1942, President Roosevelt issued Executive Order 9066, allowing the military to declare "exclusion zones" on American soil from where "any or all persons may be excluded." The order effectively gave the military the authority to single out anyone of Japanese descent—citizen or otherwise.[34] The military then forcibly detained some 110,000 people, using US Census data and other sources to seek them out and forcibly remove them from their homes in Hawaii, California, and much of Oregon and Washington.[35] They were held in internment camps run by the Department of Justice (DOJ).

The internment policy was not only popular; it also won the approval of the courts. The Supreme Court ruling against detainee Fred Korematsu in 1944 ended any hope of judicial revocation of mass internment.[36] Jerry Kang reviews the decisive role that racial ideology played in the Supreme Court rulings supporting the internment of American citizens and Japanese immigrants. He finds little else but racial stereotypes behind the decision, despite the Court's insistence that racial distinctions are "odious to a free people":

> But the curfew [or internment] that applied to Hirabayashi [a Japanese American], even though he was a United States citizen, was not enacted

solely because of his ancestry. Instead, the military had "ample ground" to be worried that ethnically-affiliated "sleeper cells" would aid a Japanese invasion. According to the Court, this was plain racial common sense. As a result, mere curfew—a relatively minor inconvenience during military crisis—was deemed a reasonable burden for Japanese Americans to bear.[37]

Kang describes the lack of accountability—stretching from the 1940s up to the present—for the racist thinking employed by the White House, the Justice Department, and the Supreme Court in the Japanese internment program. In its belated repudiations of *Korematsu*, the Court absolved itself of any responsibility in the internment policies. Essentially, the Court maintains that it was duped by the military into giving unnecessary and unjust rulings in support of internment. This means that history might well repeat itself during the next era of racialized war hysteria. The precedent set by the racist logic used to intern Japanese and Japanese Americans who ostensibly posed a threat merely because of their heritage, in other words, remains relatively unscathed in American jurisprudence, even after the formal apologies and reparations offered by the American government in the 1980s and 1990s. The bottom line is that there is no clear legal or constitutional prohibition on a new internment the next time racial thinking causes a national security threat to seem connected to a particular racialized immigrant community.

Indeed, during a terrorism scare in the 1980s, according to one DOJ document from 1986, the Reagan administration seriously considered rounding up Arab American immigrants for internment as part of a counterterrorism "contingency plan."[38] This was a frightening development that I discuss in more detail in chapter 3.

Put succinctly, the Japanese internment program had become an international embarrassment for the United States by the late 1900s. As the Cold War with the Soviet Union began, the United States sought to portray itself as a beacon of freedom for all people, but that did not square with explicitly racist American policies like internment. Partially due to this unseemly hypocrisy, and partly due to the work of civil rights advocates, and rapidly changing economic factors, immigration policies underwent a thorough reworking in the 1950s and 1960s.

By 1965, at the height of the civil rights movement, Congress had removed most of the explicitly racist quotas and exclusions in immigration laws. The 1965 Immigration and Nationality Act (popularly known as the Hart-Celler Act) remade immigration policy to one focused on attracting "hard working" immigrants of "good character," goals that remain intact after various smaller revisions to policies since 1965. In a reversal from the early part of the 1900s, professionals after 1965 had an easier time getting visas than working-class migrants. Middle Eastern immigration to America (and immigration to America in general) after 1965 has been characterized as contributing to a "brain drain" of educated professionals to the United States in pursuit of economic opportunity.[39]

The postwar generation of Middle Eastern immigrants entered the United States during the civil rights era, a time when assimilation was no longer the only viable path toward integration. Multiculturalism meant that these immigrants worked to maintain their cultural heritage by forming ethnic and cultural associations and organizations. The post-1965 generation built more churches, gurdwaras (Sikh temples), mosques, and other places of worship than ever before. Immigrants who entered the United States after the 1960s found a cultural context that was generally—though certainly not always—more willing to accept their efforts to maintain the cultural traditions they brought from their homelands.

With these linked histories, immigrants from North Africa and Southwest Asia have faced racial barriers to citizenship and inclusion throughout the history of the United States. Despite these barriers, contemporary Middle Eastern communities in America include a significant number of recent immigrants as well as millions of descendants of earlier immigrants.

Middle Eastern American communities in the 2010s face a situation that is in some ways similar to that in the early twentieth century. Now, as then, today's immigrants from North Africa and Southwest Asia face an American public that generally considers them to be from a homogenous "Middle East." No matter their actual ethnic and cultural heritage, as Middle Eastern Americans, they remain vulnerable to racist discrimination.

Middle Eastern American Communities Today

Because racism affects all Middle Eastern Americans, no matter their heritage, it is important to understand that there are many, many different communities affected by Islamophobia. It is nearly impossible to provide an accurate demographic description of the communities caught up in the Middle Eastern American racial identity. Even coming up with a simple list of the dozens of nationalities and ethnicities implied by the term "Middle Eastern" is simply not possible. This is the case for any racial category. There is no perfect list of "White" countries, or "Asian" countries—indeed, any immigrant from any country may be ascribed with any racial identity. As it always is with racial categories, the boundaries are unclear, and the list of social groups ascribed into the Middle Eastern category expands and contracts all the time.

Because of these and other complexities, producing a good description of the demographics of Middle Eastern American communities is a "daunting" task, according to Anny Bakalian and Mehdi Bozorgmehr, who produced the most comprehensive set of data on this topic to date.[40] Like most scholars who have studied these communities, they decry the dearth of reliable demographic data. Unfortunately, the situation has not improved in the years since their pathbreaking research. As they noted, there are no sources of data that adequately describe even the most visible and populous communities that make up the Middle Eastern American category.

With these constraints, it is barely possible to make even these tentative general statements about the contours of the many Middle Eastern American communities. First, despite the prevalence of Islamophobia in America, it would be inaccurate to say that these communities have been utterly marginalized and oppressed. Middle Eastern Americans have generally been quite economically successful. Indeed, several socioeconomic indicators suggest that, on average, Middle Eastern American families have higher incomes than the average American family.

The source of some multi-generational wealth in Middle Eastern American communities began with turn-of-the-twentieth-century Middle Eastern immigrants to the United States who found prosperous work as shop owners and grocers. In many places, these pioneers drew upon experiences from their home countries to fit into an economic niche left open due to anti-Black discrimination.[41] The development of this economic niche from the early twentieth century means that at the present time, there are well-established, fourth- or even fifth-generation families in Middle Eastern American communities that have enjoyed a great deal of economic success, due in part to the wealth built up by their grandparents and great-grandparents.

It is crucial to note that today's Middle Eastern communities in America include a significant number of recent immigrants in addition to these descendants of earlier immigrants. There is another cohort of young, second-generation Middle Eastern Americans represented in children of those who immigrated into the US in the 1980s. Many of them are only now reaching adulthood as members of the millennial generation.

In addition, the most recent group of new Middle Eastern American immigrants (post-1980) includes many professionals, arguably more now than earlier cohorts of immigrants. However, this latest cohort also has a number of refugees from conflicts in the Middle East along with a significant number of working class people from places like Yemen, Egypt, and other less economically developed Middle Eastern nations.[42] Many of these working class individuals spoke little English on arrival, and they have found work in skilled trades or jobs involving manual labor. In short, there is a great deal of socioeconomic class diversity among Middle Eastern Americans, with a number of very wealthy families and a number of working poor and economically struggling families as well.

All of these immigrants and their descendants find a political climate in today's United States that has some unfortunate parallels with what their counterparts experienced one hundred years ago in the 1910s. Now, as then, these families contend with an America preoccupied by racial categorization, particularly of new immigrant arrivals. As it was a century ago, today's immigrants from North Africa, Southwest Asia, and South Asia face an American public that simply sees them all as racially Middle Eastern, no matter their actual ethnic and cultural heritage.

Part of the problem, no doubt, stems from the lack of basic demographic and cultural knowledge about Middle Eastern communities. Most demographic data sources collectivize either Arab Americans or Muslim Americans rather than Middle Eastern Americans *per se*. The challenge is compounded by the uncertain classification of South Asian Americans, many of whom have been popularly classified as Middle Eastern American, but who are often formally classified as Asian or South Asian in statistical analyses, depending on the study.

To illustrate the difficulty in providing a demographic accounting of the Middle Eastern American community, consider the Arab category. It defies any attempt at definition. There is considerable disagreement among people who trace their heritage to the Arab world about whether everyone from an Arab country should identify as Arab, or whether Arab ethnicity is purely voluntary. Apart from those theoretical debates, people self-identifying as Arab Americans today include families who moved to the United States four or more generations ago, and there are also a significant number of recent (post-1980) immigrants from the more than twenty nations considered members of the Arab world due to their membership in the League of Arab States.[43] In terms of religion, Arab Americans belong to many different religious communities, including several denominations of Christianity and Islam, along with Judaism, and other faiths. The largest nationality groups among Arab Americans include Lebanese, Syrians, Palestinians, Egyptians, Iraqis and people from the Gulf states like Yemen and the United Arab Emirates. Socioeconomically, Arab Americans from families that immigrated earlier in the twentieth century tend to have higher educational attainment and income levels than the average American family, while the most recent immigrants have a wide range of socioeconomic class backgrounds.[44] But even these conclusions are tentative at best, because of the maddeningly difficult process of gathering reliable demographic data about Arab Americans.

In the 2000 and 2010 Censuses, individuals were counted as "Arab" if they self-reported any number of a long list of distinctive nationalities and ethnicities including "Arab, Egyptian, Iraqi, Jordanian, Lebanese, Middle Eastern, Moroccan, North African, Palestinian, Syrian, and so on."[45] This demonstrates a lack of understanding of the Middle Eastern American community by the Census—not all people who report "Middle Eastern" identity should be classified as Arab. For example, Druze Americans might report Jordan as their country of origin, and Chaldean Americans might name Iraq when asked for their nationality, but neither of these groups should necessarily be classified as Arabs. Similarly,

Iranian Americans might write "Middle Eastern" as their race on a survey, but they of course should not all be counted as Arabs. The Census and similar surveys fail to capture these nuances and can provide at best an inaccurate and incomplete snapshot of Middle Eastern American demographics. Among the hundreds of communities affected by this failure to recognize their distinctiveness are Assyrians, Copts, and Kurds. Simply assuming that most Iraqi Americans are Arab because of the demographics of Iraq ignores the reality that the socioeconomic, ethnic, and religious characteristics of these communities in the United States often approach the inverse of that found in their nations of origin. Minority populations in the Middle East, particularly in terms of religious identification, tend to emigrate in higher numbers.[46] Detailed demographic information about these communities is particularly difficult to find, since most surveys overlook these groups or, like the Census, simply count them as "Arabs".[47]

Furthermore, groups in the United States who trace their heritage to South Asia—a region usually defined to include Afghanistan, Bangladesh, Bhutan, India, Pakistan, Nepal and Sri Lanka—are also difficult to describe in general terms. Aside from the many national-origin groups elided under the racialized and panethnic South Asian label, there are several ethnic and national groups that are minorities in the region but are well represented in the United States. This includes Bengali, Kashmiri, Pashtun, and Punjabi American communities among others. In terms of religion, immigrants from this region belong to many denominations of Islam and Christianity, and there are Sikh, Parsi, and other religious identifications as well including many religions that have been collectivized under the Western-constructed Hindu identity.[48] Socioeconomically, South Asian Americans on average have one of the highest levels of education and income of any demographic group, but as with Arab Americans, the most recent (since 1980) immigrants from this region include many who are working class and relatively less well-off financially than those who immigrated earlier.[49]

Neither can Muslim Americans be easily categorized: there are Muslim Americans in every demographic group, and there are countless different Islamic traditions across various denominations. Simply counting the number of Muslims in the United States has proved quite a challenge. The Census does not collect data on religious identity. Recent surveys, conducted by polling the general public by telephone, place the overall number of Muslim Americans at about 2.75 million.[50] However, Muslim American advocates counted worshippers in mosques to get an estimate of "up to seven million," including non-mosque worshippers.[51] Despite the difficulty in obtaining reliable numbers, there is considerable recent literature describing a wide diversity of Muslim American demography in terms of ethnicity and nationality, socioeconomic class, geographic location, and political tendencies.[52]

There have been substantial changes in Muslim American demographics in a short time, in part due to significant immigration over the last twenty years. A 2011 survey reported that nearly two-thirds of immigrant Muslim Americans were first-generation immigrants, and more than 70% of them immigrated after 1990.[53] In terms of the proportions of Muslim Americans from various ethnic backgrounds, the same study found that the largest plurality of Muslim Americans, representing about four in ten, were born in the Middle East and North Africa, followed by people born in the United States (37%), and then South Asia (22%). The survey also reported that many Muslim Americans migrated from Europe, and it also found converts to the Islamic faith representing a vast range of heritages and backgrounds. Prior to the most recent migration of Muslims to the United States after 1990, the largest subgroup under the Muslim American umbrella were those Muslims who also identified as African Americans, groups sometimes referred to as "indigenous Muslims."[54] It appears that recent immigration has made the largest plurality of Muslim Americans "immigrant Muslims," including second- and third-generation immigrants.

Again, due to the sheer diversity of all the groups captured in the Middle Eastern racial category, any attempt to compile demographics is necessarily incomplete. Consider that looking at the demographics of immigrants from a subset of Muslim-majority nations, such as those in the Middle East, do little to elucidate the actual demographics of the many different Muslim American communities. Meanwhile, Muslim Americans from very populous countries like Indonesia and Malaysia, for example, are not included in this overview. Despite the shortcomings inherent in this exercise, I present some demographic data about the number of immigrants from Middle Eastern countries since 1965 in the tables that appear in this chapter.[55]

TABLE 2.1. Numbers of Immigrants Admitted to the United States from Selected Middle Eastern Countries, 1965–2014 *(in five-year intervals)*

Years	Egypt	Iran	Iraq	Israel	Jordan[a]	Lebanon	Syria	Turkey	Yemen[b]
1965–69	9,848	5,935	3,755	7,340	8,258	3,922	2,961	8,490	N/A
1970–74	15,197	12,901	7,244	9,733	13,474	10,131	5,199	9,567	N/A
1975–79	12,402	24,666	14,704	15,329	15,624	21,482	7,508	8,847	N/A
1980–84	14,241	56,799	13,569	16,720	15,226	17,764	9,546	11,919	1,895
1985–89	15,901	83,491	6,884	18,486	16,357	22,372	9,712	8,689	3,164
1990–94	20,243	84,042	17,458	21,868	21,475	27,265	14,108	11,528	8,082
1995–99	26,125	45,013	19,913	11,946	18,794	18,164	12,588	14,650	8,393
2000–04	23,395	49,730	21,269	17,373	18,848	19,016	12,509	16,115	7,778
2005–09	45,228	70,699	29,084	27,657	19,921	20,717	13,217	23,148	15,076
2010–14	47,515	66,398	90,062	20,295	21,218	15,689	15,260	21,026	16,596
Total	*230,095*	*499,674*	*223,942*	*166,747*	*169,195*	*176,522*	*102,608*	*133,979*	*60,984*

Note: N/A = Not Available

a Includes Arab Palestine from 1965 to 2003. Beginning in 2003, Palestine is not included and is placed under "unknown" in DHS's *Statistical Yearbook of the Immigration and Naturalization Service.*

b Prior to 1991, Yemen consisted of two separate countries (North and South Yemen) whose populations were summed up to indicate the number of immigrants for those years.

Sources: US INS (1969–1988); US DHS (2002–2014).

TABLE 2.2. Percentage of All US Immigrants from Egypt, Iran, Iraq, Israel, Jordan, Lebanon, Syria, Turkey, and Yemen, 1965–2014 *(in five-year intervals)*

Years	Total Immigrants Admitted to US	Total Immigrants from Selected Countries[a]	Percentage
1965–69	1,794,736	50,509	3%
1970–74	1,923,413	83,446	4%
1975–79	2,308,912	120,562	5%
1980–84	2,825,036	157,679	6%
1985–89	3,507,182	185,056	5%
1990–94	6,046,333	226,069	4%
1995–99	3,735,756	175,586	5%
2000–04	4,641,567	186,033	4%
2005–09	5,678,745	264,747	5%
2010–14	5,143,367	314,059	6%
Total	*37,605,047*	*1,763,746*	*5%*

Sources: US INS (1969–1988); US DHS (1996–2014).

a Yemen not included from 1965 to 1979 because data not available.

Table 2.1 shows the number of immigrants admitted from nine of the Middle Eastern nations that have sent the most migrants to the US. While it is difficult to generalize across the countries represented on this table, it is clear that the data here show a relatively constant rate of immigration from the Middle East with respect to total immigration into the United States since 1965. While the data do show some important variation driven by events in specific countries—Iran, for example, sent nearly twice as many immigrants in the five years after the 1979 revolution than it did in the five years prior—the overall amount of immigration from these countries has remained rather steady. Other than Iran, the only other exception to the pattern of a gentle rise in the number of migrants is Iraq, which sent 90,062 immigrants in 2010 to 2014, a sharp increase compared to the fewer than 30,000 who came in the two decades previous. All the other nations on the table have sent slightly more immigrants each year, on average, a difference that can likely be explained by general population increases. In terms of which countries have sent the most immigrants since 1965, Iran leads with nearly a half million, with Egypt and Iraq sending about a quarter-million each, and the rest of the countries on the table stand roughly equal in the 100,000 to 200,000 range, except for Yemen which has sent about 61,000 people since 1980.

Another way to look at the amount of immigration from these countries is to consider the proportion that they represent of all immigrants to the US. Table 2.2 shows that proportion remained mostly steady, between 3% and 6%, since 1965. Overall, the data show most of these countries have sent mostly consistent numbers of emigrants over time. Again, it is important to emphasize that even this large set of immigration data provides an unavoidably incomplete picture of the demographics of these communities. Several significant populations of Middle Eastern Americans are not well represented by this data, particularly Palestinian Americans, who are partially but not accurately represented in the immigration data from Israel, Jordan, and Lebanon. Still, the data suggest that prior descriptions of intermittent "waves" of Middle Eastern immigration between 1965 and 2014 are mostly unhelpful; immigration has been mostly steady throughout that period, with the notable exceptions of relatively high numbers of emigrants leaving Iran and Iraq in the late 1970s and early 2010s respectively.

TABLE 2.3. Numbers of Immigrants Admitted to the United States from Selected South Asian Countries, 1965–2014 *(in five-year intervals)*

Years	Afghanistan	Bangladesh	India	Pakistan
1965–69	N/A	N/A	18,327	2,704
1970–74	N/A	N/A	67,253	11,228
1975–79	929	2,921	90,334	17,282
1980–84	9,960	3,537	116,280	24,405
1985–89	14,154	7,934	137,499	31,495
1990–94	14,059	25,393	187,528	57,923
1995–99	5,525	37,641	184,397	61,850
2000–04	7,377	32,564	303,964	66,256
2005–09	15,897	66,609	332,058	87,110
2010–14	18,005	72,975	350,975	80,407
Total	*85,906*	*249,574*	*1,788,615*	*440,660*

Sources: US INS (1969–1988); US DHS (1996–2014).
Note: N/A = Not Available

TABLE 2.4. Percentage of All US Immigrants from Afghanistan, Bangladesh, India, and Pakistan, 1965–2014 *(in five-year intervals)*

Years	Total Immigrants Admitted to US	Immigrants from Selected Countries[a]	Percentage
1965–69	1,794,736	21,031	1%
1970–74	1,923,413	78,481	4%
1975–79	2,308,912	111,466	5%
1980–84	2,825,036	154,182	5%
1985–89	3,507,182	191,082	5%
1990–94	6,046,333	284,903	5%
1995–99	3,735,756	289,413	8%
2000–04	4,641,567	410,161	9%
2005–09	5,678,745	501,674	9%
2010–14	5,143,367	522,362	10%
Total	*37,605,047*	*2,564,755*	*7%*

Sources: US INS (1969–1988); US DHS (1996–2014).
a Afghanistan and Bangladesh not included from 1965 to 1974 because data not available.

Tables 2.3 and 2.4 focus on the South Asian countries that have sent the most immigrants to the US, and the data here tell a different story. First, the number of immigrants from just one country—India's 1.8 million—far outnumber those from Pakistan (441,000), Afghanistan (86,000), and Bangladesh (250,000). India has sent around one million more immigrants, or more than 56%. This is easily explained, of course, by the much larger population of India compared to its neighbors. But this discussion of sheer numbers underscores the sensitivity of conversations within these communities over the use of collective identity terms "Indian" and "South Asian," which I discuss in chapter 4. Some would argue that many of these immigrants, especially those from India, are not often caught up in the Middle Eastern racial category. Instead, they may be said to be incorporated in the Asian American racial category, or they may in fact have their own South Asian category. Discussions about where South Asians fit in the American racial landscape have been ongoing for decades, but frequent hate crimes targeting Sikhs and South Asians alongside Arabs and Muslims suggests that they may best be understood as included in the Middle Eastern racial category. The demographics data presented here will not provide much guidance for these discussions, except to emphasize the importance of these conversations, given that there are more Americans from these countries now than ever before. Table 2.4 shows that the relatively large numbers of immigrants from these four countries in recent decades generated a clear increase in the proportion of all US immigrants from South Asia. In 1965 to 1969, only about 1% of all immigrants admitted to the US were from South Asia, but by 1995 to 1999, the proportion increased to 5%, and it reached 10% by 2010 to 2014. This shows remarkable growth, and it means that South Asian immigrants made up 7% of all immigrants since 1965.

As seen in table 2.5, immigrants from the broadly conceived Middle East—including nations in North Africa, Southwest Asia, and South Asia—made up about 12% of all immigrants admitted to the US between 1965 and 2014. For the most part, the proportion of US immigration from this vast region remained consistent across those five decades, with slight dips in the early 1970s and early 1990s. The large number of immigrants from South Asia in 2010 to 2014 put the proportion to its peak, at 16%. More than one in every ten immigrants to the United States from 2010 to 2014 came from the broader Middle East.

TABLE 2.5. Percentage of All US Immigrants from Selected Middle Eastern and South Asian Countries,[a] 1965–2014 *(in five-year intervals)*

Years	Total Immigrants Admitted to US	Immigrants from Selected Countries[b,c]	Percentage
1965–69	1,794,736	71,540	4%
1970–74	1,923,413	161,927	8%
1975–79	2,308,912	232,028	10%
1980–84	2,825,036	311,861	11%
1985–89	3,507,182	376,138	11%
1990–94	6,046,333	510,972	8%
1995–99	3,735,756	464,999	12%
2000–04	4,641,567	596,194	13%
2005–09	5,678,745	766,421	13%
2010–14	5,143,367	836,421	16%
Total	*37,605,047*	*4,328,501*	*12%*

Sources: US INS (1969–1988); US DHS (1996–2014).
a Afghanistan, Bangladesh, Egypt, India, Iran, Iraq, Israel, Jordan, Lebanon, Pakistan, Syria, Turkey, and Yemen.
b Afghanistan and Bangladesh not included from 1965 to 1974 because data not available.
c Yemen not included from 1965 to 1979 because data not available.

Of course, even though immigration from these regions has re-mained generally constant since 1965, many Middle Eastern Americans were born in the United States over this time period as well. This means that the Middle Eastern American population includes a large num-ber of second-, third-, and fourth-generation immigrants, born in the United States. The best estimate of the proportion of Middle Eastern Americans who were born outside the United States comes from the American Community Survey (ACS); see the data presented in table 2.6. In 2014, ACS data shows that about 43% of Arab Americans were foreign-born, compared to 70% of South Asians, and 53% of non-Arab Middle Easterners (like Iranian and Turkish populations, for example). These proportions show that a large number of recent, first-generation immigrants have joined with a substantial number of American-born, second-, third-, and later-generation immigrants across these many communities.

TABLE 2.6. Population Size of Selected Middle Eastern American Groups, with Percentage of Foreign-Born, 2014

Ancestry/Race[a]		Population	% Foreign-Born
Arab		1,685,660	43%
	"Arab/Arabic"	322,853	52%
	Egyptian	239,010	57%
	Iraqi	143,397	75%
	Jordanian	80,120	50%
	Lebanese	506,470	22%
	Moroccan	101,211	51%
	Palestinian	122,533	38%
	Syrian	170,066	31%
Non-Arab		1,376,372	53%
	Armenian	461,076	44%
	Assyrian/Chaldean/Syriac	107,056	58%
	Iranian	452,815	64%
	Israeli	148,514	45%
	Turkish	206,911	52%
Total Arab and Non-Arab		*3,062,032*	*47%*
South Asian		4,200,435	70%
	Afghan	97,865	64%
	Bangladeshi	160,029	74%
	Indian	3,491,052	71%
	Pakistani	451,489	67%

a The population numbers of Arab and Non-Arab groups was determined from ancestry data in Census Bureau 2014a, and the South Asian numbers come from population profile data in Census Bureau 2014b.

This massive, albeit necessarily incomplete, set of demographic data is complex and hard to sum up in any general way. One thing is certain: the data show that there is endless diversity represented in the Middle Eastern racial category. New immigrants from North Africa, Southwest Asia, and South Asia have constantly arrived since 1965, providing large increases in the number of people in many of these communities. With that increase in size came even more diversity, as religious, ethnic, cultural, and national-origin subgroups continued to grow and develop. The diversity in terms of socioeconomic class, the number of languages spoken, and the large array of religious faiths, denominations, and theologies represented across Middle Eastern American communities cannot be overstated.

Making Race: Centrifugal and Centripetal Forces

It is difficult to accept that mere ideology could obscure such vast diversity and effectively lump together people from places as different in culture and history as, for instance, Egypt, Iran, and Pakistan. But that is the disturbing power of race in America.

Most new immigrants to the United States, especially those from non-Western European nations, find themselves understandably bewildered by the racial culture and politics of the United States. Many first-generation immigrants are surprised or even incredulous at the idea that Americans overlook their ethnic and cultural heritage and ascribe them with some inexplicable racial identity. As Ronald Takaki famously observed, "There are no Asians in Asia;" yet Chinese, Filipino, Japanese, Korean, Laotian, Vietnamese, and immigrants from many other ethnic and national-origin groups find themselves called by the same name: "Asian."[56] In much the same way, immigrants with heritage in Egypt, India, Iraq, Iran, Lebanon, Libya, and Yemen also find themselves called by the same name: "Middle Eastern."

Despite this racial lumping, immigrant communities have often formed cultural, ethnic, and national associations, asserting their specific heritage and ignoring (or openly defying) the racial identity ascribed to them. Asserted identities for immigrants can stem from the village of their ancestors, or from nationality, ethnicity, or religion—there are many sources of pride and heritage. Historical or political animosities between ethnic and national communities often reinforce the many divisions among different immigrant communities, making them even more keen to stand apart from the collectivized racial group.

Divisions like these, which I call "centrifugal forces," contribute to the formation of distinct social institutions and networks defined by ethnicity and nationality.[57] There are specifically Lebanese American cultural associations, churches, and mosques with predominantly Lebanese wor-shippers, and restaurants, bookstores, cafes, and other institutions with mostly Lebanese clientele. The same can be said of many Middle Eastern American subgroups. These are sustainable communities that have great networks of ethnic, national, and cultural institutions: among them are Berbers, Chaldeans, Kashmiris, Palestinians, Pashtuns, Persians, Turks, and many, many more. While many of these subgroups have no ani-mosity toward the others in the larger Middle Eastern American group, there are some communities within the Middle Eastern American ra-cial umbrella that have a great deal of bad blood between them. Thus, "centrifugal forces" exist, in effect pushing apart the communities, and pushing back against their common racialization. These individuals and groups would not easily accept any notion of a common identity.

In the 1960s and 1970s, many prominent social and political advocacy organizations for immigrant communities followed these kinds of divi-sions. Rather than having a multi-ethnic or even panethnic base, many of these organizations were based on a particular ethnic or national-origin identity, like the Japanese American Citizens League (JACL), the Organization of Chinese Americans (OCA), and the Mexican Ameri-can Legal Defense and Education Fund (MALDEF). For Middle Eastern American communities, there was the Association of Arab American University Graduates (AAUG), the National Association of Arab Ameri-cans (NAAA), and some Muslim American and South Asian organi-zations that advocated on behalf of a growing number of immigrants from the broader Middle East. These organizations took up the cause of improving rights for their communities by challenging discrimina-tory policies and beliefs. As social exclusion, economic isolation, and violent harassment based on race persisted despite the post–civil rights era promise of an enlightened America, these organizations took on in-creasingly important roles.

There is an inevitable central tension in these networks of ethnic- and nationality-based advocacy because of the power of race. The core of racist practices and beliefs is the essentialist idea of homogeneity—that is, the notion that people in any given racial group are fundamentally "all the same." Regardless of whether they come from Vietnam, China, or Japan, racist thinking concludes, all of "those Asians" have inescap-able traits that make them all equally dangerous, inassimilable, and unwanted. Similarly, Lebanese, Iranian, and Pashtun Americans have little in common culturally, but according to racist ideology, they all have the same identity and the same unwanted traits.

The pressures from discrimination, hate crimes, and racist rhetoric that falls on all of these distinct communities can act as "centripetal forces," pushing otherwise separate groups closer together. People with different cultures, languages, and religions often recognize that they face similar mistreatment based on their immutable physical appearance. To adapt, some advocates raise consciousness about race-based oppression by talking about how the problem affects all of these different communities. Some advocates will see tremendous advantages of strength in numbers if several communities successfully join together in struggle. They would achieve significant efficiency by pooling resources in coalitions of advocacy organizations. Ascribed racial identity can thus act as part of a powerful incentive to form race-based coalitions—and sometimes even camaraderie or kinship—across deep divisions along ethnic, cultural, and religious lines.

Many civil rights advocacy organizations harnessed "centripetal force" in the civil rights struggles of the twentieth century to stunning success. In fact, so successful was this model by the 1960s that race-based coalition building became established as an effective, legitimate, and mainstream method for political advocacy in the United States.[58] Black activists' successes led advocates in other racialized communities to adopt similar strategies to build political power.[59] In addition to the Civil Rights Act and Voting Rights Act, this strategy achieved reparations for Japanese internment and the expansion of affirmative action programs to Black Americans, Native Americans, Asian Americans, and Latin@s.

The strategic choice of activists to join together in race-based coalitions was not just a civil rights tactic. It had the profound effect of codifying new racial identities. The centripetal force of collectivization has been a necessary—but not a sufficient—cause for the recognition and reification of racial identity categories. Only when the ascribed identity was asserted in civil rights coalitions did racial identity categories like Asian American and Native American take hold and gain mainstream acceptance.[60] When these communities saw through the racial paradox, and co-opted the identity category they had been ascribed with, they engaged in a multifaceted and powerful racial project. They played critical roles in the formation of race.

Racial Formation

Race is a social process that makes reference to biology. It is a socially derived classification for human bodies. Race changes based on social context. It exists because of the behaviors and actions of every individual; it is simultaneously a feature embedded within social structures. Race can be observed affecting moment-to-moment experiences in the tiny microcosms of intimate relationships. Yet it also affects the promulgation of large-scale programs and policies that take shape only as decades pass. Racial formation theory, developed by Michael Omi and Howard Winant, provides some analytical tools for grappling with these complexities. The authors describe race as a *master category*, "a fundamental concept that has profoundly shaped, and continues to shape, the history, polity, economic structure, and culture of the United States."[61]

To explain how race is both part of individual lives and also part of social structures, Omi and Winant present the concept of a *racial project*. A racial project is any effort that links racial ideology to the distribution of resources. Countless racial projects coexist all the time. Racial categories are formed by the ongoing, constant reproduction of racial projects. As resources are deployed based on racial ideology, race comes to life as a cultural and institutional reality. As they unfold, racial projects draw from and add to history while projecting the legacy of racial divisions into the present and future. Racial projects, in short, serve as the building blocks of racial formation, the social process by which "racial identities are created, lived out, transformed, and destroyed."[62] The racial project is a versatile concept that can explain how race simultaneously affects individual people in their daily lives while it shapes social institutions at the same time.

Taking up a few concrete examples of racial projects—efforts that use racial ideology to distribute resources—can make the mysterious process of racial formation more understandable. First, let us consider an example of racial discourse. Casual (or formal) utterances about racial groups contribute to millions of racial projects every day. As friends and colleagues have conversations, they breathe meaning into racial concepts, and they distribute intangible resources like legitimacy and re-spect, or fear and loathing. Consider a statement like this: "White people can't dance." This seemingly simple statement, maybe part of a joke, nec-essarily recognizes and legitimizes the existence of a socially constructed racial category: White. It references history by reinforcing an old saw, a well-known and ridiculous stereotype. It projects that history into the present and future. When many millions of similar statements are made every single day, they have the collective effect of perpetuating and rein-forcing race, and giving real social power to the race concept.

Another example of a discursive racial project comes in a statement like this one: "I get nervous whenever I see a Muslim on an airplane." This statement also recognizes a racial category, even though it uses a religious term to describe it. The term "Muslim" in this context conjures a racial image. Visually recognizing that someone you do not person-ally know is a Muslim is sometimes possible without relying on racial cues, for example by noticing a certain type of religious artifact or attire, such as prayer beads or a *taqiyah* cap. In the vast majority of American conversations, however, this statement is equivalent to "I get nervous whenever I see a Middle Eastern person on an airplane." Expressions like these not only draw from and reinforce the racial image of what a Middle Eastern American supposedly looks like, but they also connect that racial image to stereotypes about terrorism in general. When mil-lions of similar statements are made all the time, they collectively act as a discursive racial project that references and perpetuates the ugly stereo-types of Orientalism. Statements like this pull all of that historical ballast into the present. In fact, this statement should be described as bigoted, in part because Middle Eastern Americans have long been subjected to prejudice and discrimination on the basis of these stereotypes. So even in the context of a casual conversation, this kind of statement can prop-erly be described as contributing to racism.

Defining racism has never been easy. Today, in colloquial use, racism is synonymous with bigotry or prejudice. Someone is "a racist" if they make a statement about Muslims on airplanes, or if they use an offen-sive epithet, hold bigoted views, or engage in overtly hateful acts. The use of the term in this way stems from a presumption that racism only manifests in individuals. In this limited view, racism in our society is the product of "a few bad apples," those anachronistic bigots who cling to outdated beliefs about the superiority of White people or the inferiority of certain racial groups. This fails to capture how racism plays out "unintentionally" through social and institutional factors. Bigotry and prejudice—while sometimes properly called racist—are not necessarily part of what creates the durable racial inequality and discrimination that is often called structural racism.

In Omi and Winant's terms, racism happens when a racial project "creates or reproduces structures of domination based on racial significations and identities."[63] When someone says they feel uncomfortable when seeing a Muslim on an airplane, they are reproducing a structure of domination: the false and racist idea that Middle Easterners are likely to engage in violence or terrorism. Discursive racial projects—the stories we tell one another, the things we say in casual conversation, as well as the rhetoric amplified in mass media—all contribute to racism, but racism does not begin or end with statements like these.

The crux of structural racism becomes evident only when examining the effects of a constellation of factors, including discursive elements along with policies and practices. Structural racism results from the amplifying combination of hate crimes, bigoted statements, microaggressions, and governmental and corporate policies that—intentionally or not—reinforce racial disparities.[64] If a policy distributes resources toward dominant groups and away from subordinated ones, it can be properly described as racist—even if the distribution along racial lines was unintended by the architects of the policy.

One such racist project involves the security screening at airports, provided by the federal Transportation Security Administration (TSA). More than thirty current and former TSA officers blew the whistle in 2013 on "racial profiling" in the TSA's so-called behavior detection program that targeted "not only Middle Easterners but also Blacks, Hispanics and other minorities."[65] Three years later, a TSA manager revealed that he was instructed by a supervisor to single out Somali Americans traveling through the Minneapolis airport.[66] These officers described widespread use of racial criteria used to determine which airport passengers to subject to additional screening. This neatly fits the definition of racism: a project that distributes resources (in this case, extra security screening) based on racial significations in a way that reinforces stereotypes and oppression. The TSA has repeatedly emphasized that it does not tolerate racial profiling. The agency conducted its own investigation in 2013, which it claimed found no evidence of racial profiling.[67] Nevertheless, Middle Eastern American airline passengers have for decades complained about discriminatory treatment at airport security checkpoints. That thirty officers stepped forward to call out the "behavior detection" program as racist gave weight to these stories as more than just anecdotes. The belief that the TSA engages in racial profiling is so pervasive that comedians frequently make jokes about having trouble getting through airport security like Ahmed Ahmed's: "I just show up in a G-string."[68]

The role of state agencies, like the TSA, in distributing resources illustrates how racial projects often intersect with state power. Omi and Winant describe the state as the key site of racial formation, where political struggles over resources combine with racial thinking in important and tremendously complex ways. The *racial state* is the battleground where the ongoing definitions and re-definitions of race push and pull against the levers of state power.[69] State policies and practices codify racial thinking, and they do so through political processes that have moved on the scale between despotism and democracy throughout American history. Political actors, by definition, make collective demands to drive resources toward themselves and their interests and away from rivals. Race tumbles around throughout this process, always there, unstable yet constant.

Advocacy Organizations and Race

The type of actor at the fulcrum of this race-making process is the advocacy organization. These are organized groups that propel collective demands that conflict with the interests of others.[70] Advocacy organizations working on behalf of marginalized communities have long been at the center of the work to protect and expand civil rights in the United States, usually by engaging with the racial state.

Using identity—racial, ethnic, religious, national-origin, gender, etc.—as a unifying "rallying cry" to hold together an advocacy organization is so commonplace that it is taken for granted today. Examples include NAACP, MALDEF, JACL, AAUG, and others. It is easy to overlook the fact that using identity as the *raison d'être* for an advocacy organization is a relatively recent innovation in democratic societies. In the past, only common belief in an issue or ideology served as a reliable cause to hold together an organization. The earliest advocacy organizations rallied around such issues as free speech, the abolition of slavery, collective bargaining for workers, and the extension of the franchise to women.[71] The innovation of using identity as the uniting factor in bringing together an advocacy organization emerged mainly from the Niagara Movement in 1905. Through the work of those Black scholars and activists to mobilize resources motivated by a common identity, that pathbreaking organization not only advocated for civil rights, but for the fundamental concept of Black unity. Identity-based organizations challenge popular conceptions of race while orchestrating changes in how resources—writ large—are distributed by the state. Whether lobbying for new housing or education; for changes in zoning ordinances, voting procedures, or tax reductions; or against a military intervention, American advocacy organizations have made use of—and changed—the social construction of race in profound ways.

Anti-slavery abolitionist organizations of the nineteenth century provide a good example, even though these organizations were not based on the identity of their members. After the constitutionally mandated ban on legislation regarding slavery expired in the early 1800s, abolitionist organizations ramped up their campaign for change. Abolition advocates, White and Black, were partly responsible for the ratification of the Thirteenth, Fourteenth, and Fifteenth Amendments to the Constitution alongside other limited successes of the Reconstruction era that followed the Civil War. Abolitionists generated sustained advocacy campaigns carried out by dedicated organizations that utilized displays of "worthiness, unity, numbers, and commitment."[72] By the turn of the twentieth century, advocacy campaigns like these became common in the United States.

Social movements for civil rights reached new peaks during the struggle against Jim Crow in the early twentieth century. Civil rights organizations mobilized thousands of volunteers to engage in consciousness raising activities, direct action, and careful lobbying and persuasion of officials at all levels of government. The movement victories in the 1950s and 1960s redefined race and changed the way Americans engaged in civil rights advocacy.

Innovative advocacy on behalf of racialized minority communities during the 1960s created new norms that defined what was appropriate for political advocacy.[73] Previously, social identity served mainly as a kind of side effect to organizing; workers wanted better wages and safety on the job, and the pride that came with identifying as a union member grew over time. The issues were what initially united the workers, not their identity as workers.

Through the civil rights campaigns of the twentieth century, racial unity became a legitimate organizing principle. Springing forth from the Niagara Movement, the National Association for the Advancement of Colored People (NAACP) brought together people in large part because they were people of color—a radical and controversial idea when the group was founded in 1909. By midcentury, identity-based civil rights advocacy organizations became a thoroughly mainstream conduit for the political expression of oppressed communities bounded by a socially constructed racial identity.

Civil rights activism united Black people from a wide variety of backgrounds—ethnic, regional, national, religious, socioeconomic class—under the umbrella of Black identity. This racial identity was as-cribed to people of the myriad nations, cultures, and religious groups across the African continent during the fifteenth and sixteenth cen-turies, a process that brutally and violently denied other identities. By the seventeenth century, few Americans or Europeans questioned the perceived existence of a firm line between the White and Black races. Race was a "master status" in the United States, where Yoruba, Igbo, Luba, and Kanuri were all considered as Black.[74] These Black people were subjected to inhuman oppression under the racial logics that lay at the foundation of the European colonialization of the Americas.

Even the savage oppression of slavery and its succeeding peculiar in-stitutions could not prevent the struggle for democracy and civil rights. The persistence of advocacy organizations shows that as a hegemonic force, racial oppression has always been vulnerable, incomplete, and contested. The centuries-old social construction of the Black race made it possible for civil rights advocates in the 1900s to *rearticulate* Black identity for organizing and recruitment into activism. Racial rearticula-tion, the process of "discursive reorganization or reinterpretation of ide-ological themes and interests already present in subjects' consciousness," was key to the Black civil rights movement.[75] Advocates rearticulated Black identity as a point of pride and as a call for coalition building.

Working at the grassroots level, organizations like the NAACP, the Southern Christian Leadership Conference (SCLC), the Student Non-violent Coordinating Committee (SNCC), and the Congress of Racial Equality (CORE) leveraged racial identity as the basis of their membership and constituency. Black churches acted as sites of mobilization where organizations could maintain local roots while establishing broad networks of staff and volunteers.[76] People of all races worked with these organizations, but their primary, defining identity was that of Black organizations working for Black civil rights.

Of course, the solidarity provided by racial identity can never result in total unity. Differences and disagreements abounded. Strategies, tactics, and goals varied widely. Some agitated for a separatist Black nationalism or for a "return to Africa." Many other groups proposed incremental but meaningful reforms, and a few made the case for an armed uprising leading to wholescale social revolution. Despite these vast differences, nearly all Black civil rights advocacy in this era relied upon a rearticulated Black identity to build grassroots support and draw attention to their cause.

Black identity thus enabled advocates to build large political coalitions that otherwise would not have been possible. Political coalitions bring together groups with similar interests in cooperation. Coalitions bring clear strategic advantages for political projects of all kinds: coordinated tactics and strategies, an efficient division of labor, and greater numbers of supporters. Coalitions can also generate the all-important intangible resource of political legitimacy. But coalition building is difficult. Coalitions require sacrifice, most notably with regard to priorities and autonomy.

Many Black activists rejected the idea of Black unity. In other words, even the centuries-old Black identity was not sufficient by itself to bring about the formation of durable political coalitions. Advocates had to actively build and maintain partnerships that relied upon Black solidarity. Leaders and community members made constant calls for various groups in Black America to join together—a necessary step to rearticulate the ascribed Black identity as a basis for political action. During this period, Black Americans experienced increasing political clout in part because so many Americans shared an ascribed Black identity.

It is impossible to overstate the significance of the work done by civil rights advocates as they produced the centripetal forces, maintained the coalitions, and succeeded in bringing real changes to culture, policy, and politics. The result of these efforts drew from old racial projects, those that created the oppressive Black identity and all of the dehumanizing stereotypes that came with it, making the identity new again by recasting Blackness, co-opting it as a source of pride and power.

The establishment of Black unifying cultural traditions and Black political and social institutions after Reconstruction contributed to the idea that Black Americans might join together on the basis of a common racial identity to seek redress for the problems of racism. The call for unity from Black advocates took on many forms, including one-on-one conversations between pastors and churchgoers, speeches at rallies, quiet conversations around dinner tables, among organizers of Black pride festivals, and through endless forms of artistic expression. "Lift Ev'ry Voice and Sing," the poem written in 1900 by NAACP activist James Weldon Johnson, became the "Black National Anthem" that was (and still is) sung to promote and emphasize Black unity.[77] For decades, leading Black advocates made direct appeals to the common racial identity while trying to build coalitions among disparate groups. Famously, Malcolm X wrote to Rev. Martin Luther King, Jr. in July 1963, urging a "United Front involving all Negro factions . . . in order to seek a common solution to a common problem caused by a Common Enemy." Meanwhile, Black advocates took up Steve Biko's proclamation: "Black is Beautiful." Nina Simone sang Master Wel's "To Be Young, Gifted, and Black." Despite countless differences separating Black communities— centrifugal forces that pushed them apart—the potential for political power made available by a unified racial identity carried enough centripetal force to enable Black advocates to sustain various coalitions of advocacy organizations along the long journey to meaningful change. In a real way, these coalitions rearticulated and reshaped race—the activism recast Blackness itself.

Race-Based Solutions to Race-Based Problems

Following World War II, the United States moved to redefine itself in opposition to its superpower rival, the ostensibly intolerant and insular

Soviet Union. Partly in response to this shift, the large, race-based coalitions made possible by Black identity successfully made the moral claim that a truly free United States would not tolerate race-based discrimination. Direct action protests organized by advocacy organizations made it impossible for federal policymakers to ignore Jim Crow segregation any longer, and they responded with reforms like the Civil Rights Act of 1964 and the Voting Rights Act of 1965. "Separate but equal" segregation policies were dismantled. The seemingly intractable system supporting Jim Crow segregation was swept away.

The defeat of the race-based *de jure* segregation known as Jim Crow was somewhat ironic in that it came through the provision of resources along racial lines. The Civil Rights Act, for instance, required official recognition of racial identity. If one was denied employment or access to public institutions based on his or her identity as a Black American, the Civil Rights Act provided restitution. To enforce the law, the federal government (and many state governments) directed newly empowered civil rights bureaus to bring lawsuits against individuals and corporations who engaged in discriminatory behavior. In some cases, the state brought police and even military resources to bear to combat entrenched racism. Thus, the allocation of state and federal resources under the Civil Rights Act can be understood as a "race-conscious" remedy to the problem of racism. This was a race-based solution to a race-based problem.

The Voting Rights Act of 1965 went even further, as it was designed not only to stop ongoing discrimination but also to prevent future racial discrimination. By designating areas of the country with a history of discrimination for added scrutiny and enhanced voting protections administered by federal agents, the Voting Rights Act required federal agencies to proactively prevent race-based discrimination. Some areas of the country, those with a history of excluding non-White voters, had to comply with even stricter requirements. This effectively allocated resources—legal, administrative, and even military—to Black communities. This radical redistribution of resources finally provided many Black Americans with reliable access to the ballot box for the first time.

In short, by the 1960s, Black Americans not only wielded significant political power for the first time since Reconstruction, but they also inaugurated a new era where identity-based organizations could legitimately stand in the mainstream political arena.

Asian, Latin@, and Native American Civil Rights

The Civil Rights and Voting Rights Acts did not cleanse American society of racism and discrimination, but this new era was nevertheless marked by a shift toward multiculturalism that haltingly invited the participation of immigrants and people of color in American culture and politics. Reforms to blatantly racist immigration policies meant that non-Western European migrants could come to the United States far easier than before. Simultaneously, cultural diversity emerged for the first time as a point of pride for most Americans, reflecting the nation's commitment to a life free from the oppression that supposedly characterized so-called Second and Third World nations. Many cultural clubs, schools, religious institutions, and political advocacy organizations that represented immigrant communities also emerged in this atmosphere.

The large majority of new immigrants from non-European nations found themselves bewildered by the racial culture and politics of their adoptive country. Many first-generation immigrants were surprised to be included in a broad racial category that did not at all match their self-identity. Chinese, Japanese, Korean, Laotian, Filipino, Vietnamese, and immigrants from many other ethnic and national-origin groups found themselves ascribed with the same name: "Oriental" (the early 1900s vernacular for Asian).

Identity-based civil rights organizations among Japanese, Chinese, and other Asian American nationality groups emerged as highly active during the mid-twentieth century. They advocated on a wide variety of issues including foreign policy, reparations and redress for Japanese Americans interned during World War II, and in favor of affirmative action to counteract discrimination affecting their communities. Many of these advocates recognized the advantages of "panethnic" coalitions, including greater numbers provided by unity, and access to the moral claim that racism is abhorrent. Their "standing claim" to legitimacy was similar to that of Blacks: Asian Americans should be understood as a racial group, and discrimination against members of this group was therefore racist and morally wrong.[78] This standing claim, in combination with the centripetal force of ascribed identity, provided Asian American advocates with a powerful argument for unity and a recruitment strategy.

Panethnic Asian American civil rights advocates successfully brought together several ethnic, national, and religious communities, leading to the eventual recognition of the rearticulated racial identity "Asian American," both in the communities themselves and in mainstream popular culture. By the 1980s, Asian American organizations were a significant force in national politics, expanding affirmative action provisions to Asian American communities. In 1988, after decades of concerted advocacy efforts by Asian American organizations, the United States apologized for Japanese internment during World War II and paid monetary reparations to former internees.

The racialization of Asians as a homogenous group contributed to bigotry and hate crimes; it is therefore remarkable that advocates were able to co-opt and rearticulate this identity as an effective organizing tool for Asian American civil rights. This achievement required the deployment of panethnicity, defined as the "development of bridging organizations and solidarities among subgroups of ethnic collectivities that are often seen as homogenous by outsiders."[79] By contributing to racial projects, panethnic organizations and activism can result from or help to create a racial rearticulation. Indeed, all racial identity categories are at root panethnic categories, and they are all brought into being by a system of racial oppression. Omi and Winant explain, "Panethnicity is a type of racialization; it is not without internal tension and conflict; it is often uneven and incomplete; it often does not liquidate ethnic difference but subsumes it; above all, it is a product of racial despotism."[80]

Dina Okamoto shows that the racial formation of Asian American panethnic identity was made possible by the social and political conditions among these communities between the 1960s and 2000s. The White majority's ascription of people of Asian descent into a single racial category was just one of these conditions. Okamoto observes that advocates pulled together communities that already had a large number of common interests despite ethnic and cultural differences. Some of those shared political interests stemmed from racial discrimination. Okamoto describes how the conditions of "racial segregation, ethnic organizing, and active leaders—can facilitate the panethnic organizing process . . . [and redefine] race by creating new opportunities that span ethnic lines, break down racial stereotypes, and challenge unfair treatment."[81] The conditions that facilitated the development of a panethnic

Asian American identity included shared experiences of discrimination, segregation in terms of geography and niches in the labor market, and the efforts of activists and advocates in Chinese, Japanese, Korean, and other communities to bring these disparate groups into coalitions.

Asian American advocates overcame the "centrifugal forces" of ethnic difference, but dividing lines still remained among Asian Americans, especially in terms of cultural, linguistic, religious, class, generational status, and political divides. None of these divisions disappeared when the racial category Asian American was recognized, but advocates were still able to rearticulate and establish an Asian American identity despite these divisions. The question that remains is whether Asian Americans were a unique case of racial rearticulation in the twentieth century, or if the work of Asian American advocates represents an option available to other civil rights advocates working in similarly situated, racially marked communities.

Yen Le Espiritu and David Lopez find that four panethnic groups—Asian Americans, Native Americans, Latin@s, and South Asian Americans (their term was "Indo Americans")—had the most "potential" for developing what they called "ethnic change."[82] Though considerable differences distinguish these various panethnic efforts, the factors that contribute to this potential are similar to the factors observed by Joane Nagel and Dina Okamoto.[83] Their analysis finds that each of the four groups had a different configuration of "structural" and "cultural" differences that might contribute to or detract from the development of panethnicity: language, religion, physical appearance, socioeconomic class, generation, and geography. For example, Espiritu and Lopez see a low degree of phenotypical variation among Asian Americans and Native Americans but a high level of "color" variation among Latin@s and South Asian Americans. They also observe some panethnic organizing in each of these four communities and note that Latin@s were "clearly the least panethnic," despite having the strongest cultural connections in terms of a shared language and religion. Because the "dominant society" did not "deem them a race apart," Latin@s struggled to forge panethnic coalitions. Meanwhile, they find that Asian Americans and South Asian Americans built several panethnic organizations. Overall, they conclude that structural conditions like class background and ascription by the wider society as a racial group have a greater influence on the development of panethnicity than cultural factors like common language or even common political goals.[84]

Along similar lines, Joane Nagel documents a threefold increase in the number of Americans reporting "an American Indian" race between the 1960 and 1990 US Census surveys. She argues that this "ethnic renewal" was attributable to a combination of federal policy, American political trends, and the activism of Native American leaders. As with Asian American leaders, these "American Indian" activists drew inspiration from the Black struggle for civil rights. They founded organizations that sought to bring together people from a wide range of ethnic, national-origin, and religious backgrounds—Lakota, Iroquois, Shoshone, and many other groups. Nagel describes the effect of direct-action protests like the occupation of Alcatraz Island, the siege at Wounded Knee, and the sit-in at the federal Bureau of Indian Affairs building in Washington:

> Individuals of Indian ancestry became more willing to identify themselves as Indians, whether or not such identification was a strategy to acquire a share of real or putative land claims awards or other possible ethnically allocated rewards (such as scholarships, mineral royalties, employment preference). It was in this atmosphere of increased resources, ethnic grievances, ethnic pride, and civil rights activism that Red Power burst on the scene in the late 1960s and galvanized a generation of Native Americans.

The success of Native Americans in gaining legitimacy as an officially recognized racial group led to a surge of "Red Power" in the 1960s and 1970s. The disruption of the federal "termination" and relocation policies in the mid-twentieth century, and the expansion of some affirmative action benefits to Native communities, were key movement victories. Even though organizations like the American Indian Movement and the National Indian Youth Council did not win monetary concessions or other tangible benefits, Nagel shows that the recognition and cultural idea of the racial, panethnic "Indian" identity were ongoing and sustainable. Even individuals who did not participate in activism were able to embrace this identity category; Nagel observes that "narrative accounts of both activists and non-activists . . . suggest that social movements exert a wider impact, affecting the attitudes of nonparticipants as well, though to a lesser extent." Nagel concludes that the ability of Native Americans to construct an identity category and engage in activism to improve their lives "reveals the role of human agency in individual and collective redefinition and empowerment."[85]

In the latter half of the twentieth century, during the post–civil rights era, panethnic, race-based coalitions built by advocates accomplished a great deal. These communities rearticulated racial identity and used it to win significant victories for civil rights.

Civil Rights and Colorblindness

Looking back at the patterns of civil rights advocacy in the United States during the twentieth century serves as a reminder of how race has exerted profound social forces throughout American history. Racist discrimination served as a necessary but not sufficient factor for advocates as they built advocacy coalitions that leveraged racial identity to gain new strategic avenues. The key component for all racial groups recognized today in the "ethno-racial pentagon"—Asian, Black, Latin@, Native American, White—has been the dedication of community leaders working in advocacy organizations. These advocates developed sophisticated strategies that recognized the impact of racial formation, co-opted ascribed racial identities, and forged coalitions. The rise of so-called identity politics transformed American political culture, establishing a new pattern for advocacy on behalf of racially marked communities in the "post–civil rights era."

Whether this pattern of advocacy holds in the case of Middle Eastern American advocates remains an open question. The last decade of the twentieth century brought significant changes to the political terrain around civil rights. Namely, serious threats to racial justice emerged in the rise of *colorblindness ideology* and the growing power of the New Right.

According to the now-dominant colorblind ideology, classifying people by race is always a "mistake." The way forward, according to this thinking, requires acting as though race does not exist—acting as though we cannot see color, like we cannot see race. The thinking is that as soon as everyone acts "colorblind," then race will cease to exist as a social force. The tremendous popularity of this view motivates countless racial projects. They extend from everyday conversations, where many Americans carefully avoid explicitly mentioning race in polite company, to political rhetoric and programs designed to prevent discrimination. Supreme Court Chief Justice John Roberts perhaps summed up the prevailing sentiment best when he famously wrote in an opinion about affirmative action: "The way to stop discrimination on the basis of race is to stop discriminating on the basis of race."[86] In other words, the only effective civil rights program is one that does not recognize race. Drawing from this reasoning, American courts have, over the past several decades, invalidated many race-based policy solutions to race-based problems.

Omi and Winant note that colorblindness was at one time perceived as a progressive, even radically progressive, position. After all, many civil rights campaigners, including Dr. Martin Luther King, Jr., believed that in the enlightened future, people would no longer recognize race. Is this not the future that we all hope for?

Recently, however, many scholars have critiqued colorblindness as naïve at best and counterproductive at worst. Neil Gotanda examined the regressive implications of colorblindness as an imperative in American civil rights jurisprudence. He found that "a colorblind interpretation of the Constitution legitimates, and thereby maintains, the social, economic, and political advantages that Whites hold over other Americans."[87] Similarly, Claire Jean Kim, in her detailed history of Black-Korean conflicts in New York, decries colorblindness as a tool to extend racial oppression by obfuscation and distraction:

> Colorblind talk furthers racial power not through the direct articulation of racial differences but rather by obscuring the operation of racial power, protecting it from challenge, and permitting ongoing racialization via racially coded methods. In all of these ways, colorblind talk helps to maintain White dominance in an era of formal race neutrality.[88]

Despite these problems, Omi and Winant insist that colorblindness should not be completely rejected. Even though colorblindness today is "an ideological framework for the effacement of race consciousness," they suggest that it might also serve as a "vehicle for *deepening and variegating race consciousness.*" They acknowledge that the New Right and other civil rights opponents rearticulated—appropriated—the concept of colorblindness, thereby "turning it into a cheap simulacrum of the movement's ideal, a parody of the 'dream.'" Omi and Winant challenge twenty-first-century civil rights advocates to once again *re-appropriate* the concept of colorblindness to further the goal of racial equality. Somehow reclaiming the dream of colorblind integration as a progressive goal might allow for a sea change in racial thinking:

> . . . such that a new paradigm of race based *both* on difference and solidarity, *both* on particularity and equality, might emerge. We would certainly not want to call such an ideal "colorblind," but we would expect it to include the possibility of overcoming racial difference, at least in part, through a creative type of consciousness and action, a radical racial pragmatism.[89]

Omi and Winant see potential advantages in using some elements of colorblindness in progressive, anti-racist work. This "radical racial pragmatism" requires a sophisticated understanding of race as something that is produced and reproduced through everyday racial projects. Using that knowledge in civil rights advocacy might enable a powerful new civil rights movement, one that recognizes racial difference when necessary to achieve reforms, but pushes an ideal of colorblind acceptance at the same time.

The discussion among scholars and advocates around colorblindness in the early twenty-first century reflects the debate around "protective panethnicity" and "strategic essentialism" from the 1990s.[90] This is the well-established pattern from the twentieth century, when aggrieved communities strategically accepted the racial identity ascribed to them, even if that identity was odious and ignorant of diversity. In many ways, this requires the opposite of colorblindness. It requires not only a recognition of race, but a positive assertion of racial identity. Rather than ignore racial ascription, this strategy co-opts racial essentialism and attempts to "turn it around," to use it as a tool for advocacy.

Consider the response to the 1982 murder of Chinese American Vincent Chin in Michigan. Disgruntled autoworkers killed Chin because they racially associated him with Japanese autoworkers who, in their view, were responsible for a loss of jobs in the American auto industry. After the vicious murder attracted international attention, civil rights advocates insisted that this was a hate crime that affected not only Japanese Americans but a large number of groups—Chinese, Filipino, Korean Americans, and everyone else perceived as Asian American— because of race. New coalitions of advocacy organizations emerged in response to Vincent Chin's murder, and they played a large part in rearticulating Asian American identity as a source of pride and political power. Civil rights advocates renewed their efforts to bring together organizations from all of these communities into coalitions under an Asian American umbrella. The work of these civil rights advocates solidified and coalesced the Asian American movement, winning recognition for the Asian American community as a group needing civil rights protections.[91]

That was then—in the 1980s. In the decade following the Vincent Chin murder, Asian American advocates used a sophisticated understanding of race and civil rights to build powerful coalitions.

What about Middle Eastern American advocates in the decade after September 11, 2001? Consider the response after the terrible murder of Balbir Singh Sodhi in Arizona. He was the first person killed in an Islamophobic hate crime after 9/11. Because of race, Sodhi's murderer believed he was exacting revenge against Muslim terrorists. Unlike what happened among Chinese, Japanese, Korean, and other Asian American advocates after Vincent Chin's murder, however, there was much less coalition building among Arab, Muslim, Sikh, and South Asian advocates looking to confront Islamophobia. That a Sikh was killed, and not a Muslim, has been remembered as a case of "mistaken identity," rather than an example of racism.

Even though a large number of Arab, Muslim, Sikh, and South Asian American advocacy organizations have been active for the past several decades, there are very few (if any) specifically Middle Eastern American advocacy organizations. Without advocacy organizations specifically working toward the recognition of the Middle Eastern American racial identity, it is unlikely that this racial category will achieve mainstream recognition alongside the "top five" racial categories in the "ethno-racial pentagon."[92] In the absence of organizations working to spur on racial projects to bring about a rearticulation of "Muslim" and Middle Eastern racial identity, mainstream recognition of Middle Eastern racial identity has not arrived. Absent that sort of mainstream recognition, it seems unlikely that new, umbrella advocacy organizations seeking to represent the whole of Middle Eastern American communities will emerge. Middle Eastern American identity, in short, is caught up in a racial paradox.

3

Islamophobia in America

Sunando Sen, a first-generation Indian immigrant, lived in New York City. He owned a small business, a copy shop on the Upper West Side. At the age of forty-six, he was murdered by a woman who reportedly admitted that she "hate[d] Hindus and Muslims ever since 2001 when they put down the Twin Towers."[1] Friends remembered Sen as a gentle and "honorable" man, who was "loved by the entire community in which he worked."[2] As Sen waited on a subway platform, he was suddenly pushed from behind, into the path of an oncoming train. He died instantly. The woman who killed him later said, "I'm prejudice[d] . . . I pushed him in front of the train because I thought it was cool." She was charged with a hate crime, and pleaded guilty to manslaughter. Her lawyer argued that mental illness led to the horrific crime while asking the court for leniency. She was sentenced to twenty-four years in prison.[3]

Too often, crimes like this one are explained away as the acts of "deranged" or intellectually disabled individuals. Even the most heinous crimes—the horrible massacre at the Sikh Temple of Wisconsin and the unconscionable murders of Balbir Singh Sodhi, Deah Barakat, Razan and Yusor Abu-Salha, and many others—have been written off in this way: the result of "one bad apple." While it is fortunately true that relatively few people have gone so far as to commit murder, the risk of experiencing violent and nonviolent hate crimes is a fact of life for Middle Eastern Americans. And, of course, Islamophobia as it manifests in America is more than just the frequency or severity of hate crimes.

Islamophobia in America is structural, systemic, and institutional. It finds expression through culture, politics, and policy. The physical nature of many hate crimes makes visible the often-invisible structures of race, but through closer analyses it becomes possible to see not only moments of racist violence but also ongoing patterns of racist discrimination and exclusion that shape life in America in ways both subtle and profound.

Like other forms of racism, Islamophobia is a multifaceted, over-determined phenomenon. Understanding its root causes requires acknowledging the elemental parts in the social production of race: racial projects. Islamophobia is best understood as a racist project, one that distributes resources in service of maintaining the race-based subordination of marginalized groups. In previous chapters, I described how race and racism happen in general terms, and I explained how the Middle Eastern American racial category has emerged through the same social processes that created all racial identities. Recognizing that racism is inherent in Islamophobia brings several advantages for explaining how it has been so durable and prominent in American culture for so long.

Part of the value of looking specifically at how race plays a key role in the production of Islamophobia comes by leveraging the explanatory power of detailed, careful analyses of White supremacy. Generations of critical scholarship have provided an account of the insidious power of White supremacy, the ideology that underpins most racist structures in the United States. Understanding that Islamophobia stems from the same White supremacist roots as other expressions of racism can clarify how seemingly separate issues—for example, stereotypical portrayals of Arabs in Hollywood films and the murder of South Asian Americans like Sunando Sen—are actually closely and deeply linked. As Andrea Smith explains, White supremacy is maintained by three central logics: slavery/capitalism, genocide/colonialism, and Orientalism/war.[4] These interrelated pillars that have supported White supremacy throughout American history can clearly be seen at work in the production of Islamophobia. Expanding from Smith's understanding of White supremacy, the anti-Islamophobia activist and scholar Deepa Iyer writes:

> . . . we could offer another pillar to [Smith's] framework, one called Islamophobia/national security that derogates Muslims and anyone perceived to be Muslim in order to preserve the illusion of collective safety. These pillars of White supremacy enable the United States to go to war; to deny people rights to their languages, histories, and homes; to militarize police forces in our cities; and to enact laws that profile, target, imprison, detain, and deport communities of color and immigrants.[5]

The very same logics that support White supremacy also lay at the center of the social processes that reproduce Islamophobia. Consider the rapid expansion of active hate groups in the United States over the past decade, many of which are specifically anti-Muslim.[6] These groups make explicit their goal of supporting White supremacy, as they combine "anti-immigrant, anti-gay, and anti-Muslim" priorities, as Iyer describes.

Understanding Islamophobia in this way reveals that there is no distinction between the racism that enables the indefinite detention of Middle Eastern Americans on suspicion of terrorism, and the racism that suppresses the voting rights of people of color, that incarcerates disproportionate numbers of Blacks and Latin@s, that perpetuates vast race-based inequities of income and wealth. There is a common ancestry in America's worst racial sins: the campaigns leading to genocide of Native Americans, the brutal reign of chattel slavery, the *de jure* system of Jim Crow segregation, Japanese American internment camps, mass incarceration, deportation, and Islamophobia. All of these stem from White supremacy.

In this chapter, I break out and analyze several key aspects of American Islamophobia. This by no means results in an exhaustive analysis, but recounting some of the problems caused by Islamophobia nonetheless clearly drives home two conclusions. First, while religion, gender, and other axes of inequality intersect and are at work here, there can be no question that Islamophobia is fundamentally a form of racism. It flows from the same well that sustains all of the forms of structural racism that have been endemic in the United States since its founding. Second, Islamophobic racism in the United States is not new; on the contrary, it has presented significant problems for a long time. These conclusions illuminate one half of the racial paradox that is Middle Eastern racial identity, showing how it is freighted with tremendous social forces in the United States. But knowing this does not by itself solve the racial dilemma—namely, whether it is beneficial for Middle Eastern American advocates to describe Islamophobia as racism. Leaving this question aside for the moment, in the remainder of this chapter I will focus on the unpleasant task of describing Islamophobia in some detail.

Islamophobia in American Culture

The common "Orientalizing" that began to reach the New World colonies as early as the 1500s deeply embedded race-based prejudice toward Middle Easterners in American culture. Though elements of the older images of an "exotic" or "backward" Orient remain, by the latter part of the twentieth century, the American popular imaginary more commonly depicted a "dangerous" Middle East. The shift in cultural representations of the Middle East from primarily "mysterious" and "atavistic" to predominantly "threatening" is a fascinating and complex topic. Melani McAlister, in her treatment of post–World War II Orientalism, identifies the 1967 war between the state of Israel and several Arab nations as a crucial turning point.[7] The representation of this war as the "Six Day War," where Israel swiftly defeated the armies of Egypt, Jordan, and Syria, helped propel in America the image of a fanatical and dangerous Middle East where "the Arabs" would shoot first and ask questions later. The popularity of this idea portended the culturally resonant "clash of civilizations" thesis, which placed the West and its allies (including Israel) against a dangerous and uniquely violent Middle East. By the end of the 1900s, this kind of thinking dominated the already racialized American discourse about people from the Middle East. Around this time, Edward Said, Nadine Naber, and other scholars noted that it was quite acceptable in polite company to make blatantly ignorant, bigoted statements about Arabs and Muslims.[8] Because of rhetoric like this, the terms "Middle Eastern," "Arab," and "Muslim" today all refer to basically the same ascribed racial identity. And, of course, this same Middle Eastern racial category has ascribed Sikhs and South Asians as well.[9]

Cultural Islamophobia before 2001

Depictions of dangerous Middle Easterners, prominent in American popular culture by the late 1960s, was supplemented with racialized representations of treacherous "oil sheiks" during the oil crisis in the 1970s. This image appeared frequently during the "oil shock" caused by the Organization of Arab Petroleum Exporting Countries declaring an embargo to protest American involvement in the 1973 war between Israel and its Arab neighbors. An oft-repeated, racially fraught image of the duplicitous Arab served as a scapegoat for Americans upset by economic recession and high gasoline prices. Blatantly racist images of these swarthy, hook-nosed "oil sheiks" appeared in countless editorial cartoons and films in the 1970s and early 1980s.[10] This "oil sheik" image was so ubiquitous that the FBI used it to set up a "sting operation" aimed at corrupt members of Congress. A trap was set by assigning covert Italian American agents, with ostensibly convincing Middle Eastern appearances, to pose as wealthy oil executives ("oil sheiks") from Lebanon and other Arab countries.[11] These undercover agents sometimes used disguises to enhance their "Middle Eastern look," and the ruse worked. Several elected officials believed that these wealthy and duplicitous "oil sheiks" would pay bribes in exchange for political favors. This led to criminal convictions against a United States Senator and various other public officials. The FBI referred to the operation as ABSCAM, short for "Arab Scam."[12] This dramatic operation served as the central plot device in a big-budget 2013 Hollywood film, a period drama set in the early 1980s, *American Hustle*.[13] The impact of the FBI lending legitimacy to the stereotypes about Arabs caused significant harm, although there has been little public outcry about questionable FBI sting operations using Middle Eastern stereotypes, before or since.[14]

Another crucial moment in the development of the "dangerous Middle Easterner" stereotype came during the 1979 Iran Hostage Crisis.[15] The American embassy in Tehran was seized by gun-toting revolutionaries who then held the embassy staff hostage for fourteen months. Television news showed these Islamic revolutionaries on a daily basis. It is difficult to overstate how much this national crisis contributed to the shift away from the Middle Eastern "oil sheik" stereotype toward the "terrorist" stereotype. Indeed, the word "terrorist" would become fully synonymous with Middle Easterners by the mid-1980s. Several horrific terrorist attacks in this era contributed to the burgeoning stereotype, including the destruction of the American embassy and a Marine barracks in Lebanon, the bombing of Pan Am Flight 103 by two Libyan citizens, multiple deadly attacks carried out by Hezbollah, the hijacking of an American cruise ship by the Palestinian Liberation Front, and many more examples. Of course, terrorist attacks were carried out by all kinds of militants throughout the 1970s and 1980s, but attacks by Middle Easterners attracted perhaps the most sustained attention in the United States.

American popular culture repeatedly reinforced the racialized characterization of Middle Easterners as eager to become maniacal, inhuman terrorists. Dozens of big-budget Hollywood films used cookie-cutter Middle Eastern villains, often shouting Arabic-sounding gibberish as they caused mass carnage in film after film. There are countless examples of dehumanization of Arabs and other Middle Easterners in every Hollywood genre, from action to romantic comedy, science fiction, and award-winning dramas.[16] The pervasive caricature appeared everywhere: on television, in film, and even in professional wrestling.[17]

It is important to emphasize that in the 1980s, the stereotypical image of a terrorist was not applied exclusively to Muslims. Instead, this blanket stereotype attached to multiple communities that were racialized in the Middle Eastern category, especially Arab Americans and Sikh Americans. In 1984, the Indian government carried out a military crackdown against Sikh militants and later that year, Prime Minister Indira Gandhi was assassinated by two of her Sikh bodyguards, partly in retaliation for the Indian Army's assault on the Golden Temple. In American discourse, these and other events were wrapped up with existing portrayals of Middle Eastern terrorism and violence, and South Asian Americans, particularly Sikhs, became thoroughly enmeshed into the racialized category of "Middle Eastern terrorists."[18] At the time, Indian government officials explicitly labeled Sikhs as "terrorists" to rally international support for their efforts to suppress the Sikh independence movement.[19] The American reaction to the violence in India again illustrates the racialized erasure of distinctions between Arabs and South Asians—and especially the racialized conflation between people of the Sikh and Muslim faiths.

By the mid-1990s, the conflation of "terrorist" with "Middle Eastern" was so pervasive that when a 1995 terror attack destroyed the Murrah Federal Building in Oklahoma City, many professional analysts, investigators, and journalists immediately assumed that the attack must have been carried out "by Arabs."[20] In reality, the perpetrators were White, Christian, and American.

The presumption that all terrorists are Middle Eastern dominated the news cycle again in 1996 when a Boeing 747 jumbo passenger jet—TWA Flight 800—exploded shortly after takeoff from New York's John F. Kennedy airport. Investigators and the media immediately began working under the assumption that terrorists from the Middle East brought down the jet. The *New York Times* ran an article under the headline "Investigators Focus Closely on Terrorism as Cause of Explosion," and it reported that a surface-to-air missile strike or a bomb were leading theories as to the cause of the disaster. The article noted that shoulder-fired Stinger missiles were "readily available in the Mideast," leaving unstated the assumption that any terrorists who would fire such missiles must have come from that region.[21] *Time* reported that the FBI and CIA asked their international counterparts in the Middle East to report any leads in regards to which terrorist group might be responsible for the loss of TWA Flight 800.[22] Eventually, the investigation revealed that there was no way a missile or bomb could have been responsible for the accident. Investigators pinpointed a design flaw with electrical wires positioned near the aircraft's fuel tank that caused a spark and the catastrophic explosion.

These examples illustrate that, by the end of the 1900s, the popular American conception of terrorism was linked deeply with the racial category of Middle Easterners, a group that included not only Arabs or Muslims but anyone who "looked Middle Eastern." This popular discourse assumed that the culture and people of the Middle East were somehow predisposed to terrorist violence. This essentialist thinking impacted Arabs, Muslims, Sikhs, and South Asians as a racist trope under which physical appearance became a crude marker of identity and an anchor for fear-inducing prejudices.

Islamophobia after 2001

The attacks of 9/11 profoundly exacerbated these racial dynamics. Within hours of the terrorist attacks, Osama bin Laden and his notorious al-Qaeda network were deemed responsible by officials and the press. A spike in reported hate crimes and discrimination against Middle Eastern Americans soon followed. Concern about "backlash" hate crimes brought the problem of Islamophobia into mainstream public discourse. President Bush and many other political leaders repeatedly emphasized that Islam and Muslims were not America's enemy, and that the nineteen 9/11 attackers did not represent Islam. On September 17, 2001, the President went to the Islamic Center of Washington, DC, and said, "The face of terror is not the true faith of Islam. That's not what Islam is all about. Islam is peace. These terrorists don't represent peace. They represent evil and war."[23] Despite Bush's persistent efforts, commentators who placed the blame for 9/11 squarely on Muslims and the religion of Islam found a large, receptive audience in the ensuing months and years.

Many held out hope that the initial spike in Islamophobia after 9/11 would give way to a return to normal, that the "backlash" would recede as memories of the attacks faded. Hate crimes occurred with frightening frequency in the months immediately following 9/11, ranging in severity— from insults shouted at people walking by, to vandalism of private homes and places of worship, to violent crimes like bullying in schools, assault, and murder. The American-Arab Anti-Discrimination Committee (ADC) received reports of more than seven hundred violent hate crimes, including several murders, in the first nine weeks after 9/11 alone.[24]

FBI statistics recorded a sharp decline in hate crimes after those initial nine weeks.[25] However, official FBI numbers notoriously undercount the actual number of hate crimes. It is therefore difficult to quantify exactly how many Islamophobic hate crimes occurred. The FBI statistics only capture those crimes actually reported to law enforcement. Even worse, before 2014, the FBI did not have separate categories for anti-Arab and anti-Sikh hate crimes, meaning that such crimes may have been counted as "anti-Other" or "anti-White," or even "anti-Muslim," depending on how the initial report was collected. Separate from the FBI numbers, many advocacy organizations (like ADC) keep a count of hate crimes reported to them, but those numbers have flaws as well. Despite these imperfections, both FBI statistics and reports to advocacy organizations support the conclusion that since 2002, there have been a persistently high number of hate crimes affecting Middle Eastern Americans—at least one hundred reports per year, compared to fewer than fifty per year before 9/11.

Some of the worst of these hate crimes include the murders of Middle Eastern Americans like Balbir Singh Sodhi and Sunando Sen, the massacre at the Sikh Temple of Wisconsin in 2012, and hundreds of acts of vandalism at private homes and at places of worship like mosques and gurdwaras. For example, in 2015, just days after the shocking murder of three young Muslim Americans in Chapel Hill, a swastika was painted on a Hindu temple, and a nearby school was tagged with the words,

"Muslims get out."[26] There have been scores of racially motivated as-saults on shopkeepers, taxi cab drivers, and people simply walking down the street. To take just one example, in September 2015, a Sikh American man in Chicago was brutally assaulted by a man who alleg-edly shouted, "Bin Laden! Go back to your country!"[27] Meanwhile, some bigots have taken to declaring their places of business as "Muslim-free zones," meaning they refuse to provide equal accommodation to Middle Eastern Americans.[28] Stories about Islamophobic hate crimes like these appear in the press on an almost weekly basis. The racial element of these crimes is usually readily apparent. Because the victims "looked Muslim," they were vulnerable to these hate crimes. Unfortunately, the hope that Islamophobia would fade away after a temporary post-9/11 moment proved unfounded. A great deal of Islamophobic discrimina-tion has persisted for more than fifteen years after 9/11.

Apart from frequent hate crimes, Islamophobic employment discrim-ination has remained a chronic issue as well. Middle Eastern Ameri-can workers from all sectors of the economy have reported that their employers failed to provide reasonable accommodation for religious and cultural practices. Advocacy organizations provided legal counsel in hundreds of workplace discrimination cases related to Islamophobia after employers unlawfully fired, refused to hire, or failed to accommo-date employees properly with regard to their religious or ethnic back-ground. Reports of discrimination against people who "look Middle Eastern" increased to such an extent following the 9/11 attacks that the US Equal Employment Opportunity Commission (EEOC) published a document specifically regarding "individuals who are or are perceived to be Muslim, Arab, South Asian, or Sikh." According to this document, complaints of discrimination by members of the groups on this list—a list explained only by the common Middle Eastern American racial category—saw "a significant increase."[29] Despite a concerted effort by advocates and government agencies to curtail this kind of discrimina-tion after September 11, 2001, EEOC statistics show that employment discrimination claims continued to increase; these claims accounted for nearly 15% of all workplace discrimination charges filed in the United States between 2001 and 2006.[30]

To sum up, Islamophobia runs through American culture in myriad ways. Here, I reviewed some of the most troubling hate crimes (violent and otherwise), a few examples of stereotypical representations in various forms of media (including the news media and popular television and film), and the seemingly intractable problem of employment discrimination that frequently affects Middle Eastern Americans. There are many other aspects of Islamophobia in American culture that deserve more attention than I can provide in the limited space available here. For now, let us turn to look at expressions of Islamophobia in American politics.

Islamophobia in American Politics

Before the 9/11 attacks, strains of Orientalism pervaded American foreign policy, and from time to time, elected leaders made outbursts that explicitly demeaned Middle Eastern Americans. After 9/11, however, Islamophobic rhetoric became a prominent feature at all levels of mainstream American politics, from local city council races to campaigns for President of the United States. In recent years, a well-funded industry of political professionals has helped to promote Islamophobic ideas in the American political sphere. Beginning in the early part of the 2000s, American politicians seemingly could not resist the temptation to use blatant Islamophobia to gain perceived electoral advantages. In other words, making Islamophobic statements was seen as a winning campaign strategy. This was more than just campaign rhetoric. It was also reflected in policy.

In the debate over "post-9/11" counterterrorism and security policy, for example, some public officials aggressively advocated for law enforcement to target Muslims for surveillance under the spurious and bigoted reasoning that Muslims are more likely to commit terrorist attacks. I discuss the impacts of Islamophobia on policies and programs later, after first focusing on the persistent hateful rhetoric in political speech and electoral campaigns.

Much Islamophobic campaign rhetoric, notably, treated Islamophobia as a "wedge issue." Often without providing any specific critique of Islam, and without promoting any particular policy, many politicians used bigoted Islamophobic rhetoric to deride their opponents as weak, to instill fear about dangerous immigrants, and to distract attention away from other issues. In this way, Islamophobia was used to generate support for candidacies and political priorities that often had nothing to do with terrorism, or Muslims. This tried-and-true political strategy to use Islamophobia as a "wedge" served as a tool to rile up the base, to drive erstwhile supporters back into the fold, and to keep attention away from potential weaknesses.

Sitting just under the surface of these efforts was a decade-long multi-million-dollar campaign that promoted using Islamophobia as a tactic throughout American politics.[31] Wealthy individuals and conservative political foundations provided some $40 million over a ten-year period to self-proclaimed "Islam experts" to travel around the United States endorsing "model legislation" to trump up Islamophobic ideas. These so-called experts produced research reports, created propaganda "documentary" films, and appeared on television news programs to promote their ideas and describe the dangers posed by Islam. In 2008, these Islamophobic activists began promulgating legislation to "ban" the Islamic canonical law, or Sharia. By 2016, seven states passed these "Sharia bans," and additional bills had been introduced in more than half of all state legislatures and in the US Congress that sought to somehow "protect America" from the nonexistent threat of Sharia. Virtually every bill proposed in all of the different legislatures used identical language designed by this network of Islamophobia activists.[32] The chief architect of the anti-Sharia bills, David Yerushalmi, admitted that the purpose of these bills was "heuristic," meaning that they would succeed not by actually banning Sharia law, but instead the process of enacting these bills would generate suspicion about Middle Eastern Americans.[33] The point of the anti-Sharia effort was to stoke suspicion, to use Islamophobia as a wedge issue.

These efforts to fuel suspicion about Middle Eastern Americans have been met with remarkable success. Consider that at least fifty-three proposed mosques and Islamic centers around the United States faced resistance in their efforts to build or expand their services between 2006 and 2012, with an especially significant increase in opposition after 2009.[34] But perhaps the most visible impact of the well-funded Islamophobia campaign was not generating policy changes or swaying the opinions of the American public, but rather the incredible frequency with which blatantly Islamophobic statements came from prominent elected political leaders, including members of Congress and the President of the United States.

Mainstream American political leaders, from President George W. Bush to New York City Mayor Rudolph Giuliani and many others, warned often about the dangers of "Islamo-facism" at home and abroad, despite a lack of evidence of a unique threat from the Middle East.[35] Terrorism perpetrated by Muslim Americans accounted for a tiny fraction—less than 1%—of violent deaths in the US for more than a decade after September 11, 2001, representing what one analyst called a "miniscule threat to public safety."[36]

In fact, the deadliest terrorists in American history have been American-born radical Christians, such as the perpetrators of the bombing of the Murrah building in Oklahoma City or members of the Ku Klux Klan and similar White supremacist organizations that carried out countless massacres throughout the twentieth century. Examples of this kind of racist terrorism abound: church arson, murderous attacks at family planning clinics, vigilante border policing, and many other hate crimes.[37] However, many mass shootings and other violent acts carried out by non-Middle Eastern Americans routinely are not discussed as "terrorist attacks," as I discuss in detail later in this chapter.

Attacks carried out by Middle Eastern Americans, on the other hand, are commonly recognized as terrorist attacks by law enforcement, political leaders, and the media. Perhaps this is because White, American-born terrorists did not constitute the kind of visible threat from outsiders that American politicians could use to energize voters to support "war on terrorism" policies. By contrast, the stereotypical image of the Middle Eastern terrorist provides tremendous political purchase. Even though it proved both reckless and immoral, many American politicians have seen it fit to intentionally fan the flames of Islamophobia.

The advocacy organization South Asian Americans Leading Together (SAALT) found that "xenophobic and racist images and language" in political rhetoric affecting "South Asians, Muslims, Sikhs, and Arab Americans" occurred with "unprecedented frequency" after 9/11.[38] SAALT collected dozens of examples of political leaders using language that portrayed these communities as a threat to national security. For example, in 2006, US Senator Conrad Burns said that the United States is up against "a faceless enemy" of terrorists who "drive taxicabs in the daytime and kill at night."[39] Along the same lines, James Inhofe, also a US Senator, stated during a 2010 committee hearing: "All terrorists are

Muslims or Middle Easterners between the age of twenty and thirty-five, that's by and large true."[40] In 2012, presidential candidate Herman Cain said that he would require a loyalty oath from any Muslims serving in his administration, explaining that "there is a greater dangerous part of the Muslim faith than there is in any of these other religions."[41]

SAALT's research also documented several instances where Middle Eastern American public officials and candidates for political office faced xenophobic attacks during campaigns. Candidates were called epithets like "raghead" and "turban topper" by their opponents and political pundits. Some faced accusations that they were "supported by Hamas" or other militant organizations. One city council candidate in Florida even suggested that if his South Asian opponent won the city council seat, terrorism would be the result, stating: "As far as I know, he could be a nice guy, but these kind of people get embedded over here. . . . You remember 9/11."[42]

In the early 2000s, rhetoric that intentionally used Islamophobia when discussing terrorist attacks became a hallmark of American political speech. Routinely, candidates for high office encouraged voters to elect a candidate who is "tough" on terrorism and not beholden to "political correctness"—in other words, willing to make blatantly Islamophobic statements. Beginning in 2007, Islamophobic rhetoric was specifically targeted at then-Senator Barack Obama, as he ran as a Democratic candidate for president. In 2007, the Fox News Channel aired a story claiming to show evidence that Obama was educated at a "radical Muslim madrassa."[43] In 2008, Republican vice presidential nominee and Alaska Governor Sarah Palin accused Obama of "palling around with terrorists."[44] This rhetoric was so effective that during the 2008 campaign, 13% of the American public incorrectly believed that Obama was, somehow, secretly a Muslim.[45] Even during his 2012 campaign for reelection, 17% of registered voters believed Obama was Muslim, even though the president was Christian.[46] The implication was that Obama's stance on terrorism would not be tough enough, or worse, that his candidacy represented an incredible conspiracy by Muslim radicals to seize control of the American military. Throughout his presidency, Obama, the first African American to win a major party's nomination for President (and, of course, election and reelection), faced persistent rumors and conspiracy theories that suggested he was Muslim and not an American citizen, even after the White House produced his birth certificate and pointed out contemporaneous birth announcements from Hawai'i.

As the Obama campaign dealt with these ridiculous and racist rumors, the 2008 Republican presidential primary campaign featured several outlandish, extreme claims based on Islamophobia. Republican presidential candidate and Congressman Tom Tancredo stated that he believed Middle Eastern terrorists were plotting to detonate a nuclear bomb inside an American city. He assured voters that, as president, he would deter such an attack by threatening Islamic religious sites: "If it is up to me, we are going to explain that an attack on this homeland of that nature would be followed by an attack on the holy sites in Mecca and Medina."[47] Since 2004, every presidential election has featured this kind of grandstanding by candidates, with many posturing to espouse the most outwardly "tough" stances toward stopping Middle Eastern terrorism. This race to the bottom of the Islamophobic gutter led to the rise of offensive statements about Muslims, including those made by Donald J. Trump and other candidates for the Republican presidential nomination in 2016. After the horrific deadly shooting at an LGBT nightclub in Orlando, Trump doubled down on his previous calls to "ban Muslims," by proposing to ban immigration from any country with a "proven history of terrorism."[48] Even though the perpetrator was not an immigrant, Trump and other Republican leaders sought to link the Orlando massacre to national policies on immigration and security by appealing to Islamophobia.

Indeed, candidates standing for nomination to become President of the United States seemingly felt a need to prove that they held Islamophobic beliefs about the "enemy," the supposedly single greatest source of terrorism. During the 2016 campaign season, many critics of the Obama administration claimed that the President had failed to protect America from the threat of terrorism, in part because he was not Islamophobic enough. Senator Ted Cruz, for example, repeatedly criticized Obama for failing to "name the enemy—radical Islamic terrorism."[49] Because President Obama refused to say that the Muslim faith contributes to terrorism, Cruz and others contended that he could not be trusted to defend America.

Political rhetoric based on Islamophobia goes beyond mere conspiracy theories and shameful pandering to voters. The racialized caricature of "radical Islamists" and "Islamo-fascism" mainly serve to legitimize and expand discriminatory state policies and practices.

Islamophobia in American Policy

After the fall of the Soviet Union in the late 1980s, numerous prominent policymakers and pundits shifted attention to the supposed threat posed by the "Muslim world" in ways that would replace the Soviets as the chief antagonist of the United States.[50] The groundwork in the late 1900s set the stage for the sweeping response to the 9/11 attacks, which saw law enforcement, intelligence agencies, and the military act aggressively in an effort to prevent another attack. Much of what would become known as the "War on Terror" resulted in policies and programs that had disparate impacts on Middle Eastern Americans.

Obviously, the government has a duty to prevent terrorist attacks. The law enforcement officers, intelligence analysts, and other officials who do the painstaking work of counterterrorism have no doubt saved many lives, and few would disagree that their work is of critical importance. Nevertheless, the imperative to improve security and prevent terrorist attacks does not provide any reason to discriminate against Middle Eastern Americans. Evidence (and, indeed, common sense) has repeatedly shown that there is no racial, ethnic, religious, or national group that is more likely to carry out violent attacks than any other. The legitimate threat posed by terrorism cannot be used to justify discriminatory policies, but unfortunately that is precisely what has taken place over the past several decades.

The War on Terror

The term "War on Terror" was not coined until 2001, when a massive shift to focus on counterterrorism across law enforcement and the military was described by President George W. Bush on September 20 in a speech to Congress.[51] But the policies that supported the War on Terror began coalescing many years earlier. As early as the 1970s, federal agencies crafted policies meant to curb terrorism that were aimed directly at Middle Eastern Americans.

The fundamental tactics of surveillance and disruption programs employed by the government that disproportionately target Middle Eastern Americans were developed even earlier, in the 1950s and 1960s. In those two decades, the Department of Justice (DOJ) undertook what came to be known as the Counterintelligence Program, or COINTELPRO, to actively undermine the work of all sorts of advocacy organizations. The program, specifically authorized by FBI Director J. Edgar Hoover in 1956, began as an attempt to expose communist (and Soviet) sympathizers, and it quickly escalated into a program that actively undermined all sorts of "New Left" political advocacy.[52] In addition to surveillance, the FBI planted *agents provocateurs* to stoke factionalism and entrap advocates into committing illegal acts. In 1976, a Congressional investigation (popularly known as the Church Committee) declared COINTELPRO "intolerable in a democratic society."[53] Even after this stinging indictment, many of the tactics developed in COINTELPRO nevertheless continued, kept alive in several federal programs that remain active today.

COINTELPRO's influence was apparent in "Operation Boulder," which began in the summer of 1972. For this clandestine program, the White House directed the FBI to target Arab American advocacy organizations and Arab American individuals nationwide. As specifically authorized by President Richard Nixon, federal agencies conducted wide-ranging surveillance and recordkeeping on all "'ethnic Arabs,' defined as all persons of Arab parentage or ancestry."[54] Immigration and customs authorities undertook special screening of Arab visitors and immigrants. Over a period of several years, the FBI interrogated many Arab American advocates and even wiretapped the telephone conversations of the president of the Association of Arab American University Graduates (AAUG), a leading advocacy organization. The program required a special screening for all nonimmigrant Arabs, such as those with student or tourist visas. Operation Boulder's apparent objective, begun in the wake of the shocking murder of Israeli athletes at the Munich Olympic Games by Palestinian extremists, was to find and monitor any organization in the United States that might sympathize with Palestinian nationalism.[55]

In the 1980s, paranoia about the possibility of Arab American-led terrorism reached such heights that President Ronald Reagan's Department of Justice even considered creating an internment camp to house "alien undesirables" while they awaited deportation.[56] One DOJ document from 1986, "Alien Terrorists and Undesirables: A Contingency Plan," estimated the total number of Arab American students currently in the US, suggesting that the FBI might round them all up as detainees. The DOJ listed "certain countries, all Arab, as being likely origins of terrorist aliens."[57] The plan had developed far enough to designate a proposed detention camp site in rural Louisiana. Fortunately, the plan was never put into action.

Arab American communities in the 1980s confronted an atmosphere of increasing "counter-terrorism" efforts directed toward them. Perhaps the most infamous example for Arab Americans came with the case of the "Los Angeles Eight." Eight political activists, seven of them Palestinian and one Kenyan, were placed under surveillance by the FBI for three years beginning in 1987, ostensibly to prevent a terrorist attack. During this time, the FBI found them distributing Palestinian magazines, yet did not observe them engaged in any illegal or dangerous activities. Nevertheless, the FBI worked with authorities from the Immigration and Naturalization Service (INS) to find grounds to deport them. Shortly thereafter, in 1987, the eight were arrested and charged with various violations of immigration law. INS sought to have them deported on the grounds that they were fundraising for an organization considered under American law to be illegal due to communist and terrorist ties, namely the Popular Front for the Liberation of Palestine. Deportation hearings kept the activists in legal limbo for years, but they were never deported. After 2001, the Bush administration kept the case alive, using new "War on Terror" powers to further the case for the deportation of the activists.[58] Finally, in 2007, twenty years after their ordeal began, an immigration judge working on a case involving two of the eight activists said that the whole ordeal was "an embarrassment to the rule of law." The Department of Homeland Security later that year finally dropped the prosecution of the remaining members of the "LA 8."[59]

Meanwhile in the 1990s, the implicit assumption that "Arabs" posed a unique threat to the United States set into place the legal and policy framework that would directly inform the response to the terrorist attacks on 9/11. In 1991, during the Gulf War, FBI agents fanned out across the country, interviewing various "business and community leaders of

Arab descent in the United States."[60] This was supposedly an effort to find "Iraqi-supported terrorists." Later, the 1996 Antiterrorism and Effective Death Penalty Act made sweeping changes to immigration policy, and gave the federal government the power to officially designate any entity as a "terrorist" organization. That designation subjected the "terrorist" organization to sanctions and prohibited Americans from providing support to it. The policy also allowed for "secret evidence" to serve as the basis for deportation proceedings, allowing the government to withhold that evidence even from lawful permanent residents facing deportation. The vast majority of cases where these powers were invoked involved Middle Eastern or Middle Eastern American organizations and individuals.[61]

Building on the framework of twentieth-century surveillance and counterterrorism strategies, shortly after the 9/11 attacks, a plethora of discriminatory policies and programs emerged. The initial wave of discrimination developed during the official investigation into how the 9/11 attacks occurred. The declaration of a "state of national emergency" made on September 14, 2001 granted new powers that spread the influence of this discrimination further, and these privileges were significantly expanded by the rapid and near-unanimous passage of the USA Patriot Act in October of that same year. The Patriot Act gave law enforcement a wide range of new authorities in the areas of surveillance, border patrols, and financial interdiction. It was renewed with little debate in 2005. Many provisions of the renewed Patriot Act expired briefly in 2015, but after just one day, the new USA Freedom Act extended most of the counterterrorism provisions until 2019. The powers granted to intelligence and law enforcement agencies under these laws led to an unprecedented expansion of the so-called security state. Some of the programs developed by these agencies, in keeping with history stretching back to the 1970s, were conducted in ways that blatantly discriminated against Middle Eastern Americans. Most of these actions were taken under the false, bigoted assumption that future terrorists would most likely emerge from Middle Eastern American communities.

The sweeping abuse of the new authorities of the "War on Terror" began within days of the 9/11 attacks. As part of the official investigation into those attacks, a roundup conducted by the Department of Justice (DOJ) and the Immigration and Naturalization Service (INS) took into custody at least twelve hundred people by October 2001. Almost all of these detainees were Arab and Muslim immigrants.[62] Various agencies detained these people on "material witness" and immigration charges. Many of those detained became known as the "Disappeared," because they would suddenly vanish from their homes after nighttime raids by the authorities.[63] Later in 2001, the Attorney General of the United States directed local law enforcement agencies around the country to conduct "voluntary" interviews with some five thousand people in predominantly Middle Eastern American neighborhoods.[64] Around this time, federal agencies launched the Terrorism Information and Prevention System, or Operation TIPS. This initiative encouraged American citizens to report any and all suspicious terrorist activity, and predictably, it resulted in a plethora of unjustified intrusions into the lives of Middle Eastern Americans. One such intrusion happened in Connecticut in November 2001, when the police received a report that two "Arabs" were talking about anthrax. In fact, the two men were Pakistani, and they were arrested at a gas station along with an Indian man and another Pakistani man who just happened to be at the gas station at the same time. One of the men, Ayazuddin Sheerazi, was detained for eighteen days.[65] Although Operation TIPS was cancelled in 2002, elements of it lived on in the form of "see something, say something" policies still active in public facilities across the country, and in the controversial Terrorism Liaison Officer program.[66] All of these policies—each resulting in the unfair targeting of Middle Eastern American communities—are rationalized as emergency efforts necessary to protect national security during an apparently unending time of crisis. Taken together, these policies (and others) resulted in fear and displacement—and a curtailment of basic civil rights and citizenship rights—for Middle Eastern Americans.

In the months after 9/11, federal agencies began to curate a "no-fly list," which barred certain individuals from boarding airplanes traveling to or from the United States. As the list continued to grow for more than a decade, with no due process or even notification given to those placed on it, evidence suggested that it contained a disproportionate number of Middle Eastern names.[67] The first successful complainant to have her name removed from the "no-fly list" was Professor Rahinah Ibrahim, an academic who lived in California. Her lawsuit in 2008 was ultimately successful, after the government admitted that an FBI agent had simply checked the wrong box on some paperwork, which led to Professor Ibrahim being inadvertently placed on the "no-fly list" and subject to loss of her rights. Despite this minor clerical error, the government vigorously fought the lawsuit for more than five years, presumably to avoid setting a precedent. Professor Ibrahim's name was finally removed from the "no-fly list" in 2014.[68] Despite constant complaints that the "no-fly list" violates basic civil rights, it and similar "watch lists" continue to remain in place indefinitely.

In addition to "watch lists" that ostensibly only affect specific individuals and not entire communities, other discriminatory programs simply affect all immigrants and travelers from Muslim-majority countries. In 2002, the INS instituted special immigration requirements that applied only to people from Muslim-majority nations and North Korea, requiring them to check into local immigration offices for photographs and fingerprinting, along with other "special registration" protocols.[69] This blatantly discriminatory program, known as the National Security Entry-Exit Registration System, continued until 2011, at which time similar biometric security measures became standard for all visitors to the United States, not just those from Muslim-majority nations.

Apart from these efforts at the border and around airports, federal agencies have found some remarkably creative ways to discriminate against Middle Eastern Americans. Beginning in 2002, the FBI and the Department of Energy conducted secret monitoring of mosques and private homes belonging to Muslim Americans in a paranoid search for hidden nuclear weapons. They found nothing of interest.[70] Later, in 2009, according to their own documents, the FBI undertook special efforts to collect as much information as possible on the "Middle Eastern and Muslim population" in Michigan under the reasoning that the relatively large size of those communities made the state "prime territory for attempted radicalization and recruitment."[71] A similar program was revealed in 2012, where the FBI used "mosque outreach" programs—intended to create an atmosphere of trust and sharing between the FBI and Muslim American communities—to conduct illicit surveillance of attendees.[72]

In the midst of all these other programs, from 2001 through 2010, Muslim American charities also came under heavy government scrutiny, which had a chilling effect on philanthropic and political donations.[73] Rather than focus investigations on the activity of the charities' managers, to see whether they clandestinely funneled money to illegal or terrorist groups, federal investigators looked at the donor lists as well. Many people who made good-faith donations to these charities reasonably worried that their names had been added to a terrorist watch list. The ACLU accused the government of violating the religious freedom of Muslim Americans, for whom giving to charity is a central tenet of faith.

Even when the laws explicitly limited government power to prevent violating constitutional protections and civil liberties, the Bush and Obama administrations ignored those restrictions to conduct blanket, dragnet surveillance. In 2005, the *New York Times* reported the existence of a clandestine program, known internally as the "President's Program," an illegal monitoring system through which various US intelligence agencies surveilled the telephone conversations and emails of ordinary Americans.[74] This program went beyond even the expansive authorities given to the intelligence agencies by the Patriot Act. When knowledge of these secret spying programs were revealed, President Bush assured the public that only "terrorist cells" were targeted for scrutiny.[75] In 2008, the "President's Program" received retroactive legal approval in the form of the Foreign Intelligence Surveillance Act (FISA) Amendments Act, which created a secret court tasked with approving surveillance requests from the government. According to classified documents leaked by former National Security Agency (NSA) contract employee Edward Snowden in 2013, intelligence services again went beyond the limits in that law, circumventing the the FISA Amendments Act and the Patriot Act as they systematically collected vast amounts of communications data.[76] Defending the controversial programs, President Obama claimed that they were needed to prevent terrorism while insisting that "America is not interested in spying on ordinary people."[77] In their justifications for these programs, both Presidents Bush and Obama relied upon the popular image of terrorists as visible outsiders, as "others." By saying that "ordinary people" would not be targeted, but "only terrorist cells," Bush and Obama effectively used a political "dog whistle" to reinforce the predominant, false belief that "terrorists" do not come from the ranks of "ordinary" Americans but instead originate from an easily recognizable group of outsiders.

This rhetoric tracks precisely how the counterterrorism policies and programs work in practice. Despite evidence to the contrary, Middle

Eastern Americans are believed to be the primary sources of terrorism, and therefore those communities need to be watched the most closely by the authorities. A recent analysis of confidential government documents found that Dearborn, Michigan—a small suburb of Detroit (population 96,000) that includes a relatively large proportion of Middle Eastern American families—is second only to New York City in the concentration of "known or suspected" terrorists on federal watch lists.[78] This analysis, like many others, definitively shows the implicit and explicit reliance on stereotypes about Muslims and Middle Easterners as dangerous outsiders active in the production of counterterrorism policies and practices.

Discriminatory Surveillance

This presumption that Middle Easterners are the sole source of the terrorism threat pervades American counterterrorism efforts at all levels. Following in the footsteps of federal agencies, the nation's largest municipal police force, the New York Police Department (NYPD), built a massive counterterrorism operation targeted directly at Middle Eastern Americans.

An investigative report from the Associated Press (AP) revealed that, beginning in 2002, the NYPD ran a clandestine program systematically targeting Muslim Americans for surveillance.[79] Known as the "Demographics Unit," a secret counterterrorism task force sent teams of undercover police officers into neighborhoods with large numbers of Muslim inhabitants. These undercover "rakers" kept records of mundane daily life at those cafes, restaurants, and bookstores where Muslims congregated. The dragnet conducted background checks on people who had legally changed their names to (or from) Muslim or Arabic-sounding ones.[80] Undercover counterterrorism officers even spied on the NYPD's own counterterrorism allies from the Muslim community, going so far as to assign agents to monitor Shaykh Reda Shata, who was a leading supporter of FBI and police counterterrorism efforts.[81] The NYPD even extended its surveillance activities to Muslim student organizations at Yale University, the University of Pennsylvania, and Rutgers University, all of which are located outside New York.[82]

According to hundreds of internal documents reviewed by the AP, devout Muslims were specifically targeted, apparently stemming from the bigoted belief that more religious Muslims are more likely to be dangerous. The AP noted that one Bangladeshi restaurant was "identified as a hot spot for having a 'devout crowd' . . . [and] was noted for being a 'popular meeting location for political activities.'"[83]

By its own admission, the NYPD's "Demographics Unit" produced no leads and no arrests in a terrorism-related case.[84] Multiple civil rights organizations called for an independent investigation of this program, and in 2013, the New York City Council passed an ordinance to require increased oversight for the NYPD over Mayor Michael Bloomberg's veto.[85] Finally, in 2014, the program was suspended after newly elected Mayor Bill de Blasio replaced the police commissioner. In 2016, the NYPD attempted to resolve before trial a lawsuit filed on behalf of Muslim Americans affected by this program, in which the department agreed to new limits on their surveillance powers.[86]

The NYPD was not the only large law enforcement agency to discriminate against Muslims and Middle Eastern Americans in its counterterrorism efforts. The FBI had an agent training program that included patently offensive materials falsely asserting that devout Muslims are likely to become terrorists.[87] One image from a slideshow used during FBI counterterrorism training is reproduced in figure 3.1. The crudely illustrated image purports to show how Christians and Jews became more "nonviolent" over time from 1400 BCE through 2010, while Muslims conversely stopped developing in 622 and have remained "violent." Shortly after *Wired* published internal FBI documents describing wildly inaccurate and patently offensive instructional materials like this image, the bureau began a "comprehensive review" of all of its reference material pertaining to religion and culture.[88] A few months later, the FBI asked the Army's Combating Terrorism Center at West Point to send experts to conduct a purge of any inappropriate training materials.[89] These bigoted training materials might have had a profound effect, because the FBI dedicated a huge amount of resources into creating a massive network of informants dedicated to spying on Middle Eastern American communities across the United States.

The FBI's program of conducting counterterrorism investigations where an informant "discovers" a terrorist plot and then FBI agents

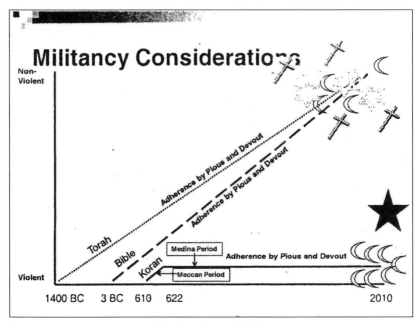

Figure 3.1. Sample PowerPoint slide from bigoted FBI "counterterrorism" training materials

make a dramatic arrest, clearly resembles police entrapment. Trevor Aaronson provides an example of this pattern in his investigation of the case of Muhammad Hussain, a troubled young man from Baltimore. Born Antonio Martinez, he spent much of his youth "angry and lost" as a small-time thief. He converted to Islam and took a new name. Eventually, he began expressing his anger on Facebook, and he "drifted toward a violent, extremist brand of Islam."[90] If he had been White and Christian, he might have been referred to counseling. But the FBI was carefully watching Facebook for expressions of violence associated with Islam. On December 7, 2010, Hussain was befriended by a man pretending to be a hardened terrorist from Afghanistan, and he was ready with a violent mission for the troubled young man. In reality, this "hardened terrorist" was a paid FBI informant. Together, Hussain and the undercover FBI agent developed a plot to detonate a bomb in a car outside an Armed Forces Career Center. The plan and the bomb were fake, and Hussain was taken into custody minutes after he pushed a button that he thought would cause a massive explosion. No one was actually harmed.

Suddenly, FBI agents rushed in and arrested the man they'd later identify in court records as "Antonio Martinez a/k/a Muhammad Hussain." Federal prosecutors in Maryland charged Martinez with attempted murder of federal officers and attempted use of a weapon of mass destruction. He faced at least thirty-five years in prison if convicted at trial.[91]

Hussain first claimed entrapment but eventually pleaded guilty to the weapon of mass destruction charge and was sent to prison for twenty-five years. The DOJ heralded the FBI's success in this case, saying, "We are catching dangerous suspects before they strike."[92] Hussain's picture appeared widely in national media reports showing that a young, brown, Muslim man was caught just before he could detonate a deadly bomb at a military recruiting center. Almost none of these news reports mentioned that this terrorist attack was not genuinely planned, but rather it was staged by the FBI. Media reports like this one, which frequently appear whenever the FBI completes a counterterrorism "sting," amplify the racial project represented by this discrimination. Photographs of the accused terrorists, almost always young, Middle Eastern men, closely associated with terrorism, appeared again and again in media reports generated by this FBI program.

Enabling these efforts is a massive web of thousands of FBI informants, operating at a scale that dwarfs even the infamous COINTEL-PRO effort from the 1950s and 1960s. The FBI's annual counterterrorism budget exceeds $3 billion, and the clandestine informants program no doubt consumes a significant portion of that amount.[93]

The FBI has consistently and repeatedly denied that it targets the Muslim community in its counterterrorism efforts. After the long-rumored secret network of FBI informants infiltrating Middle Eastern American communities was confirmed to be real, the Attorney General vigorously defended the program. At a 2010 banquet benefitting Muslim Advocates, a Muslim American advocacy organization, Attorney General Eric Holder said that the confidential informant operations "have proven to be an essential law enforcement tool in uncovering and preventing potential terror attacks."[94]

The NYPD "Demographics Unit" and this FBI "tool" both flow from the stereotype that Middle Easterners are more likely to get involved in terrorism than the average American. These programs are clear examples of racial profiling—using race to create a profile of a likely terrorist, and then distributing law enforcement resources accordingly.

Despite years of civil rights advocacy and recent protests against racial profiling, the practice remains legal in most of the United States. A Supreme Court ruling in 1996 nullified a lower court's ruling that required law enforcement to assume that "people of all races commit all types of crimes."[95] In 2012, a federal judge dismissed a lawsuit that sought to prevent FBI informants from entering mosques without a specific cause, because, he reasoned, it is sometimes necessary to "sacrifice individual liberties for the sake of national security."[96] Finally, in 2014, after years of controversy, the DOJ released new guidelines for federal law enforcement that Attorney General Holder claimed would end the practice of racial profiling and also stop discrimination on the basis of gender identity, sexual orientation, national origin, and religion. Unfortunately, the guidelines leave a massive loophole for "national security" efforts, an exception that appears to allow the controversial FBI "sting operation" program (and all other "counterterrorism" programs) to continue, even if evidence shows that they are, in fact, policies that rely on racial profiling.[97]

Defining Terrorism

Through all of these so-called counterterrorism efforts, the term "terrorism" has been deployed in ways that reinforce the racial stereotype that Middle Easterners are somehow predisposed to commit political violence. In several instances, violent actions committed by a Middle Eastern perpetrator were classified as "terrorist" even as similar actions carried out by non-Middle Easterners were not. For instance, in 2002, a lone gunman opened fire at a ticket counter at Los Angeles International Airport, killing two and injuring four others before security personnel shot and killed the assailant. The FBI concluded that this was a terrorist attack, because the perpetrator, an Egyptian American man named Hesham Mohamed Hadayet, intended to "advance the Palestinian cause . . . through the killing of civilians and the targeting of an airline owned by the Government of Israel."[98] In 2013, a similar shooting took place at Los Angeles International airport, this time carried out by a White American man originally from New Jersey, Paul Anthony Ciancia. Witnesses said that Ciancia entered the airport and opened fire on Transportation Security Administration (TSA) security guards, killing one before being captured by police. Investigators determined that Ciancia had a political motive, evidenced by a note he was carrying that denounced the TSA as a tyrannical government agency. However, he was charged with first-degree murder—not a terrorism charge—and the attack was not classified as terrorism. The attack did not appear on an official timeline of terrorist attacks maintained by the National Counterterrorism Center (NCTC).[99]

Many other similar examples, of when non-Middle Eastern perpetrators carried out violent acts that were not recognized as terrorism, suggest that in contemporary American discourse and policy, the term "terrorism" refers mainly to the Middle Eastern race of a perpetrator of a violent act. Juan Cole observed, "Arabs and Muslims who melt down are not in today's America allowed to be just 'quiet' or 'troubled' individuals. They are always seen as emblematic of their ethnic group, and one or two of them are enough to make a conspiracy."[100] All of these characterizations that apply the word "terrorism" only to acts committed by Middle Easterners serve to reinforce the bigoted idea that Middle Easterners are inherently violent.

Even after a White supremacist carried out the massacre at the Sikh Temple of Wisconsin in 2012, the official reaction was to wait for a careful analysis of all the possible motives of the attacker before labeling the attack "terrorism." Only after the investigation had proceeded for six days did Attorney General Holder declare the attack "an act of terrorism, an act of hatred, a hate crime."[101] After yet another mass casualty shooting rampage, at the Emmanuel Baptist Church in Charleston in 2015, there was finally some widespread discussion of the threat posed by White supremacist terrorism, but even then some commentators insisted that the attack may have been the result of "mental illness," and therefore not political or racist in motivation.[102]

Consider another pair of attacks, one recognized as terrorism and the other seen as merely caused by a mental instability. In 2015, Robert Lewis Dear attacked a Planned Parenthood clinic in Colorado, killing three. He was not considered to be a terrorist by most Americans. But he terrorized not only the people he personally victimized in Colorado. People around the country understandably feared a potential outbreak of similar attacks. In this instance, Dear was motivated by a political cause: to force an end to the right to choose abortion. Dear should have been classified as a terrorist, by any reasonable definition of terrorism. Instead, commentators and investigators focused on the mental health of Dear, again questioning whether he was simply mentally ill and an aberration, rather than part of a longstanding, active political movement threatening family planning clinics. This attack was not recognized as terrorism in large measure because the perpetrator was White.

Meanwhile, when married couple Syed Farook and Tashfeen Malik killed fourteen people at a San Bernardino County Department of Public Health holiday party, the attack was immediately assumed to be terrorism even before any evidence of motive was available. Eventually, the FBI found evidence that Farook and Malik were "potentially inspired" by the overall goals of organizations like the so-called Islamic State, even though they themselves were "not part of a [terrorist] network." Conclusions about their terrorist motivations were based on their "telephonic connections" with other "people of interest" in separate counterterrorism investigations.[103] The strength of this evidence was never questioned. Alternative explanations were not seriously considered for the cause of this mass shooting, which at first did not seem all that different from the many other horrific mass shooting events that took place in 2015 across the United States. Few accounts of the attack considered whether Farook and Malik suffered from mental illness or if they sought violent revenge for some personal or professional dispute. In any case, the primary reason the San Bernardino shooting was immediately and unquestioningly recognized by most Americans as terrorism is because the perpetrators were racially classified as Middle Eastern Americans.[104]

As fears of additional "lone wolf" terrorist attacks continued to animate policymakers, the Obama administration launched a new effort that once again contributed to the stereotyping of Middle Eastern Americans as predisposed to terrorism. This new effort was called Countering Violent Extremism (CVE). In part, the name CVE was developed as a replacement for "War on Terror." The architects of this program avoided using the loaded term "Islamic extremism." By changing the label to "violent extremism," the implication was that terrorism could come from any source of extremism, not just radical Islam. Critics, however, worried that despite the change in rhetoric, in practice CVE once again targeted Middle Eastern American communities for discriminatory scrutiny. Most of CVE's domestic operations center on "empowering local partners" to find "radicalized" individuals and report them to the authorities, in ways that have disturbing echoes to the failed Operation TIPS effort from a decade earlier. In support of CVE, federal agencies partnered with community centers, places of worship, and private businesses to "enhance engagement with . . . local communities who may be targeted by violent extremists."[105] Arjun Singh Sethi, with the advocacy organization Sikh Coalition, noted that in practice, the CVE program:

> . . . encourages a hypersensitivity to the mundane behavior of young American Muslims and demonizes acts that are protected by the First Amendment. Innocuous activities like growing a beard, attending a fiery sermon, protesting US foreign policy, or fraternizing with Muslim political groups become "warning signs" that are reported to police under the guise of countering violent extremism.[106]

CVE expanded throughout the 2010s, becoming a holistic effort by law enforcement and intelligence agencies to find and stop terrorists before they strike. Advocates repeatedly appealed for the basic rights of terrorist suspects, arguing that "self-radicalizing" individuals suspected of terrorism should not be arrested or imprisoned for expressing controversial attitudes. They suggested that the FBI and other agencies should make use of mental health or other support resources instead of always setting in motion a sting operation. In an attempt to respond to these concerns, the FBI issued plans to set up "Shared Responsibility Committees," which would have social workers, counselors, clergy, and other community leaders advise the FBI on potential terrorist suspects. Advocates like Abed Ayoub of the American-Arab Anti-Discrimination Committee expressed concern that these committees would actually serve mainly as yet another vehicle for FBI "intelligence gathering and surveillance."[107]

As CVE attracted controversy domestically, President Obama rapidly expanded a troubling targeted-assassinations program overseas. Assassinations of terrorist suspects were reported to have been frequently carried out by unmanned aerial vehicles (or "drones" or "flying death robots"). These "signature strikes" have been used exclusively to target Middle Easterners, including some US citizens. President Obama himself personally ordered the extrajudicial execution of Anwar al-Awlaki, an American citizen who was reputed to be a high-ranking member of al-Qaeda living in Yemen.[108] The terrifying frequency of drone strikes in his home village led Yemeni activist Farea al-Muslimi to testify before a US Senate committee:

> I have met with dozens of civilians who were injured during drone strikes and other air attacks. . . . I have met with relatives of people who were killed as well as numerous eyewitnesses. They have told me how these air strikes have changed their lives for the worst.[109]

Al-Muslimi went on to explain that in his view, drone strikes were counterproductive to the mission of preventing anti-American sentiment and terrorism. He explained that after studying in America in high school and college, he was a prominent cultural ambassador for the US in Yemen. He made it his mission to spread the word about the generosity and greatness of the American people. This work was made "almost impossible" by the drone strikes, he said.[110]

As these controversial policies unfolded, the Obama administration promoted the pervasive racial stereotype that Middle Easterners are more likely than others to become terrorists. Even though some of the Obama administration's statements won praise for doing away with the "war on terrorism" rhetoric of the Bush administration, many official statements and policies in the Obama era have either failed to adequately combat or have actively contributed to the perception that only Middle Easterners commit terrorist acts. For example, President Obama's then-Counterterrorism Advisor and later the Director of the CIA, John Brennan, gave a speech to introduce a new National Security Strategy overview in 2010.[111] His speech made it quite clear that the Obama administration had redoubled its efforts to "secure our homeland" by recognizing "the threat to the United States posed by individuals radicalized here at home." Brennan listed seven recent attacks by "radicalized" Americans, to underscore the severity of the threat posed by terrorism. Remarkably, each of the seven terrorist attacks on his list was carried out by a Muslim. Conspicuously absent from Brennan's list of terrorist attacks was any discussion of the threat posed right-wing extremists, such as the Christian Hutaree "militia," an organization that had around that time been planning coordinated, deadly terrorist attacks

in Michigan. Brennan also neglected to mention the White supremacist who opened fire at the Holocaust Memorial Museum, a terrorist
attack that claimed the life of police officer Stephen Tyrone Johns.[112]
Brennon even neglected to mention that a pipe bomb had exploded in a
Florida mosque just days before his speech, an apparent terrorist attack
that was under active investigation by the FBI at the time.[113] By neglecting to mention the mere existence of attacks like these, Brennan used
his speech to further solidify the bigoted idea that only Middle Eastern
Americans commit terrorism.

Perhaps Brennan was being intentionally ignorant. He may have
been mindful of an episode from the year prior, 2009, in which the Department of Homeland Security (DHS) issued a report warning that
"right-wing extremists"—White extremists—presented a major terrorist threat.[114] The publication of this report prompted a tremendous out-
pouring of criticism from Republican legislators, who demanded that
DHS reconsider part of the analysis that said military veterans may have
a propensity to commit violent terrorist acts.[115] The analysis cited an
FBI report that found, from 2001 to 2008, some two hundred White
supremacists who claimed to be veterans were, in fact, "active in the
extremist movement." After initially defending the report, Homeland
Security Secretary Janet Napolitano eventually apologized. After this
apology, the Obama administration carefully calibrated its messaging
and apparently avoided mentioning right-wing extremism as a potential
source of terrorism. In fact, as Brennan's speech and subsequent administration policy decisions make clear, the Obama administration seemed
almost eager to keep the label of terrorism restricted only to acts carried
out by Middle Easterners.

When Joseph Stack flew his airplane into a federal building in Austin,
the Department of Homeland Security immediately concluded—within
hours of the crash—that although they "do not yet know the cause of
the plane crash," still it was safe to say, "at this time, we have no reason
to believe there is a nexus to terrorist activity."[116] The White House reaf-
firmed this conclusion, when Obama's press secretary stated flatly that
the "plane crash" was not an act of terrorism.[117] Homeland Security Secretary Janet Napolitano concurred by explaining that Stack was "a lone
wolf" who "used a terrorist tactic," but that alone did not imply that he
was "in the same bucket" as the Oklahoma City bombing or al-Qaeda.[118]

To be clear, this was a suicide attack wherein the pilot of an airplane intentionally crashed into a high-rise office building. Internal Revenue Service manager Vernon Hunter was killed in the attack. The parallels to the 9/11 attacks could not be more obvious, nor could the political motivation be any clearer with regards to this attack on offices of the federal government. But, according to the Obama administration, this was not in any way a terrorist attack. Stack was White.

In short, reforms to counterterrorism policies initiated by the Obama administration, intended to change and improve the War on Terror policies from the Bush era, unfortunately mainly offered more of the same: racialized rhetoric that contributes to Islamophobic discrimination. All the while, everyone involved in the creation and maintenance of these policies insists that they abhor racial profiling and will not stand for discrimination. The cognitive dissonance required for leaders like President Obama and Attorney General Holder—both deeply committed to anti-racism—to uphold and expand clearly Islamophobic policies is, in part, enabled by the racial paradox that lies at the center of Islamophobia.

Islamophobia Is Racism

This review of Islamophobia has been far from exhaustive. Nevertheless, it shows definitively that Islamophobia is best understood as structural racism. It should go without saying that intersections of race, class, gender, sexuality, religion, and other axes of inequality simultaneously operate in the reproduction of Islamophobia. That does not diminish the fact that Islamophobia is a race-based problem that manifests across multiple layers of culture, politics, and policy. The racial paradox underpinning Islamophobia—the persistent refusal to acknowledge the racist logics at its very core—has allowed it to flourish in the United States even as most Americans claim to seek an end to racism.

There can no longer be any doubt that Islamophobia flows from the collective racialization of Arabs, Muslims, Sikhs, and South Asians in the United States into a Middle Eastern American racial category. This is a racial formation process borne and maintained through linked histories and shared experiences across many generations. Various threads of social divisions between Europeans and "Orientals" survived and expanded during the European Renaissance, and bigoted ideas about North Africa and Southwest Asia were transported with the original European colonists to the Americas.

Beginning shortly after the founding of the United States, the first federal immigration and naturalization policies in the 1790s codified into law the exclusion of people from regions now known as South Asia and the Middle East. Even after a shift in policy during the 1950s and 1960s put an end to explicit racism in immigration policies, Islamophobia continued to find expression in mainstream American culture. By the twenty-first century, the War on Terror relied upon the racialization of Middle Easterners in the American imagination to link the specter of terrorism to the broader Middle East—Afghanistan, Iraq, Iran, and beyond—and to denizens of the United States with heritage anywhere near those places. The worst excesses of the War on Terror—torture, drone strikes, and dragnet surveillance—were targeted at Middle Easterners in ways that legitimated and extended these durable racial logics. Islamophobia is therefore intrinsic to the racial project that establishes "Middle Eastern" as a racial identity category.

Yet the racial paradox remains. While Islamophobia is undoubtedly racism, so far it has eluded proper recognition as a key part of the American legacy of racial despotism. Without this recognition, the Middle Eastern American racial category remains in the shadows, and the full extent of Islamophobia remains hidden as well. Part of the trouble is the constant objection that Islamophobia cannot be called racism because Islam is not a race. Explicitly anti-Islamic rhetoric can be, in theory, deployed in ways that do not directly involve the Middle Eastern racial identity. Nevertheless, race is the only effective theoretical lens to understand Islamophobic discrimination, hate crimes, and discourses as they actually manifest. Understanding race as the driver of Islamophobia provides a clear explanation for hate crimes that target "Middle Eastern-looking" individuals and communities. Furthermore, race-based analyses show that discriminatory profiling policies supposedly targeting only Muslims actually impact people who "look Middle Eastern" more broadly. Nearly all references to "Muslims" in American discourses conjure a racialized image of a Middle Easterner. Policies, practices, and rhetoric that intentionally single out Muslims lend credence to this racial image. These are quintessential racial projects, efforts to distribute resources along racial lines. Because Islamophobia affects diverse communities that have been gathered under the "Middle Eastern" racial umbrella—especially (but not exclusively) Arab, Muslim, Sikh, and South Asian Americans—Islamophobia is a particularly complex race-based problem to confront. That is precisely the challenge undertaken by Middle Eastern American advocacy organizations.

At the crux of that challenge is the racial dilemma. Middle Eastern American advocates have long struggled to reconcile the racial paradox inherent in Middle Eastern identity, one that is amplified greatly by the scourge of Islamophobia. Advocates working in this arena must wade through the cacophony, the constant crisis generated by Islamophobic discrimination. Just keeping up with urgent requests for help after hate crimes and discriminatory actions is, by itself, overwhelming. Getting ahead of the crisis, finding ways to reframe the struggle against Islamophobia proactively, has been a monumental challenge for many years.

Here is the rub: simply knowing that Islamophobia is in fact racism provides no guidance to navigating the racial dilemma. In other words, even after *recognizing* that racism is inherent in Islamophobia, it does not follow that Islamophobia should be *described* as racism by advocates. It may well be better to avoid the language of racism, to gain an advantage in the fickle realms of culture, politics, and policy. In short, it is by no means clear in the twenty-first century that the most effective civil rights strategy is to call out racism by name. The racial dilemma around Islamophobia is formidable, to say the least.

4

Confronting Islamophobia

Racism affects those who fit the racial profile of Middle Eastern, yet there is scant recognition that Islamophobia is racism. This is the racial paradox at the core of Islamophobia in America. While this is a dangerous and complex situation, it is hardly unique. Many, if not most, forms of American racism remain largely ignored and unaddressed, even as they cause tremendous damage. To make a long story short, the refusal to see racism is a recurrent trend in American history.

As I have endeavored to describe in previous chapters, one of the many outgrowths of this racial paradox is the racial dilemma faced by civil rights advocacy organizations: Is it better to call out racism, or is it better to find other ways to describe Islamophobia? Given the pitfalls that open up anytime someone "plays the race card," should civil rights advocates seek to avoid the thorny and controversial topic of race altogether?

Dozens of Middle Eastern American advocacy organizations are currently at work, trying to forge a path through the racial dilemma presented by Islamophobia. Mainly, these are community-based organizations that use a particular ethnic, national, or religious identity to define their mission. These are organizations like Desis Rising Up and Moving (DRUM), the Arab American Action Network (AAAN), the Muslim Community Association (MCA), and the many other local-, regional-, and national-scope organizations seeking to represent and advocate for their communities.[1]

The strategies and tactics developed by civil rights advocacy organizations like these both draw from and produce new racial projects that have the potential to fundamentally reshape the social construction of race. As advocates conduct outreach, win reforms, and build new knowledge, they can, in a very real way, change the concept of race itself. The stakes of the struggle against Islamophobia are therefore quite high. If Islamophobia continues to expand apace, as it has over the past several decades, it will mean that the Middle Eastern racial formation process will have been mainly defined not by civil rights organizations, but by their opponents: hate groups, proponents of oppressive policies, and policymakers who openly embrace Islamophobia.

This chapter considers the recent history and current trajectory of advocacy organizations working to confront Islamophobia through profiles of six of the largest (and arguably most important) Arab, Muslim, Sikh, and South Asian American advocacy organizations: the American-Arab Anti-Discrimination Committee (ADC), the Arab American Institute (AAI), the Council on American-Islamic Relations (CAIR), the Muslim Public Affairs Council (MPAC), South Asian Americans Leading Together (SAALT), and the Sikh American Legal Defense and Education Fund (SALDEF). This enables a fuller discussion of the racial dilemma in confronting Islamophobia by beginning to describe how racial formation has shaped (and how it has surprisingly failed to shape) the orientation of these influential advocacy organizations. The chapter will show that the very existence of these organizations speaks to the ongoing relevance of the "advocacy explosion" set in motion by the great civil rights movements of the mid-1900s. At the same time, the ongoing crises presented by Islamophobia—despite the tremendous efforts of these organizations—expose the limits of the civil rights revolution, some fifty years later.

The Shape of Civil Rights Advocacy

Civil rights advocacy stems from a long, deeply American tradition, one that is full of contradictions—especially where race is concerned. Most studies agree that the social movements of the mid-1900s sparked a significant and long-lasting increase in civil rights advocacy work. In other words, the movements generated an "advocacy explosion."[2] The hundreds of organizations existing today that seek to represent the interests of myriad ethnic communities speak to this flourishing of civil rights advocacy over the past several decades.

Since the mid-1900s, advocacy for identity-based groups exists within a set of taken-for-granted expectations and "political norms," where organizations follow a legitimized script for asking for and receiving changes in response to grievances.[3] The civil rights era introduced completely new forms of advocacy into these norms. Legal protections for "protected" marginalized groups opened up entirely new ways to seek redress for discrimination. Organizations can file lawsuits based on the Civil Rights Act of 1964 and other statutes that place certain identity groups into a protected status. Advocates can appeal directly to administrative agencies for a change in discriminatory policies and practices. And perhaps most importantly, the civil rights victories in the 1900s enabled direct appeals to the public and to legislatures, because discrimination on the basis of race, gender, ethnicity, and religion became a deeply moral issue. In short, the established norms for lodging complaints about discrimination include protest actions like petition drives, boycotts, and rallies; but they also allow for lawsuits, lobbying in legislatures, and direct appeals to corporations, law enforcement, and other state agencies.

By the latter half of the twentieth century, it was accepted (and even expected) that identity-based advocacy organizations would hold rallies, file lawsuits, and demand accountability whenever members of their community faced discrimination. It is difficult to overstate the importance of this transformation in American political culture. In the space of a few decades in the mid-1900s, the entire policy and political machinery in the United States changed from open support of racism, sexism, and other forms of oppression to one that—at least on the surface—welcomed and even solicited complaints from organizations representing oppressed communities. Public agencies were set up to enforce anti-discrimination laws. Corporations moved to add anti-discrimination policies and officers. Individuals made conscious efforts to avoid overt expressions of racism and sexism. The revolution of the 1960s was just that.

It was in this context—the "advocacy explosion" set in motion by the movements of the mid-1900s—that the first Middle Eastern American advocacy organizations were established. Back then, as they do now, those organizations faced a multifaceted crisis and entrenched opposition, and as such, they had to innovate in order to advance their cause.

The Roots of Today's Middle Eastern American Advocacy Organizations

Middle Eastern American organizations have existed since the late 1800s. The earliest organizations, mostly set up by Arab and Muslim Americans, mainly provided social services and cultural activities for their local communities, but by the mid-1900s, several organizations were founded for the specific purpose of political advocacy.[4] They engaged in a wide range of campaigns to improve the lives of recent immigrants—largely Arabs from the northern Levant collectively identified as "Syrians." These original Middle Eastern American advocates espoused both foreign and domestic policy goals as they sought to affect the policy of the United States during a period of decolonization and the rise of Arab nationalism. These organizations sought to influence immigration policy and international affairs, especially the relationships between the United States and various Arab nations.

There was also a large overlap between Muslim American advocacy organizations and Black American advocacy organizations, which is of course not a surprise, considering that a large majority of Muslim Americans before the 1990s were Black. Muslim Americans engaged in a wide range of advocacy efforts throughout the 1900s, and they worked extensively in many civil rights advocacy organizations that pushed for an end to Jim Crow segregation.

The number of purpose-built advocacy organizations seeking to represent Middle Eastern American constituencies—immigrant and otherwise—expanded during the 1960s. These organizations participated in policy debates, engaged in various forms of advocacy, and also provided new, cohesive social identities and forms of expression for their communities.[5]

By 1980, the *Encyclopedia of Associations* contained information on seventy-six advocacy organizations with a Middle Eastern American constituency. These included organizations that self-identified as Armenian, Arab, Coptic, Indian, Iranian, Islamic, Lebanese, Middle Eastern, Pakistani, Palestinian, Syrian, and Turkish. Of the twenty-seven organizations that reported membership sizes, the largest was the American-Arab Relations Committee, founded in 1964 in New York City, which reported thirty thousand members. Their mission statement indicated that they worked exclusively on foreign affairs. They limited themselves to changing the United States' relationships with various Arab nations, emphatically noting that the organization itself "does not take stands on the problems of the Arab world and inter-Arab relations, or on domestic issues within the United States." Meanwhile, the largest Muslim American organization in 1980, by self-reported membership size, was the Muslim Students Association (MSA), with 6,500 members across 160 chapters. No organizations in the 1980 edition of the *Encyclopedia* self-identified as Sikh, but there were several Asian Indian organizations. The largest was the Association of Indians in America, headquartered in New York, which reported twenty thousand members. They sought to "continue Indian cultural activities in the US and to encourage Asian-Indian full participation as citizens and residents of America."[6]

Many more Middle Eastern American organizations were founded during the 1980s and 1990s. By 2004, the *Encyclopedia of Associations* contained entries on 223 Middle Eastern American advocacy organizations. Most of these organizations had a local or regional constituency, but a relatively large proportion aspired to a national presence. These included organizations that self-identified as Afghan, Arab, Armenian, Assyrian, Bengali, Chaldean, Coptic, Egyptian, Indian, Indonesian, Iranian, Iraqi, Lebanese, Middle Eastern, Muslim, Pakistani, Palestinian, Sikh, and Turkish. Among those organizations that self-reported membership numbers, the largest was the Sikh Council of North America, with 2.5 million members. According to tax filings, the organizations with the largest annual budgets were the Arab Community Center for Economic and Social Services (ACCESS), in Dearborn, Michigan, with a 2009 budget of $1.7 million, ADC and AAI, each with a 2013 budget of around $1 million, and CAIR, with a 2014 budget of $2.6 million. Most of these organizations had a legal nonprofit status that permitted them to engage in issue advocacy, but not direct electoral campaigning on behalf of candidates for public office.

Most of these advocacy organizations fit in with the form of American advocacy most common since the 1980s: they did not have true "grassroots" support. If "grassroots" means that support in the form of a large number of small donations sustains the organization, then most of these organizations would not qualify as "grassroots." Instead, the organizations generally rely upon donations from a few wealthy benefactors and seek the support of charitable foundations. The implications of this funding and membership structure on American political advocacy represents a crucial factor in the development of this field of advocacy. A few organizations can legitimately claim to have a traditional grassroots membership model, but most do not have a large number of member-donors. Despite this, these organizations typically present themselves as speaking "for the community." These are contentious assertions, but regardless, this is the state of the art in American political advocacy across all issues—not just civil rights.[7] Nearly all American advocacy organizations claiming to speak for a large number of people actually have relatively few dedicated member-donors.

There are six organizations among those with perhaps the strongest claims to actually representing a broad, national perspective of Middle Eastern American communities, namely: AAI, ADC, CAIR, MPAC, SAALT, and SALDEF. Each of these organizations has a national presence, has survived for more than ten years, and has full-time staff (paid or volunteer) for civil rights advocacy work. Here, I review some of the key developments in each organization's history, before turning to the specific question of strategies for dealing with race in chapter 5.

TABLE 4.1. Selected Arab, Muslim, Sikh, and South Asian American Advocacy Organizations with Founding Dates and Approximate Annual Budgets

Name	Founding Date	Approximate Annual Budget
American-Arab Anti-Discrimination Committee (ADC)	1980	$1 million (2014)
Arab American Institute (AAI)	1985	$1.1 million (2013)
Council on American-Islamic Relations (CAIR)	1994	$2.6 million (2014)
Muslim Public Affairs Council (MPAC)	1986	$1.1 million (2014)
South Asian Americans Leading Together (SAALT)	2000	$650,000 (2014)
Sikh American Legal Defense and Education Fund (SALDEF)	1996	$440,000 (2014)

Sources: The organizations (for founding dates); Philanthropic Research Inc. (for budgets).

Arab American Advocacy Organizations: ADC and AAI

The two most prominent Arab American advocacy organizations have deep roots in the Arab nationalism project of the early twentieth century. Arab nationalism was a significant transnational force at that time, with continuous efforts to unify countries across the Arab world, from Syria to Egypt and beyond. Hani Bawardi found that Arab nationalism influenced political organization of Arabs in the United States as far back as the 1910s, when pioneering Arab American activists founded political organizations like the Free Syria Society and Arab National League.[8] These early advocates aimed to represent their communities' political interests, but they struggled during an era when the number of Arab American immigrants was relatively small. Moreover, the tumultuous effects of decolonization, the new independence of formerly colonized states and complex relationships between various Arab nations, and the controversies surrounding the establishment of the State of Israel all spilled over into American politics. Bawardi documents the efforts of these advocates, who crafted innovative strategies through organizations like the Institute of Arab American Affairs, which "held on" until 1950.[9] They had moved to unify immigrants from Palestinian, Syrian, Lebanese, Iraqi, and other Arab nationalities into the political scene. The objective was to create a political bloc focused on Palestinian liberation and other issues important to the Arab nationalism project.

By the late 1960s, the term "Arab American" became commonly used in the mainstream, and it was an effective tool for coalition building among Syrian, Lebanese, and Palestinian Americans especially, but also North African, Iraqi, Saudi, and even non-Arab groups like Iranians and Kurds felt some affinity with this new and exciting social identity.[10] At the same time, tensions abounded in this socially constructed, transnational identity formation, even at the very beginning. Many of the most vocal proponents of Arab American identity in the 1960s shared an overarching priority—to gain support for the Palestinian liberation movement.[11] For this reason, Arab American advocacy organizations frequently faced dedicated opposition from organizations that supported Zionism.[12] In addition to their work on international affairs, especially efforts to support Palestinian liberation, many Arab American activists also recognized the need to protect Arab communities in the

United States from discrimination and hate crimes. The allocation of resources between these two top priorities—which sometimes conflicted with one another—would remain a recurrent tension throughout the history of Arab American political organizing.

As these early advocates attempted to build Arab American unity around these issues, the defeat of an Arab coalition in the 1947 Nakba War, also known as the Israeli War for Independence, signaled the final collapse of the Arab nationalism project. The effort to create a single Arab nation-state from Syria through to Egypt had ended, and meanwhile the Arab-Israeli conflict rapidly escalated with the Israeli military occupation of Gaza, the Golan Heights, the Sinai, and the West Bank in the late 1960s.[13]

Despite (or perhaps in some ways due to) the tumult overseas, the formation of Arab American advocacy organizations the 1960s and 1970s represented a crucial success in panethnic organizing, even though not all Arab Americans embraced the concept of unity. Then (and now), sizable communities of Lebanese, Egyptian, and other Arab-associated groups refused to use the identity label "Arab," preferring to identify themselves by their national, religious, or ethnic heritage (e.g., Phoenician, Melkite, Chaldean). Even taking these communities into account, the Arab American panethnic identity category can be seen as largely a successful political and social construct.

During the 1960s and 1970s, Arab American activists and scholars founded several new advocacy organizations: most notably, in 1968, the Association of Arab American University Graduates (AAUG).[14] Established in the wake of the 1967 war between Israel and its Arab neighbors, this organization was designed to express the concerns of the fast-growing Arab American community. Founding member Baha Abu-Laban recalled that the organization aimed to develop a broad base of support:

> The AAUG was an association that derived its strength from the knowledge, expertise, and deep commitment of its youthful leaders and ever-growing membership. As an association aimed at bringing together university graduates, it was, by definition, elitist, yet in appealing to all Arab-Americans in diverse disciplines and professions, there was a sense that the AAUG would be a grassroots association.[15]

Several AAUG veterans concurred with Abu-Laban's recollection in interviews. One AAUG member described his read of the political situation in the US after the 1967 war:

> Our diagnosis was, frankly, that this country doesn't have the right information about the Middle East to be able to interact properly with it, and to be able to serve its own interest with it, and so on. And so we thought it was a kind of informational problem. And so we created [AAUG], specifically to fill that vacuum. And over its lifespan it produced something like 130, 140 different pamphlets, booklets, books, textbooks, and things of that sort to try to fill that vacuum.[16]

In short, the 1967 war crystallized a nascent political awakening among both first- and second-generation Arab Americans. The AAUG quickly became the central location for Arab American political advocacy. It served both as a "think tank" and a place for grassroots organizing. This allowed AAUG to serve as an incubator for a number of new advocacy organizations that launched as the "post–civil rights era" began in the 1970s.

AAUG leaders, confronting a large amount of discrimination while also developing Arab American advocates living in cities across the country, reasoned that establishing more organizations would enable a more efficient and effective set of advocacy tools. An AAUG member who spoke with me recalled:

> In part due to the flurry of activity regarding discrimination, stereotypes, and hate crimes in the United States and regarding the rapidly devolving situation in Israel and Palestine, by 1972 the leaders of AAUG reasoned that more organizations were needed to meet demands for action. . . . So, in 1972, they . . . incorporated in Washington, DC, the National Association of Arab Americans [NAAA] specifically to do that. The nature of the two organizations are totally separate. One is a tax-exempt, not supposed to be involved in politics. One is totally political, registered as a lobby, and [set] to work on foreign policy matters on behalf of Arab Americans.[17]

While NAAA lobbied the government on international affairs, AAUG remained as a think tank with grassroots aspirations. AAUG chapters opened in various cities around the country. Elaine Hagopian noted a major effort to build coalitions to consolidate the Arab American identity—as distinct from Lebanese, Palestinian, or any other nationality—to help with marshaling political power. She cited the Federation of Associations for Arab American Relations as a coalition that existed as a third nationally prominent Arab American organization. She also estimated that some seven to eight hundred smaller Arab American organizations existed at this time, "whose activities [varied] from the social to the charitable."[18] My database, based on the *Encyclopedia of Associations*, counts only twelve self-identified "Arab" advocacy organizations active in the late 1970s, although the *Encyclopedia* notably undercounts smaller and newer organizations.

Leaders in AAUG and NAAA worked on several overlapping priorities: organizing the Arab American community politically, influencing American policy and culture around international relations with Arab nations, and advancing the domestic civil rights concerns of Arab Americans.[19] Along all of these priorities, the organizations had some success, but the potential for foreign affairs to complicate advocacy around domestic civil rights was not lost on Arab American activists.

In 1980, in part responding to the conflicts between the international and domestic advocacy priorities, Arab American leaders including James Abourezk and James Zogby co-founded the ADC. An activist present during the conversations that led to the creation of ADC said in an interview that "it was decided civil rights and work on Palestine couldn't be mixed under one roof."[20] Activists involved with the NAAA in the late 1970s debated how to deal with the "still controversial" Palestine Liberation Organization while working with the American government toward a peaceful resolution of the Arab-Israeli conflict, and also dealing with domestic civil rights.

> If we put [civil rights and foreign affairs] under the same roof, the allies we will have in terms of civil rights will be timid or hesitant to join us or include us in the civil rights movement in this country—and if the name stays "Arab American" as the lobby. So, let's separate the two. Gradually, that point of view—luckily, I think—prevailed. And ADC was formed in 1980.[21]

As it turned out, over time, ADC took up advocacy on international affairs as well. Looking at the conference programs of the annual ADC convention reveals that many of the panels, discussions, and workshops at each convention focused on international affairs—the Israeli-Palestinian conflict in particular. For example, at the ADC convention in June 2001, there were four sessions dealing with foreign policy and only one dedicated to civil rights.[22] I asked an ADC leader about this, and he confirmed that ADC often worked on international affairs. He insisted, though, that after the first Gulf War and the organization's rebuilding in the 1990s, ADC had already refocused on domestic civil rights by the time 9/11 happened.

> No doubt. Just take our program books from different conventions, and look at the speakers, and look at the shift. It is obvious. The origins of ADC are defamation of Arab American community, and ABSCAM, and so on. Defamation of the Arab community is why ADC emerged. But, it's very true that because of crises in the Middle East, from the Israeli invasion of Lebanon—it was a mess. And because of [the] high proportion of immigration from that region, that community is still extremely connected to the "old country." ADC attracted activists, in later years—and it's normal, I guess—it attracted those who are most interested in the issues of the day. Not the image of the Sheikh in the movie, or stereotypes, the issue was Lebanon, Palestine, and issues affecting their families directly. A major shift was the first Gulf War. ADC was placed in a very tight situation—an Arab country invaded another Arab country. Unfortunately . . . ADC suffered financially because of some misstatements that were made, and so on. [And a] loss of credibility, almost. But by 1997, ADC really rebuilt. That was the shift that started turning us away from foreign policy.[23]

After recovering from near-bankruptcy in the 1990s, ADC remained one of the largest and most important advocacy organizations working in the aftermath of 9/11 to represent Middle Eastern American civil rights. In 2015, ADC claimed to be "the largest Arab American grass-roots organization in the US," with more than two dozen chapters across twenty-one states.[24] It won new foundation grants in the wake of the

9/11 attacks, and continued to play a prominent role as a center for Arab American advocacy in the following decade. While the size of ADC's membership has fluctuated over time, it retains a strong claim to having the most active members of any Arab American advocacy organization.

ADC does not stand alone as the only Arab American organization with a major national presence, however. In 1985, a group of leading Arab American advocates including James Zogby and Helen Samhan founded AAI, with the goal of increasing participation of Arab Americans in electoral politics. Zogby left ADC, and one of the reasons for this move once again centered on the idea of an efficient division of labor among Arab American advocacy organizations. AAI's niche was designed to be electoral politics—developing Arab American candidates for public offices around the country, promulgating voter resources to provide guidance to voters on key issues, and engaging in efforts to get out the Arab American vote. Meanwhile, ADC would continue to lead the way on civil rights advocacy.[25] Other reasons provided motivation for the decision to split ADC, essentially, into two separate organizations by founding AAI, a development discussed more fully in chapter 5.

Unlike ADC, the structure of AAI does not aspire to a grassroots base. AAI fits squarely in the mold of "inside the beltway" lobbying firms, as a self-styled "leadership organization."[26] AAI maintains partnerships with local and regional organizations that enable a wide range of voter outreach efforts, but it does not have a large membership. Instead, AAI relies on wealthy benefactors and foundation grants for the majority of its estimated $1.1 million annual budget.[27] It resembles an Arab American "think tank" and, in addition to its electoral work, AAI also effectively contributes to debates on various issues by lobbying Congress and the administration.

In the 1980s, ADC and AAI worked alongside one another, sometimes in cooperation and sometimes separately, but generally with little public acrimony. Occasionally, however, tensions caused difficulties in cooperation. During what several ADC and AAI advocates described as a turbulent period in the 1990s, relations between these two prominent organizations became less collegial and more competitive. Once again, tensions over international affairs lay at the center of the difficulties.

The 1990s brought significant changes to ADC and AAI because of major developments in the peace process between Israel and the Palestinians. This led both organizations to react quickly after the rapid changes following the Madrid Conference in 1991 and the surprising handshake on the White House lawn between Yasser Arafat and Yitzhak Rabin in 1993, inaugurating the era of the Oslo Accords. Two advocates remembered this period as a struggle over limited and diminishing resources, in part because as the idea took hold that the peace process had actually succeeded in ending the Israeli-Palestinian conflict, the pool of active donors to AAI and ADC had shrunk.

> There was [a] shrinking of resources. Of course, shrinking of resources means more competition over scarcer resources, number one. Number two, [there were] leadership struggles, because you've got too many bosses governing or ruling over lesser and lesser territory.[28]

This impression of a competition over resources between ADC and AAI continued into the 2000s. Both organizations therefore exceeded their original mandate as designed back in 1985, as one advocate described:

> I think that between ADC and AAI, frankly, they both perceive the pool of potential supporters among the Arab Americans as very small, because most Arab Americans aren't organized and seem to be resistant to that. Therefore, one of the characteristics of ADC and AAI since their inceptions has been that while they both have clear mandates— civil rights and civil liberties on the one hand, political engagement and empowerment on the other hand—neither of them have stuck to those mandates much. And they both felt compelled on a regular basis to try to be all things to all people and try to do everything. And there's a lot of competition, a lot of one-upsmanship, a lot of when the groups do work together, it is not uncommon that one side perceives the other as having unfairly exaggerated its role in the project, and presented itself as having done the work—it's a bit like people on a tandem bicycle. The man in the front always thinks he's doing all the work, while the guy in the back thinks the guy in the front is taking a break and he's doing all the puffing.[29]

The sense of competition between ADC and AAI meant that cooperation became less common after 9/11. One advocate described "unbelievable enmity" between leaders of the two organizations over a period of "several years," especially after 9/11.[30] This tension only occasionally resulted in public disputes between the organizations, but several advocates that I spoke with expressed regret that efforts to create more stable cooperation between these two pillars of the Arab American community had repeatedly failed.

Both ADC and AAI have another characteristic that became increasingly relevant as more Muslims immigrated to the United States in the 1990s and 2000s: both have leadership historically dominated by Christian Arab Americans. While both ADC and AAI have worked closely with Muslim American communities, and both have had Muslim Americans in key leadership positions, the general impression in Arab American communities is that these two organizations are primarily run by Arab American Christians. The perceived lack of sufficient attention to the needs of immigrant Muslim communities, at least in part, led to the establishment of new, specifically Muslim American advocacy organizations in the late 1980s and early 1990s.

Muslim American Advocacy Organizations: CAIR and MPAC

The emergence of new Muslim American advocacy organizations in the 1980s and 1990s came during a time when immigration to the United States from Muslim-majority nations had increased significantly. What's more, around this same time, an "Islamic Revival" was underway.[31] As a result, it became normal and even desirable to use "Muslim American" as a social and political identity—a development that in many ways mirrored the construction of the Arab American identity in the 1960s and 1970s. Muslims in the United States and around the world increasingly asserted their faith as a central part of their personal identity. As political Islam became a significant force in many countries around the world, in cultural terms, many institutions in Muslim-majority societies underwent profound changes as well.

In the midst of this "Revival," the MSA served as the largest Muslim American organization in the 1980s, with 6,500 members in 1980. It moved to reshape Muslim American institutions in several ways. First, several MSA leaders joined with organizers of professional associations (such as the Islamic Medical Association) to form the Islamic Society of North America (ISNA) in 1982. ISNA became an umbrella organization that aspired to bring unity to all Muslim Americans, but it pointedly stopped short of engaging in political advocacy. Nevertheless, ISNA set the stage for Muslim American political advocacy by providing a forum for discussion and debate amongst Muslim Americans from all backgrounds, through its annual convention and its community outreach efforts. In 1986, ISNA leaders took a strong stand on a question that had divided many in Muslim American communities: they declared that active participation in American public and social life was important.[32] This presented a significant shift, and opened the door for the establishment of new, specifically Muslim American, advocacy organizations. Later that year, MPAC was founded.

MPAC was originally formed as a political action committee of the Islamic Center of Southern California, in Los Angeles.[33] Two years later, the organization spun off into an independent nonprofit advocacy organization. According to leaders at MPAC, the proximate cause for the founding of MPAC was a new recognition by Muslim American leaders that there had yet to be a "significant outreach" effort to Muslims by Muslims, to allow Muslim Americans to represent their own interests in the public sphere.[34]

Early issues taken up by MPAC included mainly international affairs, with some work done in the domestic political arena. Some of MPACs most visible efforts in the late 1980s and early 1990s came in its responses to major events—including the Palestinian Intifada, the Gulf War, and the Salmon Rushdie affair—and through its emphatic denouncements of terrorist attacks.[35] Apart from international affairs, MPAC's early work included "a strong interfaith dialogue effort" and a campaign in 1988 to get Muslim Americans elected as delegates to the Democratic National Convention.[36] Much of MPAC's strength grew from the close connections it maintained with policymakers and influential political and cultural elites at the highest levels. For example, MPAC co-founder and president Salam al-Marayati was nominated for a position on President Clinton's National Commission on Terrorism in 1999; although due to "intense pressure," his name was eventually withdrawn.[37] In addition to its connections in Washington, MPAC's location in Los Angeles helped it build relationships in Hollywood. The organization closely monitored the film and television media for derogatory representations of Muslims. The organization criticized problematic representations and gave awards to individuals and institutions that presented Muslims as human beings rather than just as stock villains.

Like AAI, MPAC is a self-declared "leadership organization," one that does not have wide grassroots support. Unlike most nationally prominent organizations like this, however, MPAC is not based in Washington (although after 9/11 the organization opened an office on Capitol Hill). Its domestic civil rights advocacy work expanded greatly after 2001, as reports about Islamophobic discrimination flooded in to the organization, and MPAC leaders like al-Marayati were frequently called to appear in national media. MPAC's national profile grew rapidly as it promulgated a great deal of original research, developed position statements, and initiated petition drives and similar advocacy efforts.

MPAC thus played a critical role in consolidating a new political consciousness for immigrant Muslim Americans as part of a multicultural American landscape in the post–civil rights era. Despite the vast diversity among Muslim Americans, MPAC provided a narrative of unity as the size of the population expanded rapidly in the 1990s and 2000s. As with the Arab American organizations, this effort was at best partially successful, and numerous fractures remained.[38] Still, MPAC's work— supported by an estimated $1.1 million annual budget—went a long way toward consolidating a Muslim American social and political identity.[39]

Notably, despite its mission to represent all Muslim Americans, MPAC has been limited in its outreach to Black Muslim communities. MPAC's reputation suggests that it represents immigrant Muslims, especially South Asian constituencies, without much input from Black Muslim communities. When I asked a MPAC staff member about this, he agreed that more outreach to Black Muslims was needed, and admitted that it was not currently a priority for the organization.

> Each mosque and each group we'd like to engage with more but we lack capacity. So a lot of our work is very limited in terms of trying to keep up with everybody as much as we want. However, the Shura Council has African American leadership, and we support other groups led by African

American Muslim groups. There is definitely engagement and dialogue, but we need more.[40]

The MPAC staff member referred to the Islamic Shura Council of Southern California, a religious group that has a largely South Asian and African American constituency, with which MPAC has had a long-standing partnership. Despite these admitted difficulties in reaching all segments of the large and diverse Muslim American community, MPAC remains one of the two most influential and durable Muslim American advocacy organizations.

The other prominent Muslim American advocacy organization with national scope, CAIR, also makes an ambitious claim to represent all Muslim American communities. As with MPAC, in practice this is a goal and not a reality. There is a great deal of diversity across Muslim American communities around the nation, making it very difficult to have one organization that is fully representative of the full range of diversity. CAIR might have the more legitimate claim to a truly nationally representative constituency, however, due to its decentralized, authentically grassroots structure.

CAIR, unlike MPAC, aspired from the time of its inception to build a large grassroots base of supporters. By establishing a strong presence in mosques in cities all over the country, CAIR leaders grew the organization organically, founding chapters that have a great deal of autonomy. CAIR National, meanwhile, was established in 1994 in Washington, DC, and it quickly began to follow in the footsteps of ADC and MPAC. Early CAIR statements condemned Hollywood stereotypes of Arabs and Muslims, and the new organization filed lawsuits on behalf of people who faced Islamophobic discrimination.[41] CAIR's base inside mosques allowed it to document in detail the rise of Islamophobia in the 1990s, and it began compiling statistics on the incidence rates of Islamophobic harassment. For example, after the media broadcast dozens of analysts and pundits jumping to the conclusion that Middle Easterners must have carried out the Oklahoma City bombing, CAIR issued a report in 1995 documenting the tremendous damage of their rush to judgment: they had received 222 reports of hate crimes against Muslim Americans in the days immediately after the bombing.[42]

After 9/11, CAIR expanded rapidly, opening new chapters in cities across the country, and engaging in additional outreach work. It quickly established a presence in cities across the United States through what one CAIR leader called a "franchise" model.

> We have a national headquarters, [but] different people come with their own funds to start a chapter, and then it's kind of like a franchise. It's like there's a trademark and there's some assistance for coordination. There's some logistical cooperation. But in a sense . . . each chapter is semi-autonomous, because each chapter has its own separate 501(c)(3) nonprofit status. It has its own board of directors. Each chapter hires who it wants to hire. There's no input from the national office about who the offices hire. It's strictly from the local level. And although we have a broad national agenda, each chapter addresses or comes up with certain programs based upon the needs and the demographics.[43]

Most CAIR chapters sought to represent a diverse section of the Muslim American community—not only Arab and South Asian Americans, but also African Americans as well. Various CAIR staff emphasized that the organization aspired to represent the complete diversity across Muslim American communities.[44]

The relative success of CAIR's franchise model, using a unified Muslim American religious identity to gather support and organizing in religious spaces including mosques, suggests that perhaps religion—and not race or panethnicity—was primarily operative in Middle Eastern American civil rights advocacy in the 1990s. Recall that during the 1990s, ADC faced an existential crisis and a drop in its grassroots support. Meanwhile, it was clearly the case that many Muslim Americans found their Muslim identity to be most salient in their lives, and many of them moved to support CAIR. CAIR leveraged Muslim identity in an innovative way, by gaining certification from several Muslim scholars and religious leaders as *zakat*-eligible. This means that observant Muslims can fulfill one of their obligations—giving to charity, or *zakat*—by making a donation to support CAIR. As CAIR organized in mosques, at various events including at times around Friday prayers, its *zakat* eligibility was very effective.

From interviews and informal observations at CAIR chapters in various places around the country, CAIR actually seemed to have a very diverse membership, not only Arabs or any one ethnic group. Muslims from African American, Arab American, South Asian American, and White American communities attended CAIR events and worked as CAIR volunteers and staff. Nevertheless, some local CAIR chapters have a specific ethnic "base" in one community or another.

Overall, CAIR's remarkable success in organizing at the local level gave it a legitimate and unique claim to represent the national Muslim American community—and to an extent even the wider Middle Eastern American community. Some CAIR chapters have a perceived ethnic majority, such as South Asian Americans in CAIR-LA or Arab Americans at CAIR-Chicago, but nationally the group has a reputation of a wide, multi-ethnic base of support.

Due to its widespread support, CAIR National became prominent in Washington in the early 2000s as the preeminent Muslim American organization. One way that CAIR moved to expand its influence and demonstrate its patriotism was by cooperating with law enforcement on counterterrorism while also engaging in civil rights advocacy around Islamophobia. Partly in recognition of its efforts, the CAIR Executive Director, Nihad Awad, was invited by the White House to stand directly behind President Bush during his historic speech at the Islamic Center of Washington, DC, on September 17, 2001. The FBI and DOJ worked closely with both CAIR and MPAC in the immediate post-9/11 aftermath, looking to the organizations for assistance with counterterrorism and civil rights enforcement efforts. However, CAIR leaders sometimes took positions that placed them outside of the Washington mainstream, particularly on the Israeli-Palestinian conflict. International affairs, in a familiar pattern, complicated CAIR's civil rights efforts.

As calls grew louder for CAIR and other Muslim American organizations to explicitly condemn any and all acts of terrorism and political violence, MPAC and CAIR issued repeated denunciations of terrorism in multiple ways. Nevertheless, some critics, including prominent members of Congress, began to frequently accuse CAIR, specifically, of "supporting terrorism." Some alleged that Awad and other CAIR leaders had direct connections to Palestinian militant organizations, particularly the controversial Palestinian organization, Hamas.

In 2007, the arguments of CAIR's critics were bolstered when a federal prosecutor listed the organization as an "unindicted co-conspirator" in a terrorism-related trial. The Holy Land Foundation, a Muslim American charity, was accused of sending funds to Hamas. Because the State Department had officially designated Hamas as a terrorist organization (under authorities granted with the 1996 Antiterrorism Act), providing material support to it is a serious federal crime. The prosecutor for this case listed CAIR, ISNA, and 244 other individuals and organizations as "unindicted co-conspirators" with the Holy Land Foundation, essentially making a public accusation that CAIR and ISNA had ties with Hamas. Listing "unindicted co-conspirators" is a common practice for federal prosecutors, but it is usually done as a maneuver to compel or enable testimony, for instance, or to introduce evidence. The list of "co-conspirators" is almost always provided to the court confidentially, or "under seal," to help prevent unintentional damage to the reputation of the individuals and organizations listed. After all, anyone listed as a "co-conspirator" has no access to due process to challenge the prosecutor's decision to name them, and there is no requirement to produce any evidence supporting the claim that they are "co-conspirators." In the Holy Land case, for some reason, the list of "co-conspirators" was made public. This highly unusual decision gave CAIR's many critics the ability to claim that the federal government "named CAIR as a co-conspirator" with Hamas, even though the "co-conspirator" listing did not necessarily stem from actual evidence.

The result of this controversy was that the largest, most genuinely grassroots advocacy organization in the Middle Eastern American field, CAIR—much like ADC in the 1990s—became "frozen out" of policy-making in Washington, DC. CAIR became "radioactive," meaning that almost no one in DC would meet with CAIR leaders to avoid accusations that they had worked with "supporters of terrorism." The FBI formally suspended all contacts with CAIR National headquarters in 2009, saying basically that the organization could not be trusted, in part due to the "unindicted co-conspirator" label.[45] CAIR found itself on the outside looking in, unable to get almost any direct contact with policymakers in Washington.

Almost immediately after CAIR was listed as a "co-conspirator" with ties to a terrorist organization, some CAIR supporters insisted that the DOJ had intentionally slandered the organization in a move designed to sideline the organization politically. In an interview, a federal official with inside knowledge of the Holy Land case revealed that the DOJ made the move specifically because it wanted CAIR executive director Nihad Awad to resign. He noted that the DOJ continues to work actively with ISNA—also listed as a "co-conspirator"—but not with CAIR, and he said that this was simply because the DOJ wanted nothing to do with Awad.

> CAIR is an unindicted co-conspirator. So is ISNA. We talk to ISNA. You might ask why. ISNA has new leadership. CAIR does not. Does that explain it? . . . It's Nihad [Awad]. It is Nihad. . . . But we talk to all the CAIR local chapters. There are strong relationships with many local chapters, the FBI . . . It's CAIR National [that is the problem]. . . . And the CAIR brand is hurting them. . . . The easy way [to fix this] is for Nihad to step down.[46]

According to this official, the DOJ had a clear objective behind not only the public "unindicted co-conspirator" designation, but also the policy of suspending all contact with CAIR National. The objective for DOJ was to pressure CAIR Executive Director Nihad Awad to resign. In any event, in 2010, federal courts found that listing CAIR and ISNA publically as "unindicted co-conspirators" in the Holy Land terrorism trial violated the organizations' due process rights.[47] One federal judge faulted the DOJ for making an "error" in not filing the list of "unindicted co-conspirators" under seal, as is customary.

Despite these problems, CAIR remained active and engaged throughout the 2010s, particularly at the local level. Furthermore, CAIR continued to attract a great deal of support. Looking at only the financials for the national headquarters, CAIR had an estimated budget of over $2.5 million.[48] Local chapters of CAIR also had extensive resources mostly independent from the national office, and they acted largely autonomously, reaching out to state and local authorities on reform efforts. CAIR also advocated in the courts by raising lawsuits on a wide range of issues. CAIR's broad grassroots base allowed it to make many connections with Muslim and non-Muslim communities around the country, including South Asian and Sikh organizations.

South Asian American Advocacy Organizations: SALDEF and SAALT

In racial terms, South Asian American identity has never found a clear home among the "top five" racial categories recognized in the mainstream United States. This racial confusion has no doubt contributed to the inclusion of South Asians in the Islamophobia phenomenon— lacking an established place in the racial order, these communities have often been shunted into the Middle Eastern category. In recent decades, as Asian Americans have sought to build race-based advocacy coalitions, there has been a great deal of outreach to South Asian organizations. These efforts have often constituted intentional racial projects seeking to expand the popular conception of Asians to include South Asians alongside East Asians. Meanwhile, debates have continued for decades among South Asians over how best to organize politically.

"South Asia"—as a concept—is relatively new. The huge geographic region, whose borders (as seems to always be the case) remain unclear, has also been popularly referred to as the "Indian subcontinent." Aside from the many national-origins elided under the panethnic label "South Asian," there are many ethnic groups from this region that are well represented in the United States, including Bengali, Pashtun, and Punjabi Americans. In terms of religion, immigrants from this region belong to many denominations of Islam and Christianity, and there are Sikh, Hindu, Parsi and more religious identifications as well.[49] Socioeconomically, South Asian Americans have one of the highest levels of education and income of any demographic group, but the most recent immigrants (since 1990) from this region are more often working-class and relatively less well-off financially.[50]

The development of several types of advocacy organizations among South Asian Americans is described by Prima Kurien, who notes that ethnogenesis, or the development of a panethnic identity often in relation to political advocacy, has also been advocated for specifically by some South Asian American activists. Those aligning with a non-religious South Asian identity (as opposed to a Hindu, Sikh, Muslim, or other religious-based identity) tend to work for "liberal" social justice goals, and those aligning with a religious Hindu identity typically work for "conservative" or nationalist goals. She notes that politically conservative organizations often pointedly use the Hindu identity, and they generally want to create advocacy organizations that have a pro-India, nationalistic line. On the other hand, those organizations that identify as South Asian tend to be on the left politically, and Kurien shows that these activists often seek inclusive, broad-based coalitions that unite South Asians from across India, Pakistan, Sri Lanka, and elsewhere.[51]

Another large religious group among South Asian Americans— Sikhs—have created several "liberal" advocacy organizations. Before 9/11, however, Sikh Americans had few political advocacy organizations. The *Encyclopedia of Associations* had no record of any Sikh American advocacy organization before 1980. Jaideep Singh founded the Sikh American Association in 1989, but found very little interest from fellow community members. Of Sikh Americans in the 1980s, he recalls:

> Most Sikh Americans had long believed that they were too small and in-significant a minority to become involved in the decision-making process in this country, and generally accepted being ignored by political leaders and excluded from the political process.[52]

In the 1990s, however, as the Sikh American community grew, and more second-generation activists emerged, Singh found a "natural progression" where more affluent, American-born community members began to support advocacy organizations.[53] He also found that Sikh American political advocacy "peaked" in the late 1990s, with a wide variety of projects including constructing gurdwaras, organizing unions, and countering stereotypes in media.

In 1996, several Sikh American activists founded the Sikh Mediawatch and Resource Taskforce (SMART), which began to monitor film and television for defamation.[54] SMART facilitated the connection of what Singh described as "a cadre of geographically dispersed" Sikh activists through email and innovative use of the early Internet.[55] The organization had some success, but remained volunteer-only until 1998, and even after they hired staff, they had a minimal budget.[56] Things changed quickly after 9/11.

On the day of the 9/11 attacks, SALDEF was the one of very few South Asian American organizations and the one and only Sikh American organization "that had an 800 [toll-free telephone] number that anyone could call."[57] Fortuitously, they had a staff to field calls for help. The hate crimes caused by the Middle Eastern category's racial linkages between Muslims and Sikhs led to a full-blown crisis for the Sikh American community in the months immediately after 9/11.

> Those first three to four months, our phone was off the hook twenty-four hours a day. People were calling at all times of the day and night. We were basically, at that point, reactive, which most of the other organizations were, because nobody anticipated or expected the crisis. So everyone was reacting and trying to respond to the community's needs the best they could.[58]

The early recognition that Sikh Americans would face increasing Islamophobia led to unprecedented outreach from policymakers and law enforcement agencies to SMART.

> 9/11 was not the first time Sikhs had been characterized as terrorists. [In] 1984, the incidents in India, the way the community was projected in the United States was terrorism. . . . Around 1999, 1998, SMART got a lot of recognition within the community. And we tried to stay true to our mission, which was media relations, but [after 9/11] the need was just too great for discrimination, hate crimes, harassment, school bullying, denial of public accommodation, and other sorts of things. . . . And so, 9/11 essentially gave the organization and the community a bit more credibility in the eyes of government. All of a sudden, now we're being targeted. We started getting seats at the table and voices at the table before [9/11]. But after 9/11, it was instantaneous, having a seat at the table with the DOT secretary, or the Attorney General, or the FBI director, or the President, or any of these sorts of forums. All of a sudden it was much easier for us to gain that voice. There was an interest.[59]

SMART transformed after the 9/11 attacks into a full-blown civil rights advocacy organization, dropping its initial, limited mission to educate the public about Sikhs by confronting media defamation.

By 2004, SMART had changed so much that it renamed itself the Sikh American Legal Defense and Education Fund (SALDEF), in the style of MALDEF, the iconic Mexican American civil rights organization. The organization opened a new headquarters in Washington, DC. SALDEF continued to face tremendous demand on multiple fronts, from community members who needed support, to requests for comment in the national and international press, to extensive work in diversity training programs for institutions around the country. For example, SALDEF co-produced a video with the FBI that was distributed to local police departments to assist in teaching police officers about Sikh culture.[60] SALDEF thrived in the years since 9/11. It wielded an annual budget of approximately $440,000 in 2014.[61]

SALDEF cooperated with a wide range of civil rights advocacy organizations, and even before 9/11 they gained membership in the Leadership Council on Civil Rights (LCCR), an institutional coalition of civil rights advocacy organizations that originated in 1950. The need for cooperation with non-Sikh organizations and coalitions, like LCCR, however, has been challenged by some SALDEF constituents, an issue that I discuss in chapter 5.

Meanwhile, SAALT, the largest South Asian American advocacy organization, has perhaps the most effective and aggressive panethnic outreach program of any South Asian American organization. Founded in 2000 as the Indian American Leadership Center, this organization changed its name and focus to reflect its efforts to bring together a broader South Asian constituency after 9/11.[62] It remained volunteer-only until 2004, when it hired full-time staff.[63] SAALT adopted a few unique and sophisticated policies designed to enable effective panethnic organizing drives. First, nearly all of its efforts centered on domestic policy concerns of wide interest to South Asian Americans and other communities—namely, immigration reform, civil rights expansion, and hate crime prevention. Second, and perhaps more importantly, SAALT made it a matter of policy not to engage in any international affairs.[64] These innovations stand in stark contrast to Arab and Muslim American organizations like ADC, AAI, CAIR, and MPAC, which frequently weigh in on international issues. The idea for SAALT was to remove the chance that international affairs would complicate their work to bring together people with heritage in India, Pakistan, and other places where international conflicts are ongoing. Third, SAALT engaged with local-level organizations across the country, creating a "network" of service, advocacy, and cultural organizations in a large number of cities and states. With its innovative strategy, SAALT found tremendous success in generating a multi-ethnic constituency.

With its broad base of support, SAALT built a solid claim to represent the South Asian American community as a whole, even though it remained a relatively small organization. Beginning in 2004, SAALT sponsored "local dialogs" in about nine cities, in an effort to build the organization from the local level, rather than from the top down.[65] This approach bucked the trend set by most other DC-based advocacy organizations, and it quickly helped to bring SAALT to national prominence. In 2007, SAALT launched a formal network that worked to bring together local South Asian organizations around the United States. They convened a weekend-long symposium for community advocates to discuss issues and set a "progressive policy platform" for advocacy over the coming years.[66] SAALT then brought some of these policy priorities into their advocacy work, which involved a mix of administrative and legislative approaches.[67] SAALT's work was supported with a budget of around $600,000 per year.[68] They continued throughout the 2000s and 2010s to "build bridges," as former Executive Director Deepa Iyer described:

> For many years after 9/11, many South Asian, Arab, Muslim, and Sikh nonprofit organizations existed in this cycle of crisis response, pivoting to the range of needs presented by clients and community members while also advocating against harmful government policies and divisive public narratives. But [these communities] are no longer just "post-9/11 communities." While we continue to face hate violence, surveillance, and anti-Muslim rhetoric, additional challenges lie before us as our numbers increase in America. In particular, socioeconomic differences, educational barriers, lack of accessible health care, and limited English proficiency hamper the opportunities of many community members. In addition, internal community divides along class, faith, and gender lines continue to pose challenges.[69]

As Iyer describes, the racial paradox posed by Islamophobia presents a necessary but not sufficient cause for unity among Arab, Muslim, Sikh, and South Asian American organizations.

Recognizing the Racial Dilemma

The recent history of these six organizations—AAI, ADC, CAIR, MPAC, SAALT, and SALDEF—shows just how complex the Islamophobia crisis has been over the past several decades. It metastasizes at all levels, from a shouted epithet, to mass murder, widespread discriminatory policies, and international conflicts and wars. This crisis provoked a variety of creative responses from Middle Eastern advocacy organizations.

Even as these organizations have innovated, they still largely fit the mainstream American model of civil rights advocacy. With a few important exceptions, they generally eschewed grassroots support in favor of seeking the financial backing of a small number of wealthy benefactors and charitable foundations. They largely abandoned civil disobedience as a tactic. They filed lawsuits, held the occasional rally, and engaged in direct appeals to legislators, policymakers, and the public. Yet all six of these organizations have struggled to gain traction as Islamophobic policies and practices proliferated both before and after the 9/11 attacks. As hate crimes and discrimination persist in the 2010s, these organizations remain on the front lines.

Perhaps the most pressing question facing these organizations, throughout all of their history and right up to the present, is: What do we do about race? The lack of clarity around Middle Eastern American identity has persistently complicated the work of each of these organizations. As the harm done by Islamophobia has been and continues to be tremendous and tragic, the racial dilemma at the center of civil rights work has never been more opaque.

5

Civil Rights Coalitions

Experienced advocates know that little can be achieved in politics without coalitions. Just about everything in the political arena requires building up enough strength to overcome persistent opposition, and strong partnerships are basically a prerequisite to success. Over time, as advocates build a case for change, they demonstrate the worthiness of their mission by marshaling ever-larger numbers of supporters from diverse sources. Coalitions can also generate the intangible but all-important resource of legitimacy. They can help sustain a campaign during a long and grueling journey. Even though they sometimes involve painful compromises—rearranging priorities, sharing dearly won resources, and even sacrificing some goals—coalitions have nevertheless proven essential in all areas of political advocacy. Finding the right coalition partners in the competitive and dynamic world of politics always represents a challenge. When racial identity gets in the mix, things get even more complex.

In the early part of the post–civil rights era, advocacy coalitions built on racial identity were relatively common, and many times such coalitions achieved remarkable success. As I described in previous chapters, race-based coalitions brought significant changes across the United States, and they even contributed to the formation of new socially constructed racial identities. Despite the weight of divisions—centrifugal forces spun out of diversity in history, culture, and religion—for communities within ascribed racial umbrellas, the centripetal efforts of advocates combined with persistent racial discrimination enabled the formation of sustainable advocacy coalitions.

Through until the 1980s, it was generally accepted that the reforms won by the 1960s civil rights campaigns would remain durable and effective for the long term—for decades or more. After all, the movement made racial inequality into a deeply moral issue, and when an advocate spoke up about racism, it might be perceived as racist to stand in opposition to that advocate. The framework whereby an identity-based advocacy organization files grievances has stood the test of time, but the methods available to those organizations for advocacy have changed considerably in the decades since the apex of the civil rights movement.

As it turned out, advocacy designed to expand legal protections for racialized minority communities became unconventional, or even illegitimate, at the end of the 1900s. The conservative reaction to the disruptions of the 1960s social movements meant that any discussion of special protections for racialized groups—from desegregation, busing, and affirmative action to voting rights protections—became stigmatized and controversial at best. By the 1980s, such efforts were branded as "radical," even "racist" or "reverse racist." The conservative turn of the 1970s, personified in the successful Nixon campaign to empower the "silent majority" of Americans who wanted "peace and quiet," sparked a successful counter-movement to delegitimize civil rights protections established through what conservatives derided as "identity politics."

In the face of these shifts in the political climate, anti-racist campaigns defended affirmative action policies and other anti-discrimination programs built on the legacy of the civil rights movement by relying less and less on racial identity recognition and group rights, and instead increasingly taking up issue-based approaches. Civil rights organizations began to emphasize the common benefit of their campaign for all Americans, regardless of race. In other words, a "post-racial" and "colorblind" climate emerged, and many advocates for civil rights adjusted their strategies away from the now-controversial "identity politics."

The rise of this "colorblind" ideology came about due to the profound success of conservative efforts to undo the progressive reforms of the 1960s. Government policies became ostensibly race-neutral, in contrast to earlier race-conscious programs designed to alleviate racism, set in motion by the Voting Rights Act and Civil Rights Act. The courts chipped away at many of the race-conscious provisions of civil rights protections, enforcing the ideology that only a colorblind approach would bring about a racism-free future. Conservative jurists in the federal courts enforced "strict scrutiny" in their appraisals of civil rights complaints, meaning that they required a narrowly tailored policy using the least restrictive means to achieve a compelling governmental interest. Rather than simply remaining true to midcentury interpretations of the Fourteenth Amendment which held that the equal protection clause required protecting racialized minorities from discrimination, the courts have reinterpreted "equal protection" to mean that any use of racial categories in policymaking whatsoever (even in anti-discrimination policies) is unconstitutional. This has been most clearly seen in lawsuits filed by Whites against affirmative action policies in employment and college admissions. Several landmark Supreme Court cases narrowed the legal justification for affirmative action on the grounds that Whites should not face "reverse racism." The use of "strict scrutiny" thus rendered many anti-discrimination policies enacted in the 1960s unconstitutional and invalid as early as the 1970s, and this trend has only accelerated in the twenty-first century. These developments pushed any advocacy strategy based on the affirmative use of race-based solutions to race-based problems even further outside the political mainstream.

In addition to these significant shifts in the policies and rhetoric used to justify civil rights advocacy, since the turn toward "colorblindness" in the 1970s, the use of direct action and civil disobedience protests was all but abandoned by most American civil rights advocates by the end of the 1900s. The civil disobedience—boycotts, sit-ins, and marches—seen during the 1950s and 1960s were almost completely delegitimized. When such tactics did appear, they were usually simply ignored. On the very rare occasions where such protests became impossible to ignore, mainstream commentators decried the protests as radical, violent, or ridiculous. This was seen in the 2010s when peaceful demonstrations and rallies occurred across the country as part of the Movement for Black Lives. Even the crisis caused by the frequent killings of unarmed Black people at the hands of police officers was not enough to confer mainstream legitimacy on the peaceful civil disobedience of those protests, such as the disruption of traffic on major highways.

Protests like these have been delegitimized in part because of the assumption that "the system" works. Since the 1960s, powerful actors including the state itself have emphasized how easy it is to work for change "from within," by engaging with the mainstream political system. The legacy of the social upheaval of the 1960s, it is often said, is that space has been made at "the table" where the powerful make decisions. The creation of the Civil Rights Division of the Department of Justice in 1957, along with provisions of many laws passed since the 1950s, have undoubtedly left a considerable amount of space at that figurative table for protected minority groups to seek redress by using "the system." When Barack Obama, a Black American, was elected President of the United States, that was enough proof for many that the era of colorblindness had truly arrived. It was easy to move to the conclusion, then, that there is no more need for protests to expand civil rights.

The loss of civil disobedience as a common, legitimate advocacy tactic shows (among other things) how the state is capable of exerting enormous influence over the strategies used by civil rights organizations. Aside from deploying police to physically deter street protests, the state can distribute or withhold funding, issue court injunctions to help or hinder advocates, demand financial penalties and awards, grant or refuse policy favors, and so on. In effect, the state can determine the borders of legitimate advocacy by engaging with or freezing out specific organizations. There are only a handful of exceptions when civil rights campaigners successfully used civil disobedience to win major reforms since the 1970s. Instead, the state successfully encouraged advocacy organizations to engage with "the system."

In practice, this has meant cooperating with the Department of Justice's Civil Rights Division and other state agencies specifically set up to enforce civil rights laws. Failing that, advocacy organizations have access to the courts, and ultimately, electoral advocacy—the ballot box—as the ultimate venue for pursuing reforms. Given these avenues of legitimate grievance filing, "old school" tactics like rallies, marches, and disruptive protests of all kinds have been derided as unnecessary at best, and counterproductive at worst. How have Middle Eastern American advocates done their work in this context?

Middle Eastern American Coalitions

Through "the system," there has been an arguably robust range of protections for Middle Eastern American civil rights over the past thirty years. Middle Eastern American advocates have engaged with officials at many law enforcement and counterterrorism agencies, and they have won some major reforms. Some lawsuits filed by Middle Eastern American advocacy organizations in response to discrimination have been successful. There are even examples of winning electoral campaigns supported by Middle Eastern American advocates. And yet, Islamophobia has continued to expand.

The racial paradox of Islamophobia plays a major role in the durability of discrimination affecting Middle Eastern Americans. Consider that the government uses racial logics to both conduct discriminatory surveillance on Middle Eastern Americans, and yet it uses those same racial logics to enforce civil rights protections for these communities as well. Advocates, understandably, face significant challenges in developing a coherent strategy given such contradictions. The racial dilemma, deciding how to navigate through the contradictions of caused by race, presents both a tremendous challenge and, potentially, a unique opportunity for Middle Eastern American advocates.

Considering the importance of coalitions in successful advocacy work—the tight correlation between winning reforms and building durable coalitions—perhaps the most crucial aspect of the racial dilemma is its role in coalition building among divergent communities that fall into that socially constructed racial category. Coalition building for Middle Eastern American advocates, in other words, is complicated in many ways by the racial dilemma: whether to describe Islamophobia as racism affecting a racially defined community.

If Middle Eastern American advocates use the language of racism to frame Islamophobia, then it would certainly follow that they would seek to build coalitions across Arab, Muslim, Sikh, and South Asian American organizations. After all, recognizing that Islamophobia is racism explains why Islamophobia affects all of these different communities. Given that recognition, it would make sense for Arab, Muslim, Sikh, and South Asian American organizations to come together in coalitions to confront their common enemy: Islamophobia.

On the other hand, if Middle Eastern American advocates choose the other path around the racial dilemma, and they generally avoid discussing race and racism when describing Islamophobia, then joining in such race-based coalitions makes little sense. If Islamophobia is, for example, mainly about religion, then why would Muslim American organizations join together into a coalition with South Asian American organizations? If Islamophobia affects Sikhs only because of "mistaken identity," and it is not caused by the far more intractable problem of racism, then there would be no clear reason for Sikh American organizations to want to join together with Arab American organizations. The Sikh organizations could simply assert their Sikh identity, to correct the "mistake."

Here, then, is the crucial strategic crossroads set into place by the racial dilemma. Describing Islamophobia as racism leads to coalitions across religious, ethnic, and cultural boundaries. Conversely, avoiding the topic of race while confronting Islamophobia means there would be much less of an impetus for such coalition building.

Remember that the major gains won in the 1900s by Asian Americans, Black Americans, Latin@s, and Native Americans happened in large part due to the ability of advocates to construct and maintain large coalitions of otherwise disconnected and even disparate groups. Harnessing the language of race and racism played a major part in the coalition work of these advocates, both as a cause and an effect of their efforts at coalition building.

It therefore came as a surprise to find, in my interviews with Middle Eastern American advocates, so few examples of efforts to create durable, identity-based coalitions built around a Middle Eastern American racial identity. Instead, many Arab, Muslim, Sikh, and South Asian American advocacy organizations utilized a decidedly race-neutral strategy, especially after 2001, that in many ways made it more difficult to bring together the disparate and divergent groups affected by Islamophobia. This chapter considers how and why, contrary to expectations, coalition building to leverage the common racial identity among Arab, Muslim, Sikh, and South Asian American advocates has been inconsistent at best.

To describe these dynamics, I rely upon a classification of different types of advocacy coalitions described by Rev. Dr. William J. Barber II, a leader in the influential Moral Monday movement. He has spoken often of two types of coalitions among civil rights advocates: "transactional coalitions" and "transformational coalitions." With transactional coalitions, Barber explains, cooperation ends after a short-term goal is met. "People involved . . . walk away as soon as they get their piece of the pie," he says.[1] These transactional coalitions are generally ad hoc, and they usually focus on a single issue. Transformational coalitions, on the other hand, are those that remain durable, oblige the commitment of significant resources, compel compromises and trade-offs on key priorities, and they are based on the desire to develop deep connections between organizations. Barber explains the source of strength from transformational coalitions comes from a solid connection that does not dissolve after just one setback or victory: "Our opponents need to know that if they touch one of us, they are touching all of us."[2] Transformational coalitions based upon racial identity seek to actively modify existing racial projects, and they can therefore reform how race itself operates. Strategically speaking, each type of coalition has pros and cons.

Transactional Coalitions

Transactional coalitions exist when two or more organizations jointly coordinate actions to achieve a specific policy or program goal. The transaction comes in that the organizations agree to coordinate only so long as it is mutually beneficial—all members generally have very little at stake. Usually, one issue or specific policy goal (to pass or block a certain piece of legislation, for example) serves as the main basis for the partnership. The tools of transactional coalitions are low-cost, low-reward—such as sending an open letter to a policymaker co-signed by all of the coalition members, or holding a press conference that takes place in one day, with all coalition members contributing to make the event happen.

Transactional coalitions emerge frequently among advocacy organizations, pulling together like-minded groups on a single issue of agreement. If several advocacy organizations all want some specific policy to change, they can easily engage in a short-term collaborative effort on that single issue. The buy-in only requires each organization to do what it would probably have done anyway. Usually, there is no need for sharing resources, and the division of labor or coordination of efforts among coalition members can be minimal. After the success (or failure) of their campaign for change on a single issue, the coalition can simply fade away.

Transformational Coalitions

Transformational coalitions form when two or more organizations share resources and participate in coordinated advocacy campaigns across a range of issues. These coalitions represent a significant investment for all organizations involved. Identity often serves as a rallying point and an outcome of transformational coalitions. Pride in working alongside fellow advocates—standing shoulder-to-shoulder in a broadly defined group—both draws from and reinforces collective identities like "union member," or "Asian American." Joining in coalitions in this way, identities (racial and otherwise) can be co-opted by activists to bring together organizations that ordinarily would not have any special reason to work together. These coalitions use pooled resources, even sharing key staff or financial resources to enable greater efficiency and respond to challenges. Over time, organizations develop long-term strategies with careful coordination and mutual sacrifice in choosing the shifting policy priorities of the coalition. Forming these transformational coalitions requires overcoming centrifugal forces, through careful, consistent, and dedicated organizing.

Umbrella organizations often facilitate these transformational coalitions. These enable a connection across multiple advocacy organizations, making it possible to coordinate across a wide range of strategies and tactics. These umbrella organizations typically set up a division of labor, pooling resources to achieve efficiency and to shore up weaker organizations. Unlike with transactional coalitions, these durable partnerships have a high bar—sometimes, advocates have to sideline some priorities in the short-term to coordinate efforts over the long-term. Transformational coalitions have to depend on something deeper than just a single issue or policy reform effort to stay alive. Ideological or political alignment often serves as a base, but racial identity can provide a basis to construct and maintain this kind of coalition as well.

Advocacy Strategy and Coalitions

There are marked differences between transactional and transformational coalitions, and each can be advantageous depending on the circumstances. Indeed, political scientist Hahrie Han finds that successful advocacy organizations often fluidly combine "transactional" and "transformational" work. Success depends upon moving nimbly between different strategies.[3] The key is finding ways to mobilize a dedicated set of advocates to push past opposition on the issues that matter to the organization.

The rest of this chapter looks very closely at the recent history of Middle Eastern American advocacy organizations, how they built coalitions, whether they were transactional or transformational, and the ways that race affected their advocacy strategies. The most successful and active attempts to organize transformational coalitions among Middle Eastern Americans took place in the early 1980s. By the 1990s, even as immigration from the Middle East and South Asia expanded rapidly, efforts to bring together race-based coalitions among Middle Eastern Americans suffered a serious setback. By the time that 9/11 presented an unprecedented crisis for Middle Eastern American advocacy organizations, race-based coalitions barely even registered as a potential strategy, while ad hoc transactional coalitions flourished in the first decade after 9/11. The shift in strategy away from the rhetoric of civil rights and racism and toward "rights for all" colorblindness came even as the Department of Justice moved in ways that incentivized the creation of broad coalitions of Arab, Muslim, Sikh, and South Asian American organizations. It was only after 2010, when racism and civil rights re-entered the national conversation in often dramatic and tragic ways, that significant work toward race-based civil rights coalitions begin to re-emerge among Middle Eastern American advocates. I begin to unpack these developments by looking back at the 1970s and 1980s, when the "post–civil rights era" was still new, and before the huge successes of the conservative reaction that took hold by the 1990s.

The Dawn of the Post–Civil Rights Era

Arab American advocacy rapidly expanded in the 1970s, and the terrain for civil rights advocacy was already shifting as the post–civil rights era dawned. Even in these relatively early days, advocates faced the racial dilemma. They struggled to find a strategy that would gain traction by shining a spotlight on discrimination affecting Middle Eastern Americans. Meanwhile, the strong push from conservatives reacting to the civil rights movement won significant victories. This undid many of the policies intended to make civil rights advocacy simpler and more effective. Leading conservatives like President Richard Nixon and California Governor Ronald Reagan began to use rearticulated racism to advocate for dismantling protections like equal housing and affirmative action.[4]

As these developments unfolded, a debate raged among Arab American activists over two key strategic issues. One was the perennial question of whether foreign policy advocacy was compatible with "domestic" civil rights advocacy. The other was the extent to which Arab American advocates should partner with Black civil rights organizations. Some argued against describing discrimination affecting their communities as "racism," while others recognized the potential power of the claim that stereotypes and hate crimes affecting Arab Americans were, specifically, "racist." This debate would define the development of the two leading Arab American organizations founded in the 1980s, ADC and AAI.

After 1980, James Abourezk and James Zogby leveraged the ongoing ABSCAM scandal and offensive Arab stereotypes in the media to jump-start support for the brand-new ADC. Mindful of the concern that taking a position on the Israeli-Palestinian conflict would complicate support for Arab American civil rights claims, they made the case that ADC should distinguish itself from its predecessors, NAAA and AAUG, by focusing primarily, if not exclusively, on domestic civil rights issues. The worry was based in part on the idea that some Lebanese Americans would not agree with the cause of Palestinian liberation, due to the complex and sometimes violent tensions between those two nations. Furthermore, gaining the support of longstanding Jewish American advocates for Arab American civil rights was significant, but there was a perception that they might balk if asked to also back claims for Palestinian sovereignty at the same time.

In the early years, ADC navigated the racial dilemma by taking a strong stand against "racism," using that term specifically. With its use of bold anti-racist rhetoric, the young organization quickly found support in the Arab American community and attracted a great deal of media attention. Legitimacy in elite policy circles seemed to follow. Senator Abourezk wrote letters of protest to the FBI, and various ADC supporters and board members published pamphlets about Operation Boulder and what it called "anti-Arab racism," or "the other anti-Semitism," proffering a controversial definition of "Semite" that places both Arabic- and Hebrew-speaking peoples together.[5]

In 1980, ADC "organizing drives" rolled out in eleven cities including Detroit, Pittsburgh, Dallas, and Rochester, New York.[6] Hundreds of people attended these events, and several members of Congress expressed their support.[7] The goal of these drives was to build the "ADC Network," which would mount letter-writing campaigns and "monitor local media and report instances of stereotyping and discrimination against Arab-Americans to the National Office."[8] ADC's early newsletters described "Anti-Arab and Other Racism" as a defining issue for the organization, and on December 1, 1980, ADC issued a formal statement to "combat the growth of the Klan, the Nazis, and other organized 'hate groups' in the US." The statement asserted:

> We are deeply concerned by the recent increase of anti-Semitic and anti-foreign racism emanating from numerous organized hate groups in the US. We abhor all forms of racism and discrimination wherever they occur. We commit ourselves to active opposition to these practices and to all organizations [that] advocate racism and sow the seeds of division and hatred among peoples.[9]

Figure 5.1. Photo of American-Arab Anti-Discrimination Committee (ADC) volunteer, ca. 1980

Figure 5.2. Photo of ADC co-founder James Abourezk at an anti-Apartheid event, 1980

This language—with "racism" as the frame—was typical of early 1980s work by ADC. By using rhetoric like this, ADC positioned itself as standing on the same ground as civil rights organizations active in the 1960s and 1970s: fighting against racism.

Indeed, ADC in the early 1980s worked closely with Black American civil rights organizations. ADC coordinated with one of the most successful civil rights coalitions in history, Rev. Jesse Jackson's Operation PUSH and the Rainbow Coalition.[10] A *Detroit News* article published in 1981, headlined "Blacks Urge Arabs: Join Us Politically," featured quotes from Congressman John Conyers's speech at the first ADC convention.[11] According to the article, Conyers "compared the efforts of the year-old Arab-American group to the early years of the NAACP and warned that 'pristine and intellectual' discussions are ineffective."[12] By 1984, this advice had been taken to heart, and Zogby spoke very highly of Jackson, the Rainbow Coalition leader and Democratic candidate for US President.[13] This suggests that in the early 1980s, ADC advocates saw that coalition building with communities of color was their best avenue for winning major reforms.

Figure 5.3. Photo of Rev. Jesse Jackson speaking at the ADC Convention, 1984

Some Arab Americans, however, did not support the close collaboration between ADC and Jesse Jackson. One ADC leader recalled in an interview that some Arab American donors, particularly wealthier members of the community, did not identify with the focus of ADC as combatting racism and "discrimination." In fact, some Arab Americans found this to be insulting or embarrassing:

> These guys [Arab American elites] know how to work the parties, how to work the White House. They're established. They're well-to-do. But, these guys didn't identify with the issue of discrimination. Why? These guys are all multi-millionaires, and own their companies, and own their businesses. So, they looked at it in kind of a condescending way. They viewed it as, "Why are we acting like disadvantaged people? Our grandparents came here, and carried three suitcases, and peddled until they died, and made millions of dollars, educated their kids, purchased their first home. Why are you whining? Let's do it the hard way." So, they were embarrassed by it. That's why ADC never attracted that sector of the community. So, there was a little tension there.[14]

In other words, according to this longtime advocate, some Arab Americans did not see any reason to partner with Black Americans or marginalized communities of color more generally. In their view, Arab Americans could work political connections and have success without the need for coalitions with Black Americans—coalitions that might be counterproductive. After all, they seemed to reason, why associate with a stigmatized group if instead you can become integrated into the majority?

During this period, when the racial identity of Arab Americans remained contentious, several leading Arab American advocates undertook a significant campaign to include a "Middle East and North African" (MENA) identity category on the 2000 US Census.[15] This was a remarkable campaign that bucked the political and social trend toward "colorblindness." Even as some in Congress proposed eliminating all racial and ethnic origin questions on the 2000 Census, AAI and other civil rights organizations committed to defending and expanding data collection.

Several advocates recalled heated debates in their communities around the issue of Arab American recognition on the Census.[16] Some Arab Americans expressed the idea that collecting any racial or ethnic origin data was worthless or even harmful, arguing from a "colorblindness" position. On the other hand, some Arab Americans adamantly wanted the Census to add an "Arab American" box specifically—not "MENA." Still others detested the term "Middle Eastern" because it had colonialist origins and because it obscured the national, ethnic, or religious identity that was personally important to them—such as Chaldean, Lebanese, Maronite, or Palestinian.

As the contentious discussion about race among Arab Americans continued, in 1993, Arab American advocates convened a meeting with officials in Washington, to formally discuss the addition of a "MENA box" on the 2000 Census.[17] At that meeting, disagreements among advocates about racial identity became public. The lack of unity among assembled leaders of Arab American organizations contributed to a decision by Census officials to not add any new "box" on the Census— neither "Arab," nor "MENA," nor anything else. The definition of "White" printed in the Census instructions would continue to reference North Africa and Arabs. Advocates worked with the Census Bureau to develop a list of write-in words that would be tabulated as "Arab," and the Census committed to compiling a special report on the Arab American community using this new tabulation, which it did after the 2000 and 2010 Censuses.[18]

The racial dilemma thus caused trouble for ADC and other Arab American advocacy organizations even from their earliest moments, as they were forced to choose between joining political forces with racialized minority groups or pursuing integration into the White majority. This strategic tension would persist in Arab American advocacy circles for decades. Some Arab American advocates passionately considered themselves as members of a disadvantaged minority community, demarcated by race. They recognized the value in standing alongside Black Americans and other communities of color, in coalition, using the language of the civil rights movement to describe the challenges facing the Arab American community. At the same time, many other Arab American advocates strongly disagreed with this characterization. Any discrimination (which they might argue was minor, complaining about it amounted to "whining") was not based on race, on this latter view, but based on an ignorant defamation of the Arab ethnicity and culture. Therefore, they might say, asserting that Arabs were just as American (and just as White) as the Irish, the Italians, or the Greeks was the strategy that ADC and other organizations should pursue. It would be a profound mistake to join together with people of color, on this view. The gap between these two interpretations of the roots of anti-Arab discrimination and stereotyping framed the racial dilemma that has constantly faced ADC advocates. Back in the early 1980s, ADC largely chose a race-conscious advocacy strategy, but the debate over this strategy continued.

The tensions caused by the racial dilemma may have contributed to a dramatic falling out that suddenly split the ADC co-founders, Abourezk and Zogby. The precise reasons for the division between these two Arab American icons remained contentious even in the 2000s (when I conducted my interviews with several long-serving advocates who worked closely with them). I asked almost every Arab American advocate I met about this break-up, and I heard many different explanations for what caused the divorce. Some recalled that the "two Jims" never liked one another, on a personal level. Most advocates chalked it up to "personality conflicts" rather than a substantive disagreement. Some insisted that the split was a mutual decision, but one advocate who worked closely with Zogby remembered that Abourezk "forced out" his former partner.[19] He placed the blame for the falling out squarely on Abourezk's shoulders:

> Abourezk tries to deny that Zogby put together ADC because of his personality conflict with Jim [Zogby]. But Jim [Zogby] did all the organizing. . . . Helen [Samhan] was the person who kept it all together. Abourezk was the public face, but he was also the reason it all came apart. He was so volatile. [. . .] On the one hand, he was great, Abourezk, because he raised people's consciousness, but he was a disaster on the management side.[20]

If there is a single reason that fully explains the sudden split of these two community leaders, no one was willing to discuss it with me. However it happened, the break-up coincided with a disagreement over political strategy with regards to the racial dilemma.[21] After the break-up, ADC and AAI began to diverge in their approaches to racial politics.

Just before and after the split, Zogby partnered closely with Jesse Jackson's presidential campaign and the Rainbow/PUSH Coalition. Some ADC supporters expressed concerns, finding the close political association with the increasingly controversial Jackson and other African American leaders problematic or even embarrassing.[22] Nationally, Jackson's approach to "identity politics" became a central target for conservatives as they made moves to curtail support for Democratic policy priorities by linking them to "reverse racism." Still, under Zogby's direction, the new AAI organization avidly pursued a strategy of working closely with Jackson.

Shortly after Zogby founded AAI in 1985, the organization formally joined the Rainbow/PUSH Coalition. AAI newsletters from the late 1980s frequently mention this partnership as a key strategic pathway for Arab American advocacy. For example, in early 1988, *AAI Update* included five separate news clippings describing "Arab Americans in the Jackson campaign," with headlines like "Arab American Voters Look to Jackson to Deliver Their Message on the Mideast."[23] During the run-up to the 1988 Presidential election and as AAI established itself, Zogby served as a deputy campaign manager for Jackson. Simultaneously, AAI

Figure 5.4. Photo of Arab American Institute (AAI) volunteers, 2012

undertook an effort, with the help of ADC chapters around the country, to increase Arab American voter registration and turnout and to recruit and support Arab American candidates for office. AAI also conducted widely read opinion polls of the Arab American community.[24] These efforts at highlighting the decisive role that Arab American voters could play helped to make Arab Americans an increasingly powerful electoral constituency. Campaigns for statewide offices found that Arab Americans might be pivotal constituencies in key areas. Even candidates for President of the United States looked to Arab American voters in some primary contests and in general election "swing states" like Michigan and Ohio. Due in large part to AAI and ADC's efforts, after 1988, Dearborn, Michigan became a routine stop for presidential campaigns seeking to court the Arab American vote.

Meanwhile, ADC did not entirely give up on race-based organizing, despite the 1985 split with Zogby. While it did not work as closely as AAI with Jackson's organizations, in the 1990s, ADC joined the foundational umbrella organization for race-based civil rights organizations, the Leadership Council on Civil Rights (LCCR). As a member of that transformational coalition, ADC joined numerous campaigns in collaboration with fellow members like SALDEF, NAACP, National Council of La Raza, National Congress of American Indians, Japanese American Citizens League, and the National Urban League. But during the 1990s, even more new organizations were founded in the field of Middle Eastern American advocacy, complicating the overall field's approach to the racial dilemma.

Racial Shifts after 1990

During the tumultuous 1990s, the size and shape of the field of Middle Eastern American advocacy shifted considerably. Events abroad and domestically raised the specter of terrorism to new heights not seen in the 1980s. The Gulf War, which began in 1991, the World Trade Center bombing in New York City and the signing of the Oslo Accords, both in 1993, each caused major shifts in political trade winds affecting Arab American and Muslim American advocacy organizations. ADC and NAAA fell on hard times and found themselves, in the words of one advocate, "fighting over scarce resources."[25] Several Arab American leaders told me that support from abroad and from Arab American donors for ADC and NAAA dried up as the Gulf War began and the Oslo Accords came into effect.[26] These events contributed to major rifts opening up between various Middle Eastern American communities, and they placed a harsh spotlight on the question of foreign support for Middle Eastern American advocacy organizations.

The Gulf War put ADC into a "very tight situation," according to one ADC staffer. He recalled that ADC made some "misstatements" and suffered a "loss of credibility" with regard to their stance against the war.[27] Simultaneously, both ADC and NAAA experienced a sudden drop in financial support with the apparent success of the Oslo Accords. Support for NAAA's mission waned as the Israeli-Palestinian conflict appeared (for the moment) to be winding down, and the organization was generally unable to adapt to remain relevant.[28] Several new organizations, such as the American Task Force on Palestine, emerged in the wake of Oslo, largely to fill the space left by the ineffective NAAA.[29] The dynamic political scene, due to these and other developments including conflicts between Arab governments and several terror attacks carried out by Arab militants, caused additional conflict between and among Arab American advocacy organizations. One longtime advocate recalled that the tensions in the Middle East negatively affected relationships between Arab American organizations.

The eleventh commandment was basically that we shouldn't allow events in the Middle East to spill over into the Arab American scene and divide the community. . . . And most of the time we respected that and practiced that, but over time, we became careless. So, when I'm talking about the impact of these events in the region, their impacts were mostly negative, and divisive, and sapping the energy of the community, and demoralizing the community. . . . And so the '90s presented a very turbulent period. And so there was shrinking of resources.[30]

In an effort to regroup, ADC's board brought in well-respected community leader Hala Maksoud as its new president, directing her to bring the organization back into good financial standing. She was remembered by several advocates and in ADC records as having "saved" ADC from total collapse by reorganizing its source of support, and reorienting toward the grassroots. The various ADC newsletters sent out in the 1980s, which back then were sent by postal mail to all members, pointedly did not include any direct fundraising appeals to the membership. By the middle of the 1990s, however, these newsletters came with a self-addressed, postage-paid envelope, a form for making a donation to ADC, and carefully constructed appeals for support. I asked an ADC executive about this change, and he confirmed that Hala Maksoud's team established new methods of fundraising during the 1990s. He also explained that such methods were met with limited success:

Typically, the response is, "Well, I admire what ADC does, and I wish you lots of luck, but I'm not really committed to it." This is a constant problem. That's the majority of our potential membership base. You have generational differences. Younger people tend to want to flail their arms at the existing power structure, and will take issue or umbrage with the idea that we might invite Secretary of State Colin Powell to speak at our convention. [They] think that that's an outrageous thing to do. Somebody my age has been around long enough to know that that's how you make progress.[31]

Even as Maksoud moved to shore up the organization, the strain on ADC's finances became more acute in the mid-1990s. The intermittent progress in the Israeli-Palestinian peace process, according to one former ADC leader, "divided and weakened the community."[32] In the wake of the 1995 Oklahoma City bombing, Arab American organizations failed to adequately respond to the biased assumption by law enforcement and the widespread speculation in the popular media that "Arab terrorists" must have been responsible. This represented a missed opportunity for ADC, according to several advocates working at the time. One former ADC staffer recalled:

> The Oklahoma City bombing came at a weak stage [in ADC's history]. ADC wasn't where it should have been. . . . ADC should focus down and simply keep the legal department, and grow it. No politics, no Lebanon, Syria, or anything else. But that didn't happen. Had we done that in the '80s or early '90s, by the time OKC [the Oklahoma City bombing] came along, we'd have been ready. We fought and did okay, but it could have been much better. Had we been more forceful, ADC would be ten times the size it is today. . . . A crisis like Oklahoma City was a goldmine. If we had responded affirmatively, ADC could have built itself eternally as part of the civil rights constituency in the country. . . .
>
> There were gains made after Oklahoma City, but in spite of us, not because of us. We weren't in shape to deal with that crisis.[33]

In an effort to respond to difficulties like these and splits caused by tensions in the Middle East and elsewhere, several leading Arab American advocates made an effort to re-establish coordination and cooperation among the increasingly divided advocacy organizations. One approach would have seen the reemergence of a 1970s-era umbrella organization, the Council of Presidents of National Arab American Organizations. This "loose kind of coalition" was able to provide a measure of cooperation and leadership, and "despite friction and egos and all that, it worked well in the sense it served the community well for a while."[34] That project—which leveraged a panethnic Arab American identity in an explicit way for coalition building—suffered from various challenges in the 1990s. The Council never appeared in the *Encyclopedia of Associations*, and it failed to really get off the ground. By the 2000s, all that was left of this organization was a mere email distribution list.[35]

As ADC, NAAA, and AAUG struggled, new Muslim American advocacy organizations—most notably CAIR and MPAC—emerged onto the scene in the early 1990s. In general, CAIR and MPAC did not coordinate with the existing Arab American organizations, nor did they join in transformational coalitions. Instead, the new Muslim organizations worked largely independently. One Arab American advocate remembered CAIR in the 1990s as "basically just a Muslim ADC" that competed for the same "scarce resources" as NAAA and ADC, just as those organizations scrambled to retain even basic levels of support.[36]

In the midst of the difficulties and ineffective responses to crises like the Oklahoma City bombing, one CAIR executive recalled that many saw a need for a specifically Muslim American advocacy organization—one that would stand apart from the Arab American organizations.

> Despite there being ADC, which is an Arab American civil rights organization . . . CAIR basically started off as two guys working in a small one-room office. . . . What propelled CAIR was that there was really no advocacy voice speaking for the Muslim community. After the Oklahoma City bombing . . . two guys from DC [CAIR co-founders] drove all the way out to Oklahoma. Two of the co-founders had a press conference and started coming up with media kits about the Muslim community. And then from there . . . There was a high-profile case of Nike Shoe Company. They had [a] design on the back of a shoe to look exactly like "Allah" written in Arabic—which was offensive to Muslims. And Nike acknowledged it was offensive; they discontinued the shoe.[37]

This account confirms the recollection of many advocates who felt that ADC, due to lack of funding and lack of effective leadership, was struggling to remain relevant in the mid-1990s. ADC's anemic response to the crises in the 1990s contributed to the rise of CAIR as a Muslim American alternative to the Arab American advocacy scene.

There was some limited cooperation between CAIR and ADC, following the model of transactional coalitions. For example, in 1996 the two organizations sent a joint letter to a local police chief after his officers allegedly sexually harassed two Arab American women wearing *niqab* veils.[38] Cooperation like this, the co-signing of a letter or other actions that required no long-term investment from either organization, characterized the maximum extent of cooperation between Arab American and Muslim American organizations like ADC and CAIR.

In many ways, this kind of transactional collaboration set the tone for coalition building among Arab American and Muslim American advocates in the years ahead. Rather than move toward a durable, transformational coalition, the organizations engaged in almost exclusively transactional cooperation. This strategy seemed to work extremely well for CAIR, as it grew rapidly during the 1990s to become perhaps the largest and most well-known Middle Eastern American advocacy organization, and it eventually eclipsed even the large membership size of ADC.

Meanwhile, MPAC gained a similar reputation as an organization with a valid claim to speak for immigrant Muslim communities, though it took a markedly different approach compared to CAIR. In the 1990s, MPAC did not aspire to have a grassroots presence. It was more analogous to AAI as a politically focused organization, writing opinion articles and weighing in on policy debates at elite levels.

One longtime advocate drew a sharp distinction between CAIR and MPAC in the 1990s and early 2000s. He saw CAIR as primarily religious. It was diverse, but rooted in the mosques. MPAC also took an "ecumenical" approach, but in contrast it had an almost secular orientation. While CAIR had a reputation as socially conservative, MPAC was more liberal:

> [MPAC is] not socially conservative. . . . They've kind of ended up in a sort of center liberal multicultural space—very typical of what you might get from college administrators. They're right about where your land grant college administrator might be—it's diversity, tolerance, multiplicity. . . . Their whole work, their approach, their style, the pace at which they do things, their attitude, their language, is very colored by the fact that they're LA-based and not Washington-based. The point is, I can see them in that kind of multicultural liberal space. It's a very different political space than CAIR occupies . . . CAIR is much more interested in the conservative, the traditional. The atmosphere in CAIR is often like it is in a newly arrived immigrant community's Islamic center.[39]

Interestingly, neither MPAC nor CAIR undertook much transactional coalition work in the 1990s, not between themselves and especially not with African American and Latin@ advocacy organizations. They did not follow the strategy that ADC and AAI had developed in the 1980s of using the rhetoric of the civil rights movement, and closely partnering with Black Americans and other communities of color.

Meanwhile, in the mid-1990s, the earliest Sikh American and South Asian American advocacy organizations emerged—most prominently SALDEF and SAALT. Notably, SALDEF engaged in little proactive political advocacy during the 1990s. They had the resources for some legal advice, and they remained vigilant as a media watchdog. They had a small full-time staff, but had no aspiration to take on "aggressive fund-raising or [to obtain] a floor in Washington DC or somewhere else."[40] Similarly, SAALT's early approach was analogous to that of MPAC, with SAALT acting at that time mainly as an elite "think tank" for South Asian American professionals.[41]

As the first nationally prominent Sikh and South Asian American organizations gathered strength, throughout the 1990s, the racialized image most Americans associated with Muslims had shifted. The decades-old association of Islam with Black Americans had faded, and Islam became recast as Middle Eastern in the popular imaginary. This shift happened, in part, because of rapid immigration to the United States from South Asia and the broader Middle East. As I described earlier, in chapter 2, the increasing visibility of "Arab Muslim" and "Middle Eastern" adversaries in news media and cartoonish villains in popular culture also contributed to this racial shift. Other factors included the "clash of civilizations" thesis, which was the influential prediction that the "Muslim world" and "the West" were destined for violent conflict after the end of the Cold War.[42] Policymakers, politicians, and pundits began speaking about Islam and Muslims in ominous tones. And this was all happening even before the horrific destruction wrought by the nineteen hijackers who destroyed the World Trade Center, attacked the Pentagon, and killed thousands of Americans on September 11, 2001.

Racial Pressures after 9/11

Even though the Middle Eastern American racial category had largely solidified before 9/11, the prominent advocacy organizations from Arab, Muslim, Sikh, and South Asian American communities had done very little collaborative work with one another, apart from occasional transactional moments. The failed bid by leaders at AAI and other organizations to add a MENA category to the Census, and the open opposition by some Arab American advocates to the effort at racial rearticulation, illustrate how the 1990s represented a low point for coalition building among Arab, Muslim, Sikh, and South Asian American advocacy organizations. The events on 9/11 jolted all of these organizations, causing major changes to their structures and advocacy strategies. Surprisingly, though, their increasingly race-neutral approach, featuring transactional and not transformational responses to the racial dilemma, did not change very much in the years that followed.

Even after 9/11, advocacy organizations largely stuck to their particularistic, relatively narrowly defined ethnic, panethnic, or religious communities. The ascribed racialization that projected a perception of Middle Eastern Americans as a mostly undifferentiated mass was not sufficient to bring about transformational coalition building among Arab, Muslim, Sikh, and South Asian American advocacy organizations. The oldest of the organizations, ADC and AAI, undertook varying levels of engagement with organizations representing communities of color, but even they did not actively work toward building new transformational coalitions in the wake of 9/11.

Regardless, after 2001, AAI, ADC, CAIR, MPAC, SALDEF, and SAALT were all engaged in critically important advocacy work. In general, their activities, structure, and history reflected broad national trends in advocacy strategy. They published reports on issues like Islamophobic discrimination and immigration reform, reaching out to policymakers and the general public. They partnered with corporations and government offices to provide "cultural competency" seminars and training. They ran petition drives and lobbied the government for policy changes. But like most political organizations in the US, they found little (and diminishing) support from member-donors. They claimed to represent their communities at the national level, but in general the organizations had shaky claims to an actual grassroots base of support, although CAIR was a notable exception to this pattern.

The Immediate Aftermath of 9/11

Right after the 9/11 attacks, urgent complaints about hate crimes and discrimination poured in to advocacy organizations at a rate never before seen or expected. The sudden surge in calls for help from all over the country quickly overwhelmed even the largest Middle Eastern American organizations. No organization had near enough capacity to keep up.

The fact that Arabs, Muslims, Sikhs, and South Asians were all affected by this massive spike in hate crimes and discrimination meant that the centripetal pressure on Middle Eastern American advocates to work together, which was muted in the 1990s, became impossible to ignore after 9/11. The sudden increase in demand, from requests for legal counsel, consulting opportunities with federal, state, and local authorities, constant requests for interviews from the media, and the growing need for sophisticated political lobbying to push back against the rapid rollout of discriminatory programs resulted in a renewed impetus to build coalitions wherever possible, to share the load. Simultaneously, a momentous decision by several government agencies to deal with all of the Arab, Muslim, Sikh, and South Asian American organizations as a single group also put pressure on these organizations to cooperate with one another.

In interviews, many advocates working during and immediately after the 9/11 attacks recalled the tremendous strain they faced. For months after the attacks, phones at SALDEF's offices and even the private homes of key SALDEF staff were "ringing off the hook," at "all times of the day and night."[43] An ADC leader recalled that the strain added by the post-9/11 crisis made working on coalition building "absolutely vital—beyond vital, actually."[44]

Various Middle Eastern American organizations shifted focus to join in the post-9/11 struggle for civil rights. Several formerly service- or culture-oriented organizations changed into advocacy organizations. For example, at the year-old SAALT, the events of 9/11 prompted the rapid development of political lobbying and electoral work in addition to their previous focus on "leadership development."[45] At MPAC, one staffer recalled that they used the term "civil rights" to describe their organization's work only after 9/11.[46] Prior to that, according to another MPAC staffer, that organization presented its political work as "mainstream" rather than oppositional. The events of 9/11 and the rash of hate crimes that followed it contributed to a "sense of victimization" and a "need to struggle for civil rights," he recalled.[47] Outside Washington, ACCESS, the Arab American community service organization in Dearborn, Michigan, created new advisory boards focused on advocacy and even founded a new organization—the National Network of Arab American Communities—to build coalitions and "share resources, to know what's happening in other parts of the country."[48] Along the same lines, one ADC leader characterized the post-9/11 shift at the organization by saying, "As an institution, it grew up literally overnight," continuing:

> We were almost—we were forced to mature as an organization. To learn to work with very diverse communities, to work a lot more closely with federal agencies. That was our biggest shift, our relationship with the federal government. 9/11 put us around the table, as far as federal agencies were concerned. . . . I was working here as a lawyer before 9/11. As the federal government changed after 9/11, we changed along with the government. It gave us the opportunity to be an actual stakeholder when discussions take place that are pertinent to our community.[49]

The new attention from government agencies proved to be perhaps the most long-lasting of the post-9/11 effects on these organizations. In this vein, an AAI staff member recalled that government agencies were far more responsive and proactive in working with the organization after 9/11:

> Post-9/11 work that was new was dealing with federal agencies. Because [prior to 9/11] we did not have relationships with those federal agencies. All of a sudden, every agency was putting together a citizens' task force or an advisory committee with communities affected by discrimination after 9/11. [The] FBI set up an advisory committee. Transportation and TSA set up an advisory committee [and so did] other agencies in the Justice Department, the Civil Rights Division in the Justice Department. That was new. We did not have those relationships before. We were called upon in a central way to be active in those. As you can imagine, we were stretched pretty thin.[50]

Combined with persistently high demand for help with individual cases of discrimination and hate crimes, it is not surprising that one ADC executive estimated that in the years immediately following 9/11 there was sufficient demand to keep "ten ADCs" constantly busy.[51]

Transactional Coalitions for Immigration Policy

Despite the tremendous pressure to cooperate across the Middle Eastern American spectrum, building transformational coalitions was still not seen by most leading advocates as a beneficial strategy. When I asked advocates about the coalition work they had undertaken in the years after 9/11, nearly all of the work they described fit the model of transactional coalitions. Joint actions involving more than one organization required little investment in terms of resources from the organizations, and the joint projects were almost always based on a single issue or concern. Almost all of the joint projects undertaken by the organizations disbanded after a short time.

An example of frequent transactional cooperation involving multiple Middle Eastern American organizations was crafting responses to particularly outrageous Islamophobic statements from public officials or prominent commentators. The most common response took shape in a joint letter of protest, typically written by one organization, but signed by dozens. Another similar area of cooperation came in the common practice of sending jointly signed protest letters to federal agencies, demanding changes to discriminatory policies or practices. Joint letters like this are quintessentially transactional: they happen in an ad-hoc manner, require committing almost no resources (except for the time taken to write and distribute a draft for signature), and represent a way for organizations to support one another publicly. These letters have been frequently effective in attracting attention, and they occasionally brought significant results in the form of policy changes and public apologies from officials who made Islamophobic statements.

But the area that probably best exemplifies transactional coalition building among Middle Eastern American advocacy organizations after 9/11 is joint work around immigration policy reform. Immigration policy attracts considerable attention from Arab, Muslim, Sikh, and South Asian American advocacy organizations, which of course represent largely immigrant communities.

In American politics, reforms in immigration policy are often highly dependent on other current affairs that relate only tangentially to immigration. Consider that immigration policy usually gets blamed for economic downturns, even when there is no evidence that immigration played a key role in economic disruptions. And in recent years, many policymakers increasingly linked counterterrorism with immigration reform (despite dubious evidence that the two areas are, in fact, related). Meanwhile, various legislative efforts to increase criminal and other penalties for undocumented immigration exacerbated widespread fear of deportation and imprisonment in many Middle Eastern American communities. Even visa-holding immigrants who followed proper procedures often worried that their entire lives might be contingent on the outcome of tenuous and unstable immigration policy debates.

Given the high stakes and the huge uncertainty around immigration reform in the 2000s, many advocacy organizations representing immigrant groups seized upon the immigration policy debate as an area of intense focus. Immigration policy therefore represented a major source of common concern for Middle Eastern American advocacy organizations and other advocacy organizations representing immigrant communities of color.

Most advocacy organizations' immigration policy priorities centered on quality of life issues affecting first-generation immigrants and their families. There was a lot of work on decreasing the number of people held in detention facilities for months or years at a time while awaiting hearings. Many organizations wanted to reduce long wait times for naturalization, or "citizenship delay," by streamlining application processes. Some Middle Eastern American advocacy organizations engaged in lobbying and electoral work to support candidates for office who would ban racial profiling of immigrant communities. Most of this kind of advocacy occurred under the purview of large coalitions of diverse organizations representing various immigrant communities.

The umbrella organization Rights Working Group (RWG) represented perhaps the largest of these coalitions in Washington, DC. The "working group" comprised more than one hundred advocacy organizations, including ADC, AAI, MPAC, SALDEF, Sikh Coalition, SAALT, and many others. Notably, CAIR was absent. RWG was organized with the following mission statement, which was not limited to immigration reform:

In the aftermath of 9/11, the Rights Working Group strives to restore the American commitment to protect civil liberties and human rights for all people in the US. RWG has grown a strong coalition of civil liberties, human rights and civil rights, national security, and immigrant rights organizations to work hand-in-hand to restore due process.[52]

Despite its large mission, in practice, RWG found most of its work falling into immigration reform. It seems this happened mainly because immigration reform was the area of most widespread agreement among its member organizations.

RWG won some major successes in Washington policy circles. For instance, RWG was instrumental in pressuring the Department of Homeland Security (DHS) to end a new policy instituted after the failed bombing of an airliner en route to Detroit on December 25, 2009 (the so-called "underwear bombing"). Following that incident, DHS began subjecting foreign airline passengers from a list of specific, mostly Muslim-majority countries to additional security screening—a clear act of discrimination against Muslim migrants. That policy was dropped after a coordinated advocacy campaign to highlight its problems, a campaign that involved dozens of advocacy organizations led by RWG.

In interviews with leading RWG staff, I was told that, in each of its advocacy campaigns, RWG worked on a consensus basis, providing each organization in the coalition an opportunity to veto any proposed joint action.[53] Membership in RWG was entirely voluntary, with no long-term commitment or sharing of resources among member organizations. RWG had its own staff, who engaged in a wide range of legislative advocacy activities, including petition drives, online activism, and letters of protest. RWG's funding came from the Open Society Initiative (a liberal foundation that supports nonprofit organizations) and from the Asian American Justice Center, where the RWG was housed for several years. No funding for RWG came from its constituent member organizations.

Despite appearances of a deep, lasting connection like what would be expected in a transformational coalition, in fact, RWG's efforts neatly fit into the definition of a transactional coalition. It established legitimacy by partnering with as many so-called grassroots advocacy organizations as possible and asked for little in return other than the right to add the name of each organization to its list of "members." In this way, RWG and similar "coalitions" in fact acted as independent organizations that "im-

Figure 5.5. Photo of National Capital Immigration Coalition rally, 2013

ported" a grassroots base through weak partnerships with like-minded advocacy organizations.

The strategy developed by RWG took advantage of a small "ask" for partner organizations—no need to commit any resources, no need to make any sacrifices in terms of agenda. The main "ask" was simply signatures on a membership list and on occasional joint petitions that moved forward only with consensus. Because the bonds of the coalition were weak, even though the coalition brought together organizations from across the Middle Eastern American spectrum, RWG did not contribute to the creation of durable panethnic ties as "bridging" organizations did with other panethnic groups.[54] Finally, as is common with most transactional coalitions, RWG was rather short lived. In 2016, less than ten years after it was founded, RWG disbanded.[55]

Middle Eastern American advocates worked in another transactional coalition on immigration issues, this one centered outside of Washington, DC: the Illinois Coalition for Immigrant and Refugee Rights (ICIRR). This Chicago-based organization's network of over one hundred member organizations included the Arab American Action Network, Arab American Family Services, Assyrian National Council of Illinois, CAIR-Chicago, Indo-American Center, Mosque Foundation, Muslim Women Resource Center, and several more Middle Eastern American organizations. This coalition included labor unions as well as ethnically defined advocacy organizations from an array of immigrant communities.

In 2008, ICIRR undertook a campaign to increase voter turn-out among immigrant communities of color in and around Chicago. Dubbed the "New Americans Democracy Project," the effort reportedly registered more than twenty-five thousand new immigrant voters, from "Latino, Asian, [and] Middle Eastern" communities. In addition to get-out-the-vote efforts, the New Americans Democracy Project held training sessions for dozens of "immigrant electoral organizers" from around the country.[56]

In 2008, I interviewed an organizer working with CAIR-Chicago and ICIRR, who told me that CAIR-Chicago decided to partner with ICIRR as part of CAIR-Chicago's "Project O." I was told that O stood for "Organize," not "Obama," who was a candidate for President while serving as a Senator from Illinois at the time.

"Project O" was initiated by CAIR-Chicago in 2006 specifically to improve Muslim American voter turnout. The organization sought part-ners in this effort from its inception and worked with the Mosque Foundation in 2006 to gain access to individual voters. As the effort gained steam, the immigration issue "became bigger than we thought it was going to be," according to the organizer.[57] CAIR-Chicago recognized a need to connect with other immigrant communities to effectively provide advocacy on immigration reform, as demanded by their membership base. CAIR-Chicago's grassroots members reported problems related to the visa process, civil rights in immigration detention, and citizenship delays.[58] Addressing these problems required the organization to connect to a larger national effort to enact comprehensive immigration reform. ICIRR sought out the cooperation of CAIR as a way to connect with national-level support. In collaboration with other member organizations, CAIR-Chicago volunteers combed through ICIRR databases for "Muslim names" and generated lists for canvassing and making phone calls to potential Muslim voters.[59] This kind of targeted, grassroots voter outreach to Muslim Americans was, to my knowledge and that of a CAIR-Chicago organizer, the only one of its kind in the nation in 2008. This was the product of the transactional coalition produced by ICIRR.

ICIRR differed from RWG in that nearly all ICIRR members were local organizations working on local issues based in and around one city—Chicago—rather than a national coalition based in Washington,

DC. The ICIRR organizations had a strong grassroots presence, and ICIRR required membership fees from member organizations—ranging from $110 to $500 annually—although the amount varied based on factors like the member organization's operating budget and with exceptions granted for "appropriate circumstances."[60] This membership fee provided a significant part of ICIRR's funding, suggesting a more formalized relationship between ICIRR and its member organizations than with RWG. Still, ICIRR's effort could not be called a transformational coalition because it did not require member organizations to sacrifice in terms of priorities, and its goals were all short-term—such as turning out the vote in one or two elections.

RWG and ICIRR organized transactional coalitions in that they required no sustained commitment and demanded very little sacrifice from their members. They also took a non-racial strategy toward building these transactional coalitions. The mission statements, membership, and rhetoric of these umbrella groups did not seek leverage a common identity as "people of color" or any other racialized identity. Instead, supporters were connected by their immigrant status—a status that was often—but not necessarily—racial.

Immigration policy coalitions involving Middle Eastern American advocacy organizations, while sometimes successful, did not fit the model of transformational coalitions as seen with Asian American efforts in the mid-twentieth century. Even as the Islamophobia crisis in the "post 9/11" era caused tremendous centripetal pressures to work together—not just for Arabs, Muslims, Sikhs, and South Asians, but also for all advocates working with communities of color. Even further pressure to forge transformational coalitions was applied on leading Middle Eastern American advocates directly by the federal government.

The State Tries to Make Race: Interagency Meetings with the "Post-9/11 Community"

In the years after 9/11, Arab, Muslim, Sikh, and South Asian American organizations were apparently not keen on building transformational coalitions, but they all nevertheless had to contend with essentially the same issues and demands with regards to discrimination. They all confronted the Islamophobia crisis in their own dynamic ways. Each organization was often stretched to the limit (or beyond the limit) in terms of capacity. It is no small irony that it was only at this time of greatest crisis that these organizations finally received sustained attention from the federal agencies they had been attempting to influence for decades: law enforcement and counterterrorism agencies, especially those housed in the Department of Justice and the new Department of Homeland Security.

In various different ways, state actions generated centripetal pressure, encouraging the disparate Middle Eastern American organizations to work together. In a sense, many so-called counterterrorism polices instituted in the 1990s and 2000s, which had a disparate impact on Middle Eastern American communities, provided some indirect motivation to these advocacy organizations to work together. When discriminatory policies contributed to the racial projects that lumped all those communities together, the conditions were set for cooperation between different groups in the Middle Eastern American umbrella.

In addition to those indirect, nebulous centripetal forces was a clear, direct encouragement by state agencies to bring together what became known around Washington, DC, as the "post-9/11 community." This was a shorthand for a specific list of communities, which can only be explained by referring to the Middle Eastern racial category: Arab, Muslim, Sikh, and South Asian Americans. Various efforts by federal agencies in the months and years after 9/11 had the effect of pushing together those disparate and diverse advocacy organizations representing these "post-9/11 communities."

Law enforcement and security agencies played a large part in providing encouragement toward building transformational civil rights coalitions across the "post-9/11 community." The FBI and other agencies in the Department of Justice (DOJ) conducted extensive efforts to protect the civil rights of Middle Eastern Americans. Their mission was to enforce existing civil rights statutes, and they saw the Islamophobia crisis as one of their top priorities. This may seem contradictory, given the extensive role the very same agencies had in building and carrying out discriminatory "counterterrorism" programs. Even as discriminatory programs were ongoing, top federal officials declared that a primary goal of law enforcement and anti-terrorism efforts was to "build trust" with Middle Eastern American communities. The apparently hypocritical statements by top leaders from DHS and DOJ claiming that their agencies were "working alongside" Middle Eastern American leaders were met with suspicion by some advocates. But some of the most egregiously discriminatory "counterterrorism" programs—including the FBI's undercover informants and "sting" operations—were kept secret, and were not definitively known about until the late 2000s and early 2010s. Without hard evidence of these clandestine programs, many Middle Eastern American advocates openly embraced the opportunity to work with counterterrorism and law enforcement as part of a strategy to show their clear renunciation of terrorism. During the years that some of the worst abuses were kept secret, there was a great deal of effort from advocacy organizations and federal agencies alike to work cooperatively to "build trust," prevent terrorism, and enforce civil rights protections.

One of the most interesting policy questions for enforcing civil rights policies after 9/11 was determining the extent to which Middle Eastern Americans qualified under anti-discrimination statutes that protect racialized minority groups. Officials at the DOJ, the EEOC, and the Labor Department took the position right after 9/11 that anti-discrimination statutes protecting racial and ethnic minorities clearly applied to Arab, Muslim, Sikh, and South Asian Americans, despite the unclear legal "protected class" status of these groups. After the decision was made to include Middle Eastern Americans as a protected class, a wide range of resources became available for the federal effort to protect the civil rights of the "post-9/11 community."

Perhaps the most far-reaching and impactful effort at civil rights enforcement came under the auspices of an interagency working group convened by the DOJ on "post-9/11 community" concerns. In fact, the focused attention from the DOJ given to Arab, Muslim, Sikh, and South Asian American organizations in this manner was nearly unprecedented.

Right after 9/11, reports of hate crimes targeting Middle Eastern Americans began pouring in to FBI field offices throughout the country, often from advocates seeking assistance. Concerned about a lack of effective contacts within Arab, Muslim, Sikh, and South Asian communities, the Civil Rights Division of the DOJ immediately began a new effort to bring together representatives from any and all relevant federal agencies to meet regularly with Middle Eastern American advocates.

The authority for convening this interagency working group was set by the Civil Rights Act of 1964 and by Executive Order 12250, which was signed by President Carter in November 1980. These policies empowered the Attorney General to enforce anti-discrimination measures by requiring all federal agencies to cooperate with the DOJ to combat racial discrimination in any federal program or policy. Thus, multi-agency meetings convened to discuss anti-discrimination enforcement are often referred to as "12250 meetings." Using this authority, in late 2001, Assistant Attorney General for Civil Rights Ralph Boyd directed the DOJ's National Origin Working Group (NOWG) to coordinate a response to 9/11 "backlash discrimination" by ordering a 12250 meeting.[61]

This quickly transformed the relationship between the DOJ and advocacy organizations representing Middle Eastern Americans. Boyd personally met with leaders from organizations representing these groups, and multiple federal agencies including Health and Human Services and the Equal Employment Opportunity Commission joined in a series of community roundtables where they heard from community advocates and the general public.[62] The first roundtable was held in the Chicago area on October 9, 2001, "to address the concerns of that area's sizeable Arab, Muslim, Sikh, and South Asian American communities," according to a DOJ newsletter.[63] Similar forums were convened in Dearborn, Michigan, and Arlington, Virginia, in the months immediately following 9/11.

I spoke with a former DOJ staff member who described the early development of the idea for an interagency working group specifically for Arabs, Muslims, Sikhs, and South Asians. The obvious racial component in Islamophobic hate crimes spurred staff attorneys at the DOJ to bring together many organizations from a wide range of ethnic and religious groups to enforce anti-discrimination statutes.

> In weeks and months after 9/11, I know that there were a number of outreach efforts to Arab, Muslim, Sikh, South Asian groups. The reason I say Sikh and South Asian is because there were hate crimes immediately after 9/11, as you know. The Justice Department's Civil Rights Division saw the spike in these hate crimes. Persons . . . that were the victims of these hate crimes were not always Arab or Muslim. They were in the "perceived to be" Arab or Muslim category, which is where Sikhs and

many South Asians fell. Dark skin, speak with an accent, the story goes on from there. . . . [The decision was made] to convene a bimonthly meeting where groups could bring cases and issues, concerns. The DOJ meeting brought the Equal Employment Opportunity Commission, FBI, the forming parts of Homeland Security, Immigration, the visa office at State, [and] other offices that had equities in these groups' issues. That's where it began, [and] it's followed since, with every assistant AG [Attorney General], through today.

The idea for these interagency meetings came when a small group of Middle Eastern American staff attorneys advocated for it. The DOJ Civil Rights Division moved quickly and effectively to respond to the perceived crisis in hate crimes. The former staff member continued:

> The Civil Rights Division at DOJ . . . took it upon themselves to extend all the protections of their office, from getting information out on how to file complaints to [becoming] a listening board to take in what national community groups were saying. The Civil Rights Division worked with the FBI to enforce those federal statues [and] to prosecute when necessary. And so, they began a really constructive, proactive outreach. At the same time, community groups were reaching out to the Justice Department and FBI, [saying] "Look, the FBI was pounding on these doors," or "The community was being racially profiled here." Or, "There was graffiti on our house of worship" or on community centers. You know, "Government, come protect us."[64]

Even though the advocacy organizations had not specifically asked for a large meeting involving all the different groups affected by Islamophobia, the DOJ decided that the most efficient way to deal with the post-9/11 civil rights crisis was to bring them all together. Beginning in late 2001, on a regular, bimonthly basis, representatives from Arab, Muslim, Sikh, and South Asian American organizations came into the DOJ building and sat together for a meeting with the DOJ.

This represented a major intervention by the state, in a way that applied direct pressure on Middle Eastern American organizations to form transformational, race-based coalitions. This follows the expected pattern in racial formation theory. The state often acts to distribute resources, to codify racial ideology. The DOJ saw the racial nature of Islamophobia, and they moved decisively to bring resources to these disparate communities because of race. The DOJ, in short, was encouraging race-based thinking to solve race-based problems.

The first interagency meeting to discuss hate crimes and discrimination was held in Washington on November 1, 2001.[65] At this initial meeting and at the regularly scheduled meetings that followed, representatives from several Arab, Muslim, Sikh, and South Asian American advocacy organizations met in person with officials from the DOJ Civil Rights Division, the FBI, and other federal agencies.

Several people who regularly attended these interagency meetings told me about the proceedings.[66] Generally, a few days or weeks before each meeting, advocacy organizations were asked to submit a list of topics they wished to discuss. The DOJ then reviewed the proposed topics and contacted any relevant federal agencies to request investigations or to summon an agency representative to attend the meeting. DOJ staff then prepared an agenda that was shared with all meeting participants. During the closed-door meeting, advocacy organizations then spoke directly with policymakers and administrators from across the federal bureaucracy, including at various times representatives from Treasury, Secret Service, Census, State Department, Department of Homeland Security, Department of Defense, and others.

A representative of the Department of Homeland Security's Civil Rights and Civil Liberties office, a regular participant in these interagency meetings in the late 2000s, met with me in July 2009. I asked him whether this sort of interagency coordination with civil rights advocacy organizations was unique to the Islamophobia crisis. He indicated that the "post-9/11 community" interagency meetings were not at all unique, saying "there are always working groups in the government. Every administration always meets with constituency groups." He mentioned Latin@ community organizations that advocate on immigration issues as an example. Upon further reflection, however, he said that the form of the Arab, Muslim, Sikh, and South Asian interagency group was unique because it was designed specifically to allow advocacy organizations to air grievances across the federal government.

It's unique in this sense that the needs of the community, in terms of what their ask for government is, as well as what the government needs to understand and define the issues of Arab, Muslim, Sikh, [and] South Asian communities are completely unique to the circumstances at present, and the days after 9/11. That uniqueness—both sides wanting and needing to understand information, deliver a message to their constituencies—was so unique that it warranted something that didn't happen regularly. ICE [Immigration and Customs Enforcement] and Hispanic groups talk all the time over immigration. But the quarterly meeting, the forum, with issues brought, panel discussed, this is fairly unique. The only one of its kind that I'm aware of.[67]

Here, the DHS official notes that the government wanted to send a message that it was proactively trying to stop post-9/11 discrimination. In his view, "both sides"—meaning advocates and government officials—wanted these meetings to show good-faith effort at engaging with the problem.

These high-level meetings between the federal government and advocacy organizations served several purposes for the state. First, several advocates from Arab, Muslim, Sikh, and South Asian organizations told me that these interagency meetings were one of the only times when representatives from various advocacy organizations were able to meet face-to-face to discuss issues that affected the entire "post-9/11 community." Thus, the Department of Justice managed to facilitate coalition building between Arab, Muslim, Sikh, and South Asian community organizations. Second, federal agencies used these meetings for recruitment in "building trust" initiatives, trying to keep open communication lines. Several former advocates left their positions in advocacy organizations to work in the DHS and DOJ, partly through connections made in meetings like these. Third, the government used interagency meetings to gather information about Middle Eastern American communities. Though the meetings themselves provided little information that would be of use to law enforcement or counterterrorism intelligence, one participant told me that the DOJ has used the interagency meeting to ask community representatives to report any information on suspicious behavior that they hear from grassroots activists. In this way, the government used these interagency meetings as an example of its ability to hear about potential threats "on the ground" while remaining responsive to concerns about discrimination.

Whether or not they produced effective reforms or met any other practical goals, these meetings show active work by the state to integrate diverse communities according to racial ideology. Organizations considered to represent constituencies that fit with the racialized "post-9/11 community" were able to request and receive policy changes, investigations, and even funding from the executive branch through these meetings. Organizations representing communities that fell outside of this racialized category did not have this kind of access—for example, specifically African American Islamic organizations did not appear to be included in the interagency meeting. This indicates that race had a powerful impact on anti-discrimination policymaking in the wake of 9/11. The "post-9/11 community" was a racial construct born out of the recognition that a wide range of ethnic, national, and religious communities were affected by hate crimes and discrimination fueled by racism. Through these meetings, the state codified racial thinking directly into policy and practice—a striking example of a racial project in action. This underscores the importance of the interface between advocacy organizations and the state to the social construction of race, writ large.

Other levels of government also made race-conscious efforts to confront Islamophobia. At least two state governments—Maryland and Michigan—have followed racial thinking in establishing specifically Middle Eastern American agencies. In 2007, Maryland's governor added a Commission on Middle Eastern American Affairs to a range of similar commissions on racial and ethnic community affairs. Governor Martin O'Malley remarked that "it is important to recognize the Middle Eastern American community which plays a vital role of moving the state forward."[68] I spoke with a staff member at the commission, who explained that one of their primary objectives was to determine to what extent Middle Eastern Americans qualified for state and federal assistance for members of protected minority groups.[69] In other words, the Commission was actively working to include Middle Eastern Americans under the rubric of affirmative action. The commission was led by a Pakistani American, which might lead some observers to conclude that the commission is actually limited in scope to South Asian Americans.

But the staff member I spoke with made it clear that the use of the racial term "Middle Eastern American" was quite deliberate. The commission sought to include people who identified with many categories, "from Arab Americans to Muslim Americans, South Asians, and others," she told me.[70] A primary objective was securing minority business contracts and support from the state of Maryland for Middle Eastern American entrepreneurs.

In 2015, the state of Michigan followed Maryland in setting up a state-level Commission on Middle Eastern American Affairs, which had a mandate to "monitor, evaluate, and provide recommendations . . . regarding issues facing the Middle Eastern American community."[71] Prior to this, Michigan had a longstanding office on Arab and Chaldean American Affairs, but Governor Rick Snyder changed that office's name and expanded its scope, in recognition of the racial connections that lumped together not only Arabs and Chaldeans but many other communities as well.[72]

All of the efforts made by the Department of Justice—and the state governments of Maryland and Michigan—to consolidate civil rights work using racial thinking represent clear cases of the government pushing disparate groups together by making use of racial ideology to distribute resources as described in racial formation theory. Coming at the same time as all of the post-9/11 Islamophobic discrimination and rhetoric, there were tremendous centripetal forces acting on Middle Eastern American advocacy organizations. Only occasionally did these centripetal pressures lead to the creation of transformational coalitions, however.

Building Transformational Coalitions

Only a few Middle Eastern American advocates working in the years after 9/11 actively worked toward building transformational coalitions, efforts that would seek to leverage strategic advantages around racial formation. Leaders at SAALT and SALDEF, for example, sought to build coalitions along a wide range of ethnic and religious groups in the early 2000s. When asked about building connections between South Asian American communities and Arab American and Muslim American groups, one SAALT leader recalled:

> [Those links have] been developed over time. There was an absolute need after 9/11, even from the community's perspective, for Arabs, Muslims, Sikhs, and South Asians to have a response to what was happening.[73]

Note that she implicitly mentioned that most of SAALT's constituents would not ordinarily expect to join in with a transformational coalition with Arabs, Muslims, and Sikhs, when she says "even" the community saw a need for such coalitions. In other words, only the extraordinary crisis spawned by the 9/11 attacks produced enough impetus for rank-and-file SAALT constituents to see the need for transformational coalitions.

Another SAALT leader described how racial and religious identity affected her organization's work.

> We [SAALT] work closely with local and national organizations on issues pertaining to all groups, Muslim, Hindus, Sikhs, as well as other religions. We really try to use national-origin as the way to identify as South Asian, but we see that there are a lot of specific issues that affect different religious groups. The way that it relates to our work as South Asians, we either work on those issues or we work with organizations that do.[74]

These two leaders both found that the best strategy for navigating the racial dilemma was to build broad coalitions that transcended religious divisions. She did not mention race, specifically, but SAALT's National Coalition of South Asian Organizations produced several documents that expressed a clear call for racial justice.[75] For example, SAALT's National Coalition gave nine specific policy recommendations, including calls for greater political participation and voter organizing; work toward economic justice, gender equity, health care, immigrant rights, and LGBTIQ rights; and a specific plan for "Civil Rights and Civil Liberties."[76]

SAALT's work on this National Coalition provides a clear example of an effort to create a transformational coalition for Middle Eastern Americans. The effort continued beyond its initial meetings in 2008, with regional events taking place around the country called the "One Community United" campaign. In May 2010, a "One Community" event took place in Chicago that involved two Arab American organizations, an Asian American organization, a Muslim American organization, and a number of immigrant rights organizations.[77] The goals of meetings like this, to build durable connections between racially linked communities based on shared priorities, fits the mold of transformational coalition work.

SALDEF also attempted to bring together a transformational coalition by partnering with Arab and Muslim American organizations. I asked an executive at SALDEF to describe those efforts, and he at first responded by cautioning that some members of the Sikh American community vocally opposed coalition work with Muslim Americans. Some of his members expressed an opinion that SALDEF should just loudly assert that "we're not Muslims" through an educational outreach campaign.[78] SALDEF leaders effectively pushed back against this idea while continuing to engage in coalition building. One leader described how the organization took on the difficult task of pushing the idea of transformational coalitions on a skeptical membership:

> Over time, the community has had its own perception, and SALDEF has tried to break away a little bit. . . . We're a community with a voice. We don't necessarily have to bind with the Muslim Community or the Asian community to advocate for our issues. We have the connections and relationships now. Many members of the community don't want us to work at all with the Muslim community. They say, "Why are you working with them? Muslims are the problem." It's a bit understandable. The fact is, we're not attacked because we're Sikhs, we're attacked because we're perceived to be Muslim. Which is worse, in a way. If we're attacked because we're Sikh, we can deal with that on our own. But if we're attacked because we look Muslim, they're not only attacking the Sikh community but also the Arab and Muslim [communities]. Three communities. It's a delicate balance, but we tell our community that we have to. We're all in this together. We're going to be all in this together for a while, until we can change the culture in this country.[79]

I asked whether the attitude that "Muslims are the problem" was widespread in the Sikh American community. He assured me that this opinion belonged only to a "small, but vocal minority." This kind of struggle—between community members who argue for a distinct identity and organizers looking to foster broader commonalities—is a hallmark of durable coalition building. It shows how advocates play a key role in overcoming centrifugal forces when trying to forge transformational coalitions between distinct and different community groups.

SAALT and SALDEF's efforts to create transformational coalitions were rewarded with additional recognition and cooperation from larger advocacy organizations and the government. LCCR admitted both SAALT and SALDEF as members after 2001, and the Department of Justice invited both organizations to join in the regular interagency meetings of the "post-9/11 community." These organizations built a strategy based on the recognition that race brought them together with Arab and Muslim Americans, and they made attempts to build transformational coalitions along those lines.

These efforts were successful, but they remained isolated. There are very few other examples of nationally prominent Middle Eastern American organizations besides SAALT and SALDEF engaging in this kind of work. SAALT staff and a few other advocates that I interviewed mentioned that they had seen more efforts at building transformational coalitions in specific localities around the United States. The work of Linda Sarsour to join together Arab Americans with #BlackLivesMatter and other "people of color" coalitions in New York and elsewhere is perhaps emblematic of those efforts. Nevertheless, despite all of the centripetal forces generated by Islamophobic racism, no nationally prominent, transformational Middle Eastern American coalitions took hold in the decade after 9/11. Instead, most advocacy organizations seemed to avoid discussing a Middle Eastern American racial identity as much as they could.

Avoiding Race: Transactional Coalitions after 9/11

Most Middle Eastern American advocates I interviewed did not know of any significant coalition work that sought to bring together Arab, Muslim, Sikh, and South Asian American groups into transformational coalitions. Instead, when I asked advocates working at the six largest Middle Eastern American advocacy organizations about coalition work, I heard mainly about transactional efforts that cropped up on the sidelines of the DOJ interagency meetings as the only occasions that these organizations engaged in coalition-based strategies. Moreover, nearly every organization that I studied eschewed the language of race and racism in their public advocacy work.

Unlike ADC and AAI in the 1980s, which frequently used the word "racism" while actively participating in civil rights coalitions, Middle Eastern American advocacy organizations after 9/11 instead usually crafted their messages in pointedly race-neutral language. Rather than insist on strong protections for minority communities facing racial discrimination, most Middle Eastern American advocates advocated for equal treatment for all. This rhetorical shift may seem small, but it reflects significant developments in the field of civil rights advocacy across the board.

The CAIR leader, whom I described in chapter 1, argued against using race as a matter of public policy. Recall that he insisted that a race-conscious approach to civil rights would be harmful, as it would only serve to "separate Americans" by religion and ethnicity. Describing CAIR's involvement in advocacy coalitions, he went on to explain that staying away from identity politics provided a strategic advantage:

> There is an element [of race and racism] there, but it is not the main driving force. The reason for that is our allies are so diverse. Some are driven by principles. Those who defend civil liberties, that is the issue. Those who are religiously oriented: progressive Jewish groups, progressive Christian groups, they're driven again by the strive to establish justice, fair treatment of all people.

Essentially, this CAIR leader sees that describing Islamophobia as racism and working to build coalitions on the basis of race would preclude the participation of allies from religious and other social justice organizations. When I asked this leader directly whether race affected CAIR's advocacy strategy, I received a complex answer:

> The American Muslim community doesn't consider itself a unique racial group in America. For one reason. If you go to any mosque now, you'll see the diversity that America represents at that mosque. You'll see the Mexican Muslim, the Pakistani Muslim, the Anglo Muslim, the Latino Muslim, the African American Muslim, [the] Chinese Muslim. You'll be

sitting there and you'll see like what you see outside, but inside. Obviously, with a larger Arab and Pakistani ratio, but what I mean is: you don't see one race.[80]

He went on to explain that because Muslims come from many different backgrounds, it makes little sense to discuss Islamophobia as a form of racism affecting Muslims. I pointed out that Sikh Americans and Muslim Americans who "look Muslim" tend to face Islamophobia as well, because of their physical appearance. I suggested that this was because of racism and asked whether this fact influenced CAIR's relationship with the Sikh American community. He replied: "I'm not sure I understand the question, to tell the truth."[81] The concept that Sikhs and Muslims shared an ascribed racial identity had not even occurred to him, despite all the many incidents of Islamophobia affecting South Asians and Sikhs. This leader, and others I spoke with at CAIR and MPAC, expressed the belief that a coalition for civil rights based on a broad racial identity that included Sikhs and other non-Muslim groups did not make much sense for their membership. They insisted that the best strategy for tackling Islamophobia was showing how Muslim Americans deserved the same rights as Christian and Jewish Americans—not showing how Muslim Americans suffer from racist oppression as communities of color.

In keeping with this strategic orientation, another CAIR executive who spent time in the CAIR National headquarters told me that CAIR oriented itself as a mainstream political organization seeking to improve rights for all, rather than as an organization arguing for minority rights.

> I don't see the constituency in terms of ethnic groups. The membership is attracted to CAIR because of its broad appeal and effectiveness. . . . We don't go after controversy, but instead we will take a brave stand for the benefit and good of all.

He described a CAIR national strategy meeting where the organization voted on a proposal to engage in a "non-Muslim type of advocacy," meaning advocacy on issues that would benefit everyone, not just Muslim Americans.

> The CAIR legislative advocacy agenda is one among four or five issues we voted on this year. We want to work on national issues, not Muslim-specific issues. Racial profiling and immigration reform. Citizenship delay, specifically. These take the front seat in our legislative advocacy, and they're not specific to Muslims. When we talk about these issues, we're talking about a racial issue, [and its effects] generally, not just [on] Muslims. . . . I was present at the meeting where we discussed talking about a non-Muslim type of advocacy. It passed with flying colors.[82]

Despite this new push toward "non-Muslim advocacy," I saw little to suggest that CAIR engaged in any significant transformational coalitions in the early 2000s. CAIR's approach, by and large, remained race-neutral.

Rather than challenge colorblindness ideology by pointing to race as a central cause of discrimination, most advocates I interviewed expressed opinions like these CAIR leaders, saying that racism is "not the main driving force" in Islamophobia. MPAC, for example, seemed to have a similar strategy as CAIR. Transactional coalition work between MPAC and other advocacy organizations—on those occasions where it happened—was based on events and issues, not on a transformational concept like redefining racial identity. Indeed, one MPAC executive sounded almost exasperated when I asked how MPAC worked with other community groups in coalitions:

> We've had great relationships [with other community organizations]. SALDEF. Interfaith. Christian-Muslim cooperation group. We're on a number of immigrant rights and other advocacy coalitions in DC. There are a lot. Almost too many meetings with these coalitions [*laughing*].[83]

Here, the MPAC leader is describing a wide range of coalition work, but just a few days later, a different MPAC leader contradicted this statement, telling me that the organization did not even try to coordinate coalition work with regular meetings. The only time he recalled meeting with Arab, Sikh, and South Asian American organizations was on the sidelines of the DOJ interagency meetings.

> There's nothing across ethnic or religious organizations. But at the DOJ interagency meeting, we all sort of become aware of the issues that all of

us are working on, and then we schedule a conference call when issues arise.[84]

A version of that statement—"we schedule a conference call when issues arise"—was repeated in various forms by many of the staff that I spoke with at all Middle Eastern American advocacy organizations. When I asked about cooperation among Arab, Muslim, Sikh, and South Asian American organizations, I almost always heard something along these lines. One executive at SAALT described coalition work by saying, "With those organizations [CAIR, MPAC, ADC], it's not weekly or monthly meetings. We do work closely with them as issues arise."[85] Some advocates viewed coordination with other organizations as unnecessary. One staff member at AAI put it bluntly: "I feel like I'm on every flipping working group in the city," adding that such meetings were a "waste of my two hours." She emphasized that most of AAI's coalition work with other organizations came on an "as-needed basis." [86]

What these advocates describe is a landscape where cooperation across the Middle Eastern American spectrum—crossing the many diverse lines between Arab, Muslim, Sikh, and South Asian American communities—was confined to short-term, transactional efforts. This work avoided controversy by rejecting calls for special civil rights protections or "identity politics." Instead, these organizations emphasized how they pushed an agenda to benefit "all Americans." Partnerships among organizations involved in transactional coalitions emerged on a case-by-case, temporary, and as-needed basis. Each organization worked mostly independently, joining together only briefly when a particular policy priority or crisis moment brought them together. Their efforts required few compromises or sacrifices, and little sharing of resources.

One former ADC leader frankly told me that absolutely "no coordination" existed between ADC, AAI, MPAC, and CAIR. "None at all," he said.[87] Another former ADC executive confirmed this account:

Political and social activism in this country has its up and downs. And right now, we're at a down. One or two [Arab American] organizations are functioning okay, three or four are barely functional, and the rest are dysfunctional. There are many reasons for it. Definitely, I think 9/11 has had some serious impact on the community. We didn't see it clearly at the time, in the middle of the crisis. But it did sap the energy of the community, and it had what we warned against immediately after the crisis: a chilling effect. It took us years to bring Arab Americans to the forefront, to convince them to identify as such. And get active socially and politically as such [as Arab Americans]. And now, many of them have retreated.[88]

According to this advocate, the "chilling effect" of 9/11 caused the Arab American community to back away from identity-based civil rights activism to avoid controversy. In the current context, he believed that racial identity was no longer effective as a political organizing tool.

Even though the existing, fragile Arab American advocacy coalitions collapsed after 2001, new opportunities opened up for those same organizations to coordinate with other groups advocating for the civil rights of people of color more broadly. One ADC leader told me about a rush of coalition building immediately after the 9/11 attacks.

Maybe because it's attractive to work on post-9/11 issues. After 9/11, NAACP, La Raza, all the other guys, they started looking to work with us more closely. "Make sure ADC is signed on letters," and so on. That wasn't always the fact all the time before 9/11, at least from my experience. That helps us. And it makes it easier. When LCCR [Leadership Council on Civil Rights] gets a Ford Foundation grant to look at Islamophobia and anti-Semitism in Europe, [LCCR President] Wade Henderson makes sure that [ADC Executives] are on the delegation.[89]

In addition to its work with LCCR, ADC also worked with the Asian American Justice Center on several campaigns after 2001. This work helped ADC win grants from the major charities including the Ford and Carnegie Foundations.[90]

Overall, what the leaders of these organizations found is that the best strategy for confronting Islamophobia after 9/11 was to leverage color-blindness ideology. They found it most beneficial to continue along the line established by the conservative reaction to the civil rights movement: all Americans should be treated equally under the law, and the only way to achieve that is to ignore racial identity. On occasion, the leading Middle Eastern American organizations formed transactional coalitions, but only on an ad-hoc basis. This strategy produced success-ful interventions into Islamophobic processes in the years after 9/11, but the persistence of hate crimes, discrimination, and the expansion of Islamophobic rhetoric in American politics has continued to frustrate these advocates for many years afterwards.

Finding the Way Forward

The decade after 2001 saw a lack of durable cooperation and coordina-tion between the most influential Middle Eastern American advocacy organizations. This was surprising because the civil rights protections of the mid-1900s were supposed to make it easy for disparate communities similarly affected by racism to join together to demand redress. Instead, most of the best and brightest advocates—each of whom has dedi-cated their lives to improving civil rights—found that the best strategy for stopping racist Islamophobia was to ignore race. The way forward, according to these long-time advocates, was to present their community as full-fledged Americans, worthy of the same rights as any other citi-zen. Despite the tremendous centripetal forces exerted by Islamophobia over the past several decades, almost no organizations have emerged aiming to represent the entire set of communities underneath the Mid-dle Eastern American racial umbrella.

The colorblind strategy undertaken by most Middle Eastern Ameri-can advocacy organizations all but precludes participation in transfor-mational coalitions based on racial identity. By actively trying to avoid framing Islamophobia as racism, there is simply no foundation for co-alitions between diverse and disparate groups—Arabs, Muslims, Sikhs, and South Asians.

The advocates that I spoke to offered several reasons why they found it advantageous not to engage in the kind of transformational, race-based coalitions that defined twentieth-century movements for civil rights. I heard these five reasons most often cited by those advocates who expressed skepticism about such race-based coalitions.

First, many advocates insisted that their community was large and powerful enough on its own to accomplish its goals without investing in transformational coalition building. Advocates from several different communities made this same argument, including even relatively small communities like Chaldean Americans and Sikh Americans.[91] While most advocates recognized the value of coalitions based on achieving specific policy goals, or coalitions of organizations representing the same ethnically or religiously defined community, a coalition based on race seemed unnecessary at best and counterproductive at worst. These advocates believed they could achieve their goals with their own community, alone.

Second, some advocates expressed skepticism that a coalition would accept their specific political priorities. Many discussed how their foreign affairs issues would not get a fair hearing in a broader coalition based on racial identity. For example, several Arab American advocates I spoke with described that the top priority of their constituents was the plight of Palestinians living under occupation. In their view, most Arab American supporters of ADC, AAI, and other organizations would insist on this as the top priority even at the expense of domestic civil rights and most other political concerns. Other advocates pointed out that ongoing conflicts between nations in the broadly conceived Middle East (including in North Africa and South Asia) would necessarily strain or even prevent alliances between American communities with ties to these nations. They worried that conflicts like those between India and Pakistan, within Iraq, Syria, and Lebanon, and between Iran and the Arab world more generally, would spill over and unavoidably complicate any serious effort at a transformational coalition of Middle Eastern Americans.

Third, some advocates suggested that unlike Native Americans and Asian Americans, too few people identified with the Middle Eastern racial category in the United States to mount a successful race-based campaign for unity. That is, a "critical mass" of people who already identified as Middle Eastern American did not exist. Unlike the first reason, which holds that there are enough members in any one ethnic community to provide political clout, this argument instead suggests that Middle Eastern Americans do not make up a large enough proportion of the overall American population to achieve recognition as a racial group.

Fourth, some experienced DC insiders made the case that race-based coalition building was not recognized as legitimate in today's elite policy circles. For example, some advocates said that foundation grants would not go to organizations working on an explicitly race-based campaign.

Due to colorblindness ideology and to the effective demonization of affirmative action as "reverse discrimination," advocates who spoke about racial justice did not feel that it would be attractive to funders (both wealthy individuals and charitable foundations) if they led their organizations into "people of color" coalitions.

Finally, a few advocates that I interviewed believed that Islamophobic discrimination was just not a big enough problem to act as a powerful centripetal force that would push together the diverse and disparate groups under a single Middle Eastern American umbrella. While several long-time advocates said that Islamophobia did present a major issue, many noted that the socioeconomic status of Arab, Muslim, Sikh, and South Asian Americans was higher, on average, than that of most other communities. Given the "success" of some in these communities in attaining a middle class (or wealthy) lifestyle, how could they argue that Islamophobia posed a serious, existential threat to their well-being? This was not a majority opinion among the advocates that I interviewed, but I did hear it from time to time.

These arguments, in one combination or another, appeared most frequently when I asked advocates about the lack of race-based coalitions among Arab, Muslim, Sikh, and South Asian American organizations. The implication is that even the phenomenon known as Islamophobia—extensive and deep-rooted—combined with pressure from the government to form into a "post-9/11 community" have not generated sufficient centripetal forces to overcome the centrifugal forces keeping these organizations apart.

The lack of successful transformational coalitions among Middle Eastern American organizations struggling against the prominent controversies of Islamophobia signals a major shift in American civil rights advocacy. The dominance of colorblindness ideology shows the success of efforts to roll back the protections won by the civil rights movements of the mid-1900s. Middle Eastern American advocates have found that it no longer makes strategic sense to band together in advocacy coalitions based on identity. The racial formation of Middle Eastern Americans has been profoundly affected by these racial politics. The methods and strategies of the 1900s no longer apply in the 2010s, which leaves open the question about whether a new civil rights era is about to dawn.

6

Toward a New Civil Rights Era

In the summer of 2010, a major international scandal erupted around the planned construction of a community center in New York City that would include a space for Muslims to worship. The center would also feature a performance art space, sporting equipment, and conference facilities. The building was set for construction on Park Place in lower Manhattan, not far from where the World Trade Center's iconic Twin Towers once stood.

In May, plans for the community center completed a lengthy approval process after a public hearing. This generated some attention from a small but influential network of conservative activists.[1] They began spreading the idea that because "Muslims attacked" the United States on 9/11, a building that had a place for Muslims to worship so close to the World Trade Center site represented a blatant attempt at a morbid celebration. In several blog posts, they proffered a conspiracy theory, warning that the construction of this particular community center lay at the heart of a secret plot for the "conquest" of the United States by nefarious Muslims.

Remarkably, only a short time after these blog posts appeared, newspapers and television news bureaus around the country began conducting in-depth investigations on the proposed community center, which was at the time named Cordoba House. In their reports, however, the news media mostly used a moniker for the community center promoted by the small group of conservative activists: the "Ground Zero mosque." Shortly after the scandal over the "Ground Zero mosque" reached the front page of newspapers around the world, public officials including members of Congress, state governors, and even the President of the United States and other heads of state spoke out on the issue of this proposed building. The issue of the community center's construction weighed heavily in the 2010 Congressional elections as a wedge issue.[2]

The small band of conservative activists opposed to the Cordoba House had successfully used Islamophobic rhetoric to create a huge scandal.

Perhaps the most memorable opinion given in support of the community center came from New York City Mayor Michael Bloomberg, who spoke on August 3, 2010:

> The World Trade Center site will forever hold a special place in our city, in our hearts. But we would be untrue to the best part of ourselves—and who we are as New Yorkers and Americans—if we said "no" to a mosque in Lower Manhattan. Let us not forget that Muslims were among those murdered on 9/11 and that our Muslim neighbors grieved with us as New Yorkers and as Americans. We would betray our values—and play into our enemies' hands—if we were to treat Muslims differently than anyone else. In fact, to cave to popular sentiment would be to hand a victory to the terrorists—and we should not stand for that. For that reason, I believe that this is an important test of the separation of church and state as we may see in our lifetime—as important a test—and it is critically important that we get it right.[3]

Bloomberg's widely quoted enunciation of the American value of religious freedom, enshrined in the First Amendment to the Constitution, failed to sway the wide majority of Americans who explicitly opposed the construction of this particular community center. A CNN telephone poll of the American public taken between August 6 and August 10, 2010 found that only 29% favored, while 68% opposed, the plan to build "a mosque two blocks from the site in New York City where the World Trade Center used to stand."[4]

The controversy over the proposed community center in New York City contributed to a wave of opposition and protests at mosques around the United States, sometimes escalating into threats and violence.[5] In Tennessee, for example, a mosque already under construction in 2010 encountered sudden and heated opposition. Arsonists attacked the construction site, and the question over whether the mosque should be built became a major issue in the election for the state's governor.[6] Meanwhile, in May 2010, a pipe bomb exploded in a mosque in Jacksonville, Florida, causing extensive damage. Thankfully, no one was hurt.[7] In several other places during the summer of 2010, mosques were vandalized. Whether such hate attacks on Muslims were definitively more numerous in 2010 than in other years is unclear, because of the difficulty in keeping accurate statistics on hate crimes like these. What is clear, however, is that the attention given to Islamophobic attacks was much greater in 2010 than it had been at any time since 2001.

Even with all this extra attention on the civil rights of Muslim Americans, the voices of Middle Eastern American advocates were heard only rarely in the media. Despite editorials and op-eds published in newspapers around the world on the issue—and the nearly nonstop coverage of the controversy on 24-hour cable news networks—there seemed to be very little time to allow civil rights advocates to be heard. Instead, it was the voices of commentators who advocated *against* building mosques that dominated the discussion in the press.

There are many reasons that might explain the absence of civil rights advocates in the media narratives, and certainly editors and producers are partially responsible for not giving adequate space for those voices. Christopher Bail found that a powerful "fringe effect" amplified the voices of anti-Muslim organizations after 2001, enabling them to "dominate the mass media."[8] Consider that if "earned media" (or, for that matter, paid media) can be considered a resource available for deployment by advocacy organizations, then Middle Eastern American advocacy organizations and their allies lost a huge opportunity in 2010. The voices of Islamophobic commentators handily won that round of the media battle.

That a small group of conservative activists generated so much controversy over the community center in lower Manhattan exemplifies the large space still available in mainstream American discourse for attacking Middle Eastern American civil rights. After the Islamophobic mania over the "Ground Zero mosque" faded, several other manufactured controversies emerged, with yet more political candidates making blatantly Islamophobic statements, particularly during the 2012, 2014, and 2016 election cycles. There is a measurable impact of all of this Islamophobic sentiment, combined with fears after various violent episodes that were said to be "terrorist attacks" coinciding with the rise of the so-called Islamic State in the mid-2010s. At the end of 2015, AAI conducted a poll that found even higher levels of "unfavorable" opinions toward Middle Eastern Americans than in 2010. In 2015, only 33% reported having a "favorable" opinion of Muslim Americans, compared with 48% who held a "favorable" opinion in 2010.

In short, Islamophobia continues to be popular and mainstream, with no end in sight. The enunciation of deeply Islamophobic rhetoric and blatantly discriminatory anti-Muslim policy proposals by Donald J. Trump in the 2016 presidential election played a large part in his many victories at the ballot box. Furthermore, hurtful and widespread discriminatory policies, such as the FBI's "sting operations," continue. By any measure, Islamophobia lives on as a major problem in America.

The hope that Islamophobia would fade as the emotional memories of 9/11 receded into history has, unfortunately, been dashed. Islamophobia, it seems, is only getting worse. The space within which Islamophobia continues to operate would have been much smaller if Middle Eastern American advocacy had gained more traction in the years before and after 9/11.

The Racial Dilemma and the Durability of Islamophobia

The lack of traction for Middle Eastern American advocates has much to do with the uncertainty caused by the racial paradox and the racial dilemma. The racial paradox obscures the fact that the Middle Eastern American racial identity exists. This severely complicates the racial dilemma that Middle Eastern American advocates must contend with. Without the ability to clearly and concisely describe Islamophobia as a racist phenomenon that affects a racialized group, it becomes much more difficult for advocates to speak about Islamophobia as racism. This, in combination with increasingly weak protections against discrimination in American culture, politics, and policy, makes avoiding the topic of race and racism an appealing strategic option for Middle Eastern American advocates.

But what does it mean for American civil rights advocacy as a whole that most advocates avoid describing Islamophobia as racism? It means that the so-called post–civil rights era may be over. In the late-twentieth century, co-opting racial identity for civil rights gains was almost always a good strategic option for advocates. If a civil rights advocate from the 1970s travelled through time to the 2010s and heard about the kinds of discrimination, hate crimes, and rhetoric directed at Middle Eastern

Americans today, that advocate would expect there to be protests, boy-cotts, and rallies organized by race-based, transformational coalitions. Indeed, the lack of such actions does not align with what would be ex-pected according to racial formation theory and the examples provided by campaigns in the late-1900s for Asian, Native, and Latin@ American rights. Yet here we have Middle Eastern American organizations that, for the most part, decided to eschew race-based coalitions while they avoided discussing racism in favor of a colorblind strategy.

This continued even as the government put pressure on Arab, Mus-lim, Sikh, and South Asian communities to join together into race-based coalitions. In addition to blatantly discriminatory policies and programs that generated centripetal forces, the Department of Justice (DOJ) and other agencies used a race-conscious approach to civil rights enforce-ment in an effort to deal with all Middle Eastern American communities as one. These offices recognized how racial discrimination affected all of the different communities under the Middle Eastern umbrella, and as such they sought to deal with all of them at once. AAI, ADC, MPAC, SAALT, and SALDEF were invited to work together with the Civil Rights Division at the DOJ. Yet, even with the government giving major incen-tives to join race-based coalitions, these organizations worked together almost exclusively in transactional ways. They did not form durable, transformational umbrella organizations, and they had very little proac-tive coordination at all.

Perhaps the main reason that the race-neutral strategy was adopted by Middle Eastern American advocates was mainly due to the dominance of the colorblindness ideology in American politics. The prevalence of colorblindness in American political and legal narratives has been documented by a wide range of scholarship.[9] On the colorblind view, simply acknowledging that race exists is a problem—talking about race perpetuates racism. The solution to racism, then, is to just ignore race entirely. Even keeping simple statistics on race, such as the number of people from different racial groups living in a particular city or attend-ing a particular school, for example, serves only to contribute to racism, on this view. The best way forward, according to colorblind ideology, is to pretend that race does not matter. Since the 1990s, a legal framework supporting this idea has been rapidly spreading throughout the United States. California voters approved a constitutional amendment in 1996 (known as Proposition 209 or the "California Civil Rights Initiative") that made it illegal for state institutions to acknowledge race, sex, or ethnicity, with very limited exceptions. Similar laws passed throughout the country in the 1990s and early 2000s. These new policies have been supported by the courts. Judges have steadily added more limits to affirmative action programs, and they have imposed a strict "intent requirement" on discrimination claims. These steps foreshadowed a landmark 2013 Supreme Court decision that nullified most of the iconic Voting Rights Act of 1965.[10]

The narrowing of civil rights protections in American jurisprudence has carried profound impacts for Middle Eastern Americans. Even as federal agencies and advocacy organizations filed lawsuits in an effort to prevent Islamophobic discrimination, the courts placed more and more hurdles to clear before it accepted that racial discrimination was to blame. For example, in *University of Texas v. Nassar*, the Supreme Court in 2013 found that Dr. Naiel Nassar, a Middle Eastern American man, did not face intolerable working conditions after a supervisor singled him out for scrutiny and openly stated in his presence her belief that "Middle Easterners are lazy."[11] When another doctor of Middle Eastern descent got a job at the hospital—despite that supervisor's objection— she lamented that they had just "hired another one." These blatantly racist statements were not enough to prove that the discriminatory intentions of Dr. Nassar's supervisors were intolerable. The Supreme Court, in a 5–4 decision, ruled that discrimination on the basis of race, religion, or ethnicity was not the only reason that he lost his job. Because there were other motivating factors, the Court said, the protections of the Civil Rights Act did not apply. This ruling, once again, narrowed the legal terrain upon which civil rights claims stand.

Given the rapidly shrinking ground on which civil rights advocates can claim that racial discrimination affects their communities, should it really be a surprise that Middle Eastern American advocates by and large chose to avoid the language of race?

The dominance of colorblindness represents a significant shift in American life, and it has enabled a major rollback of the legal and political framework put in place by the 1950s and 1960s-era civil rights movement. The knock-on effects of this shift on civil rights advocacy are only now becoming fully apparent. The change in the work of the American-

Arab Anti-Discrimination Committee (ADC) is very instructive. Recall that in the 1980s, ADC worked closely with the Rainbow Coalition and Operation PUSH against what they jointly called "racism." By 2001, ADC's rhetoric had changed, and most of its post-9/11 statements talk about protecting rights for "all Americans," including minority groups. Similarly, the Council on American-Islamic Relations (CAIR) avoided using the term "racial profiling" to describe a new TSA airport screening program in 2010, instead calling it "religious and ethnic profiling." Advocates sometimes go out of their way to make sure they do not run afoul of colorblind conventions.

Middle Eastern American advocates have, by and large, chosen to ride the wave of colorblindness. The results of this choice are debatable, but the strategy itself has not been debated much among many of the advocates I spoke with. Instead of vibrant debates about whether to take up the rhetoric of racism, a strategy compatible with colorblindness was mostly taken for granted. This shows that advocacy tactics that explicitly discuss race to stake a claim for civil rights have very little legitimacy in contemporary political circles. The colorblind approach is usually seen as the only viable option for advocacy.

The inability to clearly refer to Arab, Muslim, Sikh, and South Asian Americans as a racialized group—because of the racial paradox that has captured the Middle Eastern American identity—has made it all too easy to ignore or deny the racism inherent in Islamophobia. It is easy to point to the overlapping causes of Islamophobia—particularly religion, gender, socioeconomic class, immigration status, and geography—as an excuse to ignore race altogether. A mantra of colorblind ideology is: "It's not race, it's class." Of course, race always interacts with other social forces, but that does not mean that race is irrelevant. The racism in Islamophobia is obvious, but an endless debate rages over even this simple fact, mainly because of colorblindness ideology.

The dominance of colorblindness over Middle Eastern American advocacy strategy is complicated by one additional factor that may prove pivotal in the coming decade—the boundaries of Whiteness and the contours of civil rights advocacy in the coming "majority-minority" era.

Whiteness and Middle Eastern Americans

The existence of the Middle Eastern racial category does not deny agency to the individuals and groups ascribed with it. Many people who find themselves frequently ascribed with a Middle Eastern identity take great effort to reject that classification. Several scholars have described in detail how many Middle Eastern Americans "pass" as White.[12] In this way, many people intentionally downplay or even hide their heritage in an effort to join in the American mainstream, complete with a White racial identity. John Tehranian concluded that, while individuals stand to gain the benefits of Whiteness by "passing," this means the broader community loses the ability to describe the discrimination affecting them as racism. Thus, Tehranian describes a "Faustian pact with Whiteness," what Deepa Iyer calls "the racial bribe."[13] Similarly, Andrew Shryock argues that the status quo, with the ambiguous racial position for Middle Eastern Americans, carries certain advantages for political clout, advantages that would be lost in an overt identity politics campaign.[14] Tehranian and Shryock both recognize the shrinking terrain of race-based civil rights protections.

Of course, people are not only sociological subjects but also the subjects of their own lives. Middle Eastern Americans have recognized the profound racial contradictions in America, and they are attempting to live within them. This has led them, both as individuals and as collectivities, largely to eschew identifying themselves along racial lines, but instead to insist both on their internal diversity and their civil liberties under the Constitution. In many ways, this is a profound effort that should prove successful. The question ultimately boils down to whether colorblindness can ever actually produce effective anti-racist change.

The debate over identity politics has been particularly relevant and long-lasting for Arab Americans. The vast diversity among Arab Americans has always complicated political organizing in these communities, and today many Arab American families have been in the United States for four or more generations. Several studies find that many Arab Americans believe strongly that they are White.[15] Perhaps the Census definition of Whiteness—"having origins in any of the original peoples of Europe, the Middle East, or North Africa"—makes this White identity obvious.[16]

Recently, however, a renewed effort by Arab American advocates to add a Middle East and North Africa (MENA) category on the Census may have broad impacts. This development emerged despite a great deal of suspicion in Middle Eastern American communities toward the Census. This suspicion is reasonable. Consider that after the September 11 attacks, the Census controversially provided detailed data to the US Customs Service about Arab American populations in 2002 and 2003. AAI's earlier effort to gain official Census recognition was shelved in the early 2000s amid concerns over how that effort might contribute to profiling by law enforcement and counterterrorism agencies.[17]

By 2010, however, concerns over Census data had subsided enough to allow for new campaigns led by Arab American advocates encouraging the community to participate in the 2010 Census survey. Some Arab American activists, who were notably not affiliated with AAI or ADC, encouraged Arab Americans filling out the Census survey to "Check it right, you ain't White!"[18] This effort reflects an understanding among some younger Arab American advocates of a strategic value in a "people of color," non-White identity. The campaign intended to show the Census Bureau that Arab Americans should not have the instruction on the Census form to check the White racial identity by having large numbers of Arab Americans instead check "Some Other Race" and write-in "Arab American." In an interview, one Arab American advocate explained that this "you ain't White" effort was "intended to be something that would appeal to the young crowd," adding that this slogan was

> certainly not the message that we in the established organizations necessarily would have chosen to send. Because the issue is not so much that people from the MENA region do not identify with the White racial category. The issue is that many of them do, but the undifferentiated White category is insufficient. Hence, our campaign to . . . encourage the Census Bureau to disaggregate the MENA data from the White population.[19]

AAI has been emphatic in making the Census reform push about recognizing an ethnicity category, not a racial category. In an effort to increase buy-in, and to provide the easiest bureaucratic path to acceptance, AAI insists that the MENA category is an ethnicity, and that people can identify as both White and MENA. This approach, intended to maximize participation in the Census and thereby get a large number of people checking the MENA box, also conforms neatly with colorblind ideology. If Arab American advocates effectively articulate a "colorblind" perspective in the construction of the MENA Census category, such that MENA identity is understood as ethnic and specifically not racial, that might further serve to legitimate similarly "colorblind" strategies for advocates in the 2020s.

This all illustrates how the decades-old debate among Arab American advocates over racial identity shows no sign of reaching any definitive conclusions. In recent years, some leading Arab American advocates—like Linda Sarsour—have suggested that a non-White identification with "people of color" would be more valuable, despite frequent opposition from within the community.

As these debates raged, some young Arab American scholars and activists began to openly challenge what they perceived as the "old guard," the leadership in organizations like ADC and AAI. At the annual ADC Convention in 2014, a panel titled "Racial, Religious, and Ethnic Self-Identification" featured young Arab American scholars who gave contentious presentations about the need for "race-based activism."[20] Khaled Beydoun, an ADC activist and law professor, implored ADC members to recognize a racial coalition with "people of color." Similarly, Hisham Aidi, author of several books on race and diasporic Muslim communities, spoke critically of "ethnic activism" by ADC and AAI, while noting that "younger activists" wanted racial identity—not ethnic or religious identity—at the core of their political work. Aidi and Beydoun both explained the potential strategic political value for ADC if it adopted a race-based orientation. Several audience members strongly rejected this concept during a question-and-answer session. One ADC member in attendance stated flatly, "I'm not going to accept an identity just for the convenience of the political structure." Others spoke expressively about their self-identification with a specific national, ethnic, or religious identity, such as Palestinian or Muslim, that for them was far more salient than any racial category. The panel ended without much in the way of resolution. More than anything else, the discussion at the convention seemed to confirm the persistence of the controversy among Arab American leaders and activists around the issue of racial identity.

As a liminal group—one that has always had an ambiguous position in the American racial system—Middle Eastern Americans face the brunt of the impacts of shrinking civil rights protections. The belated recognition that these communities have faced racialization for decades has come just as the so-called post civil rights era might very well be drawing to a close.

The Future of Civil Rights

In March 2015, I attended an event titled "Living In America: Islamophobia" hosted by the All Dulles Area Muslim Society (ADAMS), just outside Washington, DC. Community members packed the main prayer room to listen to comments and analysis from scholars and advocates Linda Sarsour, Dalia Mogahed, Saeed Khan, and Ajenai Clemmons. The ADAMS Main Center is an important hub for many Muslim American communities in the DC area. It attracts a multi-ethnic, diverse crowd every Friday. That night was no exception. The event came shortly after yet another brutal and tragic Islamophobic hate crime—the murder of three young Muslim Americans in Chapel Hill, North Carolina. Many came to hear something uplifting in the wake of that devastating news.

The standing-room-only crowd heard speeches discussing the impacts of hate speech on lesbian, gay, bisexual, and transgendered communities, and the rising tide of reactionary legislation like photo identification laws for voting, restrictions on the right to have an abortion, and paranoid anti-Sharia bills. The speakers drew links between Islamophobia and discrimination affecting many other communities of color in the US, with further references to the historic and ongoing persecution of groups like Catholics, Irish, Blacks, and Latin@s. The speakers on the panel uniformly encouraged a broad view of civil rights. "We need to speak out on bigotry whenever we see it, not just when it affects our own community," Clemmons said. "It is imperative that we row in sync. I'm including White Muslims in this too, because if all Muslims were blonde-haired and blue-eyed, we wouldn't even be having this conversation," she added, to thunderous applause.

The panel generated a sophisticated, powerful analysis of racism, including Islamophobia. Questions from the audience centered on ways that community members can advocate for change, and the answers emphasized the need for transformational coalitions that connect Middle Eastern Americans with other communities of color. The receptive crowd listened attentively, but no representatives from CAIR, MPAC, or the other nationally prominent advocacy organizations were there. This conversation happened at a time when Middle Eastern American advocacy strategy remained at a crossroads. The strategic choices these advocates faced had everything to do with race. Yet any consensus among advocates about how to get beyond the racial dilemma remained far in the distance.

What is clear, however, is the coming demographic shift to "majority-minority" in the United States. By the 2040s, "people of color" will make up more than half of the American population. How will civil rights for "people of color" communities work in that context? How will the contours of the racial dilemma shift? While it is difficult (and mostly pointless) to predict how unstable racial classifications will transform over the next three decades, one safe prediction is that there will be change. The status quo around racial identity and racial politics has never remained static over the long term.

In studying this question, Jennifer L. Hochschild sketches six possible racial futures stemming from the transition to "majority-minority." She compares the coming changes with the massive transformation in racial thinking between 1900 and 1968. She argues that by the 2050s, it is likely that race will have transformed again in equally profound ways. She worries that "a few more terrorist attacks" could bring "a powerful nativism tinged with religious and ethnic hostility" that would rapidly affect Middle Eastern American racialization in profoundly disturbing ways.[21]

Many other scholars of race have considered how Americans will come to understand race in the new "majority-minority" era. Some foresee a racial binary—White/Non-White or Black/Non-Black. Others imagine a tripartite division, with Patricia Hill Collins proposing a White/Black/Indigenous framework, Nadia Kim and Claire Jean Kim imagining a tripartite White/Black/Asian split, and Eduardo Bonilla-Silva similarly predicting a White/ Honorary White/ Collective Black "tri-racial order."[22] None of these analyses adequately accounts for the position of the Middle Eastern Americans, in part because their position in the racial order has always been unclear.

If Hochschild is correct, and if the unthinkable happens, another terrorist attack on the scale of 9/11 carried out by extremists marked by a Middle Eastern racial identity, then today's Islamophobia crisis may get even worse. That scenario would likely bring a more rigid racial regime, and what might be called a complete eviction from Whiteness for Middle Eastern Americans. But it seems equally possible that by 2040, the memories of 9/11 will have faded as other existential crises besides terrorism (climate change, unemployment, the latest season of *Dancing with the Stars*) rise to the fore. In that scenario, as racist stereotypes about terrorism fade into the background, perhaps Middle Eastern Americans will become fully White, similar to the path taken by the Irish in the early-1900s. As unlikely as that seems today, racial dynamics are unpredictable, and nearly anything is possible.

While it can be entertaining to speculate about how racial categories will shift over time, the more important question is whether civil rights will remain protected at all in the 2040s, after Whites no longer have an outright majority. The rule of White supremacy has never required a numerical majority—there are plenty of examples from around the world of minority groups (particularly White minorities) holding social, cultural, and political power. If the current trajectory of narrowing protections for civil rights continues, it seems possible that the color line will remain *the* American problem throughout the twenty-first century.

The strategies that civil rights advocates have developed for rearticulating the color line have been critical in providing some of the most powerful and longstanding changes in American culture. The advocates of the mid-1900s risked everything to push against the prevailing wisdom that endless war, brutal Jim Crow segregation, and oppressive patriarchy would never be dismantled. As Michelle Alexander described in her groundbreaking analysis of the "New Jim Crow," there are parallels between the present moment and the 1960s in civil rights advocacy— but there are also important differences between these two eras. She acknowledges the changes in the political climate since the 1960s, including the rise of colorblind ideology, that provide a challenging environment for today's advocates. She concludes that in order to discuss policy changes in a pragmatic way, advocates must "talk about race openly and honestly."[23] She acknowledges the "temptation to avoid race," especially because White people have a "striking reluctance" to "talk about or even acknowledge race."[24] She worries that "pollsters and political consultants who have become influential in civil rights advocacy" will insist that colorblindness is the only pragmatic way to win policy changes.[25] Alexander admits that it will take "courage" to overcome the temptation to fall in line with colorblind ideology, but concludes that:

> Seeing race is not the problem. Refusing to care for the people we see is the problem. The fact that the meaning of race may evolve over time or lose much of its significance is hardly a reason to be struck blind. We should hope not for a colorblind society but instead for a world in which we can see each other fully, learn from each other, and do what we can do respond to each other with love. That was [Dr. Martin Luther] King's dream—a society that is capable of seeing each of us, as we are, with love. That is a goal worth fighting for.[26]

Alexander notes that transformational coalitions of the 2010s must include not only Black Americans and not only people of color, but White Americans as well. This is the most crucial difference between the 2010s and the 1960s—the prevailing racial order today provides no real benefits to anyone. We are all worse off because of racism, because of Islamophobia. The challenge for Middle Eastern American advocates is to find ways to build transformational coalitions, to somehow rearticulate racial identity and colorblindness at the same time. However it happens, if there is to be a "new civil rights era," there is no doubt that Middle Eastern American advocates will be central in making it happen.[27]

The trials and tribulations of Middle Eastern American advocacy organizations in the here and now provide crucial clues for determining the future arc of race in America. These organizations may yet find leverage with Middle Eastern racial identity, using it to build new coalitions to gain advantages in their negotiations with the racial state. They might develop an innovative new advocacy strategy that redefines and extends colorblindness as a progressive ideology, thereby helping to usher in a new civil rights era that transcends the efforts of their forebears. Whatever shape this work takes, the tireless efforts of these advocates to improve civil rights should more than suffice, if Americans truly do want to live in a society that rejects racism. If something as controversial and damaging as Islamophobia continues unabated, then there can be little doubt that racism of all kinds will long endure in America.

METHODOLOGICAL APPENDIX

From ethnographic descriptions of a single office to a longitudinal survey of activists across hundreds of organizations, there are a wide range of options for investigating questions like the ones posed in this book. Before settling on the mixed-methods approach described in this appendix, I initially considered an especially detailed case study of one or two organizations, perhaps using ethnographic methods. While such an ethnographic study would have a great deal of value, I quickly rejected this possibility as it seemed incapable of thoroughly examining the linkages and fractures between the many organizations serving the disparate constituencies under the Middle Eastern identity umbrella.

INTERVIEWS

The initial sample of interview respondents was obtained by simply calling, writing, or visiting the organizations' offices. After meeting with the first wave of contacts, I pursued a purposive snowball sampling method (that is, I asked to be introduced to other respondents at the end of each interview). In a very short time, this provided an extensive list of further interview contacts. I did not limit the pool of potential interview respondents according to their institutional affiliation, but instead took an approach where I would speak to anyone affiliated with any advocacy organization. This led to a sample that spans many more organizations than the six specified for focused analysis. This technique allowed for a more complete picture of connections (and disconnections) between organizations across the field, while also developing a very adequate picture of the history of the six largest organizations that were the original focus of my research. A full list of interview subjects appears in table A.1.

In preparation for each interview, I constructed a customized list of topics to bring up during the course of the conversation based on what I already knew about the individual and her or his organization. These in-depth and qualitative semi-structured interviews gave respondents the ability to direct the course of the conversation. Even though these interviews involved a basic level of trust, it is possible that some respondents withheld information or misremembered events. There are ongoing debates among qualitative methodologists over how interview data can best be used as a source for empirical data. To support each of the conclusions I make in this book, I have more than one source of data. I attempted, where possible, to cross-reference between an interview and my content analysis. I note in the text when I rely on only one source.

Four of my respondents worked with the government (working directly on Middle Eastern American civil rights issues). In addition to the advocates, two were members of the clergy (one was a Christian priest and one was a Muslim imam). Eight interviews were with volunteers and community organizers who did not want to be affiliated with any one advocacy organization. Most interviews were conducted in person, either in the respondent's office or at a restaurant, café, or other similar location. Several interviews were conducted by telephone. Most of the interviews were audio recorded and later transcribed. For the interviews where audio recording was not possible, I took notes during, or immediately after, the interview. After collecting notes and creating transcripts, I looked for common themes in the interviews through a systematic qualitative analysis process.

I was aware of my role as an outsider to the communities directly served by these advocates. I worried about being perceived as not only naïve and untrustworthy, but maybe even dangerous as well. Fortunately, these concerns proved to be unfounded. The vast majority of my respondents were quite eager to share their insights and opinions. Many, especially leading advocates and those who had worked in the advocacy field for a long time, were accustomed to giving interviews to researchers and journalists. A few had even met with American presidents and other heads of state, so they were hardly intimidated by my friendly (if persistent) requests to take up some of their time. In fact, two of my respondents revealed that they had been under active law enforcement surveillance in the past (one had actually seen his FBI dossier, years after it had been created). Both of them told me that they were knowledgeable about government espionage and knew right away that I was not an imposter. On a few occasions, the advocate asked to see my academic bona fides before agreeing to speak with me. I was once asked to provide proof of my academic status, and a bit of conversation and the presentation of my business card sufficed. Some respondents asked me about my personal beliefs, my political views, and my motivations for this research before I began asking questions of them. In all cases, I introduced myself with my academic affiliation to assure my respondents that I was a legitimate researcher, and I gave everyone my contact information in case of any concerns or questions after our meeting. This project, which involved human subjects, obtained an exemption from the University of California, Santa Barbara Institutional Review Board. The proposal number for this project was 20080322. At Dickinson College, this project received an expedited review from the Institutional Review Board, and it was approved. The protocol ID number was 97.

TABLE A.1. List of Interviews

Number	Organization	Date (as referenced in text)	Technical notes	Location of interviewee
1	MSA	April 2005a	In person	California
2	None	June 2005a	In person	Michigan
3	Palestine Office	June 2005b	In person	Michigan
4	Arab American and Chaldean Council (ACC)	July 2005a	In person	Michigan
5	ACC	July 2005b	In person	Michigan
6	ADC	July 2005c	In person	Michigan
7	Mosque (clergy)	August 2005a	In person	Michigan
8	None	August 2005b	In person	Michigan
9	MSA	August 2005c	In person	Michigan
10	ADC	August 2005d	In person	Michigan
11	Church (clergy)	August 2005e	In person	Michigan
12	ACCESS	August 2005f	In person	Michigan
13	CAIR	December 2007	In person	California
14	CAIR	January 2008d	In person, not recorded	District of Columbia (DC)
15	CAIR	January 2008a	In person	DC
16	ADC	January 2008c	In person	DC
17	MPAC	January 2008b	In person	DC
18	ISNA	January 2008e	In person	DC

Number	Organization	Date (as referenced in text)	Technical notes	Location of interviewee
19	MPAC	February 2008f	In person	DC
20	ADC	February 2008b	In person	DC
21	SAALT	February 2008d	Phone	DC
22	ADC	February 2008a	In person	DC
23	SALDEF	February 2008e	In person	DC
24	AAI	February 2008c	In person	DC
25	National Association of Muslim Lawyers (NAML)	February 2008g	Phone	DC
26	United Sikhs	February 2008h	In person	DC
27	ADC	March 2008a	In person	DC
28	ADC	March 2008b	In person	DC
29	CAIR–Chicago	March 2008c	Phone	Illinois
30	NAML	March 2008d	In person	DC
31	SALDEF	April 2008a	In person	DC
32	None	April 2008b	In person	New York
33	None	April 2008c	In person	DC
34	Karamah	May 2008c	Phone	DC
35	AAI	May 2008a	In person	DC
36	American Task Force on Palestine	May 2008b	In person	DC
37	None	June 2008g	Phone	DC
38	CAIR–Chicago	June 2008e	Phone	Illinois
39	RWG	June 2008c	In person	DC
40	RWG	June 2008d	In person	DC
41	SAALT	June 2008b	Phone	DC
42	CAIR–Chicago	June 2008f	In person, not recorded	DC
43	ACCESS	June 2008i	Phone	Michigan
44	ICIRR	June 2008g	Phone	Illinois
45	ADC	June 2008j	In person, not recorded	DC
46	AAI	June 2008a	In person, not recorded	DC
47	NNAAC	July 2008a	Phone	Michigan
48	MPAC	September 2008a	Phone	DC

Number	Organization	Date (as referenced in text)	Technical notes	Location of interviewee
49	CAIR	October 2008a	Phone	California
50	Government official	February 2009a	Phone	Maryland
51	CAIR	July 2009b	Phone	Minnesota
52	ADC	July 2009c	Phone	DC—Follow up interview
53	DHS Official	July 2009a	In person	DC
54	ADC	August 2009b	In person	Michigan
55	CAIR	August 2009a	In person	Michigan
56	LCCR	August 2009c	In person, not recorded	Michigan
57	SAALT	October 2010a	In person, not recorded	DC—Follow up interview
58	SAALT	October 2010b	In person, not recorded	DC—Follow up interview
59	Federal official (agency withheld)	February 2012a	In person	DC
60	None	October 2012a	In person, not recorded	DC
61	RWG	June 2013a	In person	DC—Follow up interview
62	CAIR	June 2013b	In person, not recorded	DC
63	DHS	October 2013a	In person, not recorded	DC—Follow up interview
64	DOJ	October 2013b	In person	DC
65	ADC	December 2013a	In person, not recorded	Michigan
66	ADC	June 2014a	In person, not recorded	DC
67	Government official	November 2014a	In person, not recorded	DC—Follow up interview
68	None	December 2014a	Phone, not recorded	DC—Follow up interview
69	NNAAC	March 2015a	In person, not recorded	DC
70	AAI	September 2015a	Phone, not recorded	DC—Follow up interview

CONTENT ANALYSIS

The sample of documents in the analysis was obtained in three ways. First, I downloaded all information from several organizations' publicly available websites including all linked documents in several electronic formats multiple times between 2008 and 2015 using desktop web archival software. The software package, WinHTTTrack, followed hyperlinks from the organizations' homepages and downloaded all linked documents to my computer. Second, I visited the headquarters of several organizations between 2007 and 2010, and I made digital copies of documents with a portable electronic scanner. Finally, I registered for the email newsletters of several organizations at various points between 2005 and 2013, and some of the newsletters delivered to me were added to the sample of documents. In a few instances, specific collections of documents were sent to me by officials at the organizations. In all, I obtained more than ten thousand documents. Even this number is not a representative sample of all of the work done by the organizations in the study, but they nevertheless provide a relevant sample describing the public-facing efforts of these advocacy organizations.

To analyze the documents, I used optical character recognition software to enable computer-assisted keyword searches. Each keyword search produced a series of sentences containing my search terms. I read through these sentences, coding relevant "hits" into several different categories. These coded sentences became a pool of information describing organizational activity. When discussing the results of my analysis in the book, I provide a citation to each document as published by the organizations. The process of compiling the documents informs my analysis in other ways as well.

DATABASE

My goal was to construct a database that contained information about all active Middle Eastern American advocacy organizations operating at any point between 1980 and 2010. To obtain data for this project, I first developed a list of keywords to use to search the index of the *Encyclopedia of Associations*. This list of keywords was developed over several iterations, after I discovered archaic words (e.g., "Moslem" for "Muslim") in use during the 1980 edition. The final list of keywords, used to search both the 1980 and 2004 editions, is found in the list below.

After searching the index, and obtaining a list of organizations and the location of their entries, I then copied the data from each entry into a Microsoft Access database. I did not code or otherwise alter the information as it was presented in the *Encyclopedia* for this initial step. This process produced information on 159 organizations surveyed in the 1980 edition of the *Encyclopedia* and 382 organizations in the 2004 edition. Later, additional data on organizational finances was added from the Guidestar service to supplement the 2004 database.

LIST OF KEYWORDS USED TO SEARCH THE *ENCYCLOPEDIA OF ASSOCIATIONS*

Afghanistan	Islam	Punjabi
Albania	Jordan	Saudi
Arab	Kurd	Shia
Armenia	Kuwait	Sikh
Asian Indian	Lebanon	Somali
Asiatic	Libya	South Asian
Assyria	Malaysia	Sri Lanka
Bangladesh	Maronite	Subcontinent
Bedouin	Melkite	Sudan
Bengali	Middle East	Sufi
Bhutan	Morocco	Sunni
Chaldean	Moslem	Syria
Copt	Muslim	Tunisia
Desi	Near East	Turkey
Druze	Nepal	Turkmenistan
Egypt	Oriental	Urdu
India	Pakistan	Wahhabi
Indonesia	Palestine	Yemen
Iran	Pashtun	Zoroastrian
Iraq	Persian	

NOTES

CHAPTER 1. THE RACIAL DILEMMA

1 Orlando and Sullivan 2013.
2 Walsh 2003.
3 Not all expressions critical of Islam or Muslims are examples of Islamophobic bigotry. It is possible to criticize Islamic religious leaders, express disagreement with certain Islamic beliefs, or even plainly denounce the basic tenets of Islam without engaging in Islamophobia. Equating thoughtful discussion of Islam (or any religion) with racism would effectively silence legitimate debate and scholarship. That said, for the past several decades, comments critical of Islam as they appear in American discourse frequently have been rooted in a racialized bigotry.
4 FBI 2013.
5 I will use Middle Eastern and Middle Eastern American when referring to the racial category, but I will also refer to Arab, Muslim, Sikh, and South Asian American communities as well.
6 Marvasti and McKinney 2004.
7 Oxford English Dictionary 2015.
8 See Aidi 2014; Bakalian and Bozorgmehr 2009; Beydoun 2014; Marvasti and McKinney 2004; Meer 2013; Rana 2011; Volpp 2002; Werbner 2005.
9 Bakalian and Bozorgmehr 2009; Saito 2001; Whidden 2001.
10 MPAC 2012; Kurzman 2011; 2015.
11 Perliger 2013.
12 Interview June 2008a.
13 Aaronson 2013; Human Rights Watch 2014.
14 Center for Human Rights and Global Justice 2011.
15 Aaronson 2013; Center for Human Rights and Global Justice 2011; Human Rights Watch 2014.
16 Aaronson 2015.
17 Human Rights Watch 2014.
18 Aaronson 2013.
19 Sanchez, Pérez, and Prokupecz 2015; Lichtblau 2016.
20 Omi and Winant 2015.
21 Hollinger 2006.
22 O'Reilly 2016.
23 Rau 2010.

24 Meer 2013, 386.
25 For excellent analyses of recent "Islamophobia scholarship" and the overall lack of a discussion of race in the academic literature, see Meer 2013; Garner and Selod 2014.
26 Skrentny 2006.
27 Berry and Wilcox 2009.
28 Trump 2015.
29 Moore 2016.
30 Diamond 2016.
31 Moore 2016.
32 SAALT 2010a, 12.
33 King 2011.
34 SAALT 2010a, 19.
35 Somander 2010.
36 Media Matters 2013.
37 Ali et al. 2011.
38 Sherman 2014.
39 Quoted in Sherman 2014.
40 Here and throughout the book, I have obscured identifying details to maintain the confidentiality of people who spoke with me in interviews for this project. Where possible, I identify the specific organization that the person works for; their role, gender, and nationality; the month and year of the interview; and other pertinent details. When necessary some minor details have been changed or omitted to maintain confidentiality. In this instance, I have omitted the advocate's specific role at CAIR, because otherwise I would inadvertently identify him. On rare occasions, and only when given express written permission, I identify someone I interviewed by name.
41 Interview December 2007.
42 Hattaway Communications 2012, 3, 4.
43 CAIR 2010.
44 Ahlers 2010.
45 Quoted in Hing 2014.
46 This research was funded in part by a grant from the National Science Foundation, Grant No. 0802767. Any opinions, findings, and conclusions or recommendations expressed in this material are those of the author and do not necessarily reflect the views of the National Science Foundation.
47 Minkoff 1991.
48 Guidestar is a product of Philanthropic Research Inc.
49 Jackson 2005; McCloud 2014.
50 Naber 2012; Cainkar 2009.

CHAPTER 2. THE RACIAL PARADOX

1 Quoted in Yoder 2013.
2 Bakalian and Bozorgmehr 2009, 68; Kayyali 2013; Census Bureau 2011a.

3 Alsultany 2012; Nacos and Torres-Reyna 2007.

4 For example, consider Hanson 2001.

5 Asbridge 2011.

6 Grosfoguel and Mielants 2006; Qureshi and Sells 2013; Said 1978.

7 Kahf 1999, 31.

8 Said 1978.

9 Edwards 2000.

10 Little 2002, 3.

11 Albrecht 2015; Bawardi 2014; Naff 1993; Suleiman 1999.

12 Shaheen 2003, 192.

13 To be clear, even though the most common term in use in the 2010s to refer to the racial identity formed by the socio-historical process described here is "Muslim," it is not quite accurate to assume that all Muslim Americans are classified into the same racial group. Rather, a racial identity that includes some Muslims has been constructed.

14 Diouf 1998; GhaneaBassiri 2010; McCloud 2003, 160; Naff 1993; Suleiman 1999.

15 Beydoun 2014; Naff 1993; Suleiman 1999.

16 Leonard 1997, 39–84; Mehdi 1996, 249.

17 Moore 1995, 47–67.

18 Ibid., 29.

19 Roediger 2005.

20 Beydoun 2014; Gualtieri 2009; Tehranian 2007.

21 López 2006; Moore 1995, 47–67; Suleiman 1999, 7.

22 López 2006, 48.

23 *In re Najour*, 174 F. 735 (N.D. Ga. 1909).

24 López 2006, 49.

25 López 2006, 167; *In re Ahmed Hassan* 48 F. Supp. 843 (E.D. Mich. 1942).

26 *Ex parte Mohriez*, 54 F. Supp. 941 (D. Mass. 1944).

27 Moore 1995, 56, 57.

28 *United States v. Thind*, 261 US 204 (1923).

29 Moore 1995, 59.

30 Ibid., 47.

31 Hitti 1924, 89.

32 Cahn 2008.

33 Gualtieri 2004, 63.

34 Levine 1995.

35 Selzer and Anderson 2001; 2007.

36 *Fred Korematsu v. United States*, 323 US 214 (1944).

37 Kang 2005, 258.

38 Dempsey and Cole 1999.

39 Aswad 2003, 273.

40 Bakalian and Bozorgmehr 2009, 66–96.

41 Marvasti and McKinney 2004, 6; Gualtieri 2009.

42 Gallup 2009.
43 Suleiman 1999, 1–24.
44 Kayyali 2006, 33–34.
45 Census Bureau 2003.
46 Howell and Shryock 2003, 446.
47 Marvasti and McKinney 2004, 3–8.
48 Kurien 2001, 263–293; Leonard 2006, 91–114.
49 Leonard 1997, 77, 82.
50 Pew Research Center 2011.
51 Bagby 2012, 4.
52 Haddad 2004; Moore 2007, 116–132; Leonard 2003.
53 Pew Research Center 2011.
54 Jackson 2005, 23.
55 The structure and design of these tables is drawn directly from Bakalian and Bo-zorgmehr 2009, 72–86. The authors present additional demographic data as well.
56 Takaki 1998, 502.
57 Omi and Winant 2015, 44; Espiritu 1992; Okamoto 2014.
58 Berry and Wilcox 2009.
59 Omi and Winant 2015, 150.
60 Espiritu 1992; Okamoto 2014.
61 Omi and Winant 2015, 106.
62 Ibid., 109.
63 Ibid., 128; emphasis removed.
64 Feagin 2014.
65 Schmidt and Lichtblau 2012.
66 Nixon 2016.
67 Johnston 2013.
68 NPR 2006.
69 Omi and Winant 2015, 137–158.
70 Andrews and Edwards 2004, 481.
71 McAdam, Tarrow, and Tilly 2001.
72 Ibid.
73 Winant 1995, 176.
74 Omi and Winant 2015, 131.
75 Ibid., 164.
76 Morris 1986, 4.
77 Roberts 2012, 254.
78 Tilly 2006.
79 Espiritu and Lopez 1990, 198.
80 Omi and Winant 2015, 131.
81 Okamoto 2014, 4, 6.
82 Espiritu and Lopez 1990, 198–200.
83 Nagel 1995; Okamoto 2014.

84 Espiritu and Lopez 1990, 200–203, 218, 219.

85 Nagel 1995, 956, 958, 961.

86 *Parents v. Seattle School District*, 551 US 701 (2007).

87 Gotanda 1991, 3.

88 Kim 2000, 17–18.

89 Omi and Winant 2015, 264; emphasis in original.

90 Spivak 1987, 281; Espiritu 1992.

91 Espiritu and Omi 2000.

92 Hollinger 2006.

CHAPTER 3. ISLAMOPHOBIA IN AMERICA

1 Santora 2012.

2 Rosenberg 2015.

3 Ibid.

4 Smith 2006.

5 Iyer 2015, 104.

6 Ibid., 24.

7 McAlister 2001, 82.

8 Said 2001; Naber 2000.

9 Axel 2001; Ballantyne 2006; Rana 2011; Volpp 2002.

10 Gottschalk and Greenberg 2007, 118–125.

11 Shaheen 1980.

12 Maitland 1980.

13 Russell 2013.

14 Shaheen 1980.

15 Mahdavi 2006.

16 Shaheen 2003, 171–193.

17 Rahmani 2007.

18 Axel 2001; Ballantyne 2006.

19 Axel 2001, 79–120.

20 Michel and Herbeck 2001, 249.

21 Knowlton 1996.

22 Fedarko et al. 1996.

23 Bush 2001b.

24 Ibish 2003.

25 Kaplan 2006.

26 Kim 2015.

27 Kaplan 2015.

28 CAIR 2015.

29 EEOC 2002.

30 Malos 2010.

31 Ali et al. 2011.

32 CAIR 2013.

33 Elliott 2011.
34 Pew Research Center 2012a.
35 Kurzman 2011.
36 Kurzman 2013.
37 Southern Poverty Law Center 2009.
38 SAALT 2010a; 2014.
39 SAALT 2010a, 7.
40 Ibid., 11.
41 SAALT 2014a, 11.
42 SAALT 2010a, 21.
43 ThinkProgress 2007.
44 Phillips 2008.
45 Pew Research Center 2009.
46 Pew Research Center 2012b.
47 Noah 2007.
48 Detrow 2016.
49 Greenberg 2015.
50 Said 2001; Mamdani 2004; Rana 2011; Kumar 2012.
51 Bush 2001a.
52 United States Senate 1976.
53 Ibid.
54 Shah 1986, 2.
55 Shah 1986.
56 Dempsey and Cole 1999, 37.
57 Ibid.
58 Cole 2003.
59 Weinstein 2007.
60 Belkin 1991.
61 Elaasar 2004, 80; Nimer 2002, 178.
62 Wilgoren 2001.
63 Iyer 2015, 37.
64 Maira 2004.
65 Iyer 2015, 38.
66 Priest and Arkin 2010.
67 Bakalian and Bozorgmehr 2009, 182–184.
68 Kravets 2014.
69 ADC 2009; RWG 2012.
70 Kaplan 2005.
71 ACLU 2013, 14.
72 ACLU 2012.
73 ACLU 2009.
74 Risen and Lichtblau 2005.
75 Lichtblau and Risen 2005.

76 Greenwald 2013.
77 Obama 2013.
78 Scahill and Devereaux 2014.
79 Apuzzo and Goldman 2011a.
80 Apuzzo and Goldman 2011b.
81 Sullivan 2011.
82 Hawley 2012.
83 Apuzzo and Goldman 2011c.
84 Goldman and Apuzzo 2012.
85 Goodman 2013.
86 Shamsi 2016. Notably, the NYPD admitted to no "fault or liability" in the settlement.
87 Ackerman 2011a.
88 FBI 2011.
89 Ackerman 2011b.
90 Aaronson 2013, 20.
91 Ibid., 22.
92 Ibid., 23.
93 Aaronson 2013, 16.
94 Henderson 2010.
95 *United States v. Armstrong*, 517 US 456 (1996).
96 Kim 2012.
97 United States Department of Justice 2014.
98 FBI 2005.
99 National Counterterrorism Center 2014. As an aside, the official website for the NCTC shows in profound ways how the government generally classifies attacks as terrorism based on the identity of the attacker, rather than the motives. A "content note" dated August 15, 2014 on the website (www.nctc.gov) offers a disclaimer on the "spelling of Arabic names and terms," which explains that transliteration from Arabic into English is difficult. The unstated assumption is that most terrorism information on their webpage will contain names and terms from the Arabic language. Following this is a brief explanation of the "Islamic calendar," which again leaves implicit the idea that this information is somehow relevant to counterterrorism. Finally, the "historic timeline" that lists terrorist attacks is weighted heavily toward events in the Middle East, and violence carried out by Middle Easterners in the West. Not mentioned are a large number of shootings of civilians with political motives who are not Middle Eastern or Muslim.
100 Cole 2013.
101 Bankoff 2012.
102 See Lysiak 2015; cf. Chu 2015.
103 BBC News 2015; Serrano, Bennett, and Karalamangla 2015.
104 Farook was a second-generation Pakistani American, and Malik was a first-generation Pakistani American by way of Saudi Arabia.

105 United States Executive Office of the President 2011, 2.
106 Sethi 2015.
107 Currier and Hussain 2016.
108 Scahill 2015.
109 Quoted in Friedersdorf 2013.
110 Friedersdorf 2013.
111 White House 2010; Brennan 2010.
112 Ruane, Duggan, and Williams 2009.
113 Hannan 2010.
114 DHS 2009.
115 Thompson 2009.
116 CNN 2010.
117 Gibbs 2010.
118 Hsu 2010.

CHAPTER 4. CONFRONTING ISLAMOPHOBIA
1 Bakalian and Bozorgmehr 2009, 97–124.
2 Berry and Wilcox 2009.
3 Marquez 2001, 230.
4 Bawardi 2014.
5 Wright 1995.
6 Quoted in Gale Group 1980.
7 Minkoff, Aisenbrey, and Agnone 2008; Skocpol 1999; Putnam 2000.
8 Bawardi 2014, 3.
9 Ibid., 291.
10 Naff 1993; Suleiman 1999; Joseph 1999; Saliba 1999; Bawardi 2014; Naber 2012; Gualtieri 2009.
11 Suleiman 1999.
12 Bawardi 2014; Saliba 1999.
13 Aburish 2004.
14 Abu-Laban and Suleiman 1989; Kayyali 2006, 106.
15 Abu-Laban 2007, 47.
16 Interview February 2008a.
17 Ibid.
18 Hagopian 1975, 109.
19 Kayyali 2006.
20 Interview February 2008a.
21 Ibid.
22 ADC 2001.
23 Interview February 2008b.
24 ADC 2015.
25 Interviews May 2008a; February 2008a; February 2008c.
26 AAI 2015.

27 Philanthropic Research Inc. 2013.
28 Interview February 2008a.
29 Interview March 2008b.
30 Interview February 2008a.
31 Roy 1994; Haddad et al. 1991.
32 Leonard 2003.
33 MPAC 2015.
34 Interview September 2008a.
35 MPAC 2015; Interview September 2008a.
36 Interview September 2008a.
37 MPAC 2015.
38 cf. Bilici 2012.
39 Philanthropic Research Inc. 2014.
40 Interview September 2008a.
41 Nimer 2002; Leonard 2003.
42 Brooke 1995.
43 Interview January 2008a.
44 Interview January 2008a; January 2008b; March 2008c; October 2008a.
45 Abrams 2009.
46 Interview February 2012a.
47 CAIR 2012.
48 Philanthropic Research Inc. 2014.
49 Kurien 2001, 263–293; Leonard 2006, 91–114.
50 Leonard 1997, 77, 82.
51 Kurien 2003, 263–265.
52 Singh 2008, 4.
53 Ibid., 5.
54 Interview February 2008e; April 2008a.
55 Singh 2008, 4; Interview April 2008a.
56 Interview April 2008a.
57 Ibid.
58 Ibid.
59 Interview February 2008e.
60 United States Department of Justice 2007.
61 Philanthropic Research Inc. 2014.
62 Kurien 2003, 269; Interview June 2008b.
63 Interview June 2008b.
64 Kurien 2003, 269; Interviews June 2008b; February 2008d.
65 Interview June 2008b.
66 Interview February 2008d.
67 Interview June 2008b.
68 Philanthropic Research Inc. 2014.
69 Iyer 2015, 112.

CHAPTER 5. CIVIL RIGHTS COALITIONS

1 Quoted in Bean 2013.
2 Quoted in Bean 2013.
3 Han 2014.
4 Perlstein 2008.
5 ADC 1981; Shah 1986.
6 ADC 1980a.
7 ADC 1980b.
8 ADC 1980a.
9 ADC 1980b.
10 ADC 1984a; 1987.
11 Gebert 1981.
12 Ibid.
13 ADC 1984b.
14 Interview February 2008a.
15 Samhan 1999; Kayyali 2013; Aidi 2014.
16 Interviews November 2014; June 2014; December 2014.
17 Interviews November 2014a; December 2014a.
18 Interview November 2014a.
19 Interview May 2008a.
20 Interview May 2008a.
21 One community advocate who worked closely with ADC and AAI told me that the split between Abourezk and Zogby did not come about because of a disagreement over the strategy of partnering with Black Americans, and that the split was instead entirely about non-strategic, "personal" issues (Interview September 2015).
22 Interviews February 2008a; May 2008a.
23 AAI 1988.
24 Interviews May 2008a; February 2008c.
25 Interview February 2008b.
26 Interviews January 2008a; February 2008a; May 2008a; September 2008a.
27 Interview January 2008c.
28 Interview February 2008a.
29 Interview May 2008b.
30 Interview February 2008a.
31 Interview March 2008a.
32 Interview February 2008b.
33 Ibid.
34 Interview February 2008c.
35 Ibid.
36 Interview February 2008a.
37 Interview August 2009.

38 ADC 1996.

39 Interview March 2008b.

40 Interview April 2008; Singh 2008.

41 Interview June 2008b.

42 Huntington 1993.

43 Interview April 2008.

44 Interview February 2008b.

45 Interview February 2008d.

46 Interview January 2008b.

47 Interview September 2008a.

48 Interview July 2008a.

49 Interview January 2008a.

50 Interview February 2008b.

51 Interview February 2008a.

52 RWG 2010.

53 Interviews June 2008c; June 2008d.

54 Espiritu 1992.

55 Rights Working Group Executive Committee to RWG Supporters mailing list, March 10, 2016.

56 ICIRR 2008.

57 Interview June 2008e.

58 Interview June 2008f.

59 Interview June 2008e.

60 ICIRR 2010.

61 United States Department of Justice 2002, 2. The interagency working group on post-9/11 discrimination and hate crimes came about due to the work of Arab, Muslim, and South Asian American attorneys working at the DOJ Civil Rights Division on 9/11, who immediately recognized the need for an innovative response. They pressed Boyd and other top officials to organize various efforts to deal with the crisis of Islamophobic backlash in the days right after 9/11. Their knowledge of advocacy efforts and connections in their communities were instrumental in causing the Civil Rights Division as an institution to undertake outreach and enforcement efforts including the interagency meeting. These actions were definitive in enabling Arab, Muslim, Sikh, and South Asian Americans to have status as protected classes under anti-discrimination statutes.

62 Kaplan 2006, 21; United States Department of Justice 2002.

63 United States Department of Justice 2002, 2.

64 Interview February 2012a.

65 United States Department of Justice 2002.

66 Interviews January 2008c; February 2008b; February 2008d; February 2008e; February 2012a.

67 Interview July 2009a.

68 Maryland Office of the Governor 2007.

69 Interview February 2009a.
70 Ibid.
71 Michigan Office of the Governor 2015.
72 Associated Press 2015.
73 Interview June 2008b.
74 Interview February 2008d.
75 SAALT 2008; 2010b.
76 SAALT 2008.
77 SAALT 2010b.
78 Interview February 2008e.
79 Ibid.
80 Interview December 2007.
81 Ibid.
82 Interview January 2008a.
83 Interview January 2008b.
84 Interview January 2008b.
85 Interview June 2008b.
86 Interview June 2008a.
87 Interview March 2008b.
88 Interview February 2008a.
89 Interview February 2008b.
90 Interview February 2008b.
91 Interviews July 2005b; February 2008h.

CHAPTER 6. TOWARD A NEW CIVIL RIGHTS ERA

1 Elliott 2010.
2 Sargent 2010.
3 Bloomberg 2010.
4 CNN Opinion Research 2010.
5 Goodstein 2010.
6 BBC News 2010.
7 Hannan 2010.
8 Bail 2012; 2015.
9 See Ansell 2006; Bonilla-Silva 2014; Carr 1997; Kim 2000.
10 *Shelby County v. Holder* 570 US ___ (2013).
11 *University of Texas Southwestern Medical v. Nassar* 570 US ___ (2013). Coinciden-
   tally, this decision was handed down the day before the landmark *Shelby County*
   decision that nullified much of the Voting Rights Act, and that is likely why it
   received less attention than it deserved.
12 Maghbouleh 2017; Naber 2000; Tehranian 2008; Read 2008.
13 Tehranian 2008; Iyer 2015, 104.
14 Shryock 2008, 104.
15 Abdulrahim 2008; Read 2008; Samhan 1999.

16 Census Bureau 2011b.

17 Clemetson 2004; Interview December 2014a.

18 Aidi 2014.

19 Interview December 2014a.

20 ADC 2014; Interview June 2014a.

21 Hochschild 2005, 75.

22 Collins 2000; Nadia Kim 2007; Claire Jean Kim 2000; Bonilla-Silva 2004.

23 Alexander 2012, 237.

24 Ibid., 238.

25 Ibid., 240.

26 Ibid., 243.

27 Sunaina Maira (2016) describes a "new civil rights movement," where younger Middle Eastern Americans have built "cross-racial alliances." Deepa Iyer's (2015) analysis finds similar trends. Perhaps the most recent efforts by advocates and activists described by these two scholars portend significant developments in the near future.

REFERENCES

AAI (Arab American Institute). 1988. "Vote '88: Press Roundup." *AAI Update* 12. Washington, DC: AAI.

———. 2015. "American Attitudes Toward Arabs and Muslims." *AAI.org*, December 21. Accessed at http://www.aaiusa.org on June 10, 2016.

Aaronson, Trevor. 2013. *The Terror Factory: Inside the FBI's Manufactured War on Terrorism*. New York: Ig Publishing.

———. 2015. "How This FBI Strategy Is Actually Creating US-Based Terrorists." *TED.com*, June 4. Accessed at https://www.ted.com on July 8, 2015.

Abdulrahim, Sawsan. 2008. "'Whiteness' and the Arab Immigrant Experience." In *Race and Arab Americans Before and After 9/11*, edited by Amaney Jamal and Nadine Naber. Syracuse, NY: Syracuse University Press.

Abraham, Nabeel. 1994. "Anti-Arab Racism and Violence in the United States." In *The Development of Arab-American Identity*, edited by Ernest McCarus. Ann Arbor: University of Michigan Press.

Abrams, Joseph. 2009. "FBI Cuts Ties with CAIR Following Terror Financing Trial." *FOXNews.com*, January 30. Accessed at http://www.foxnews.com on July 8, 2015.

Abu-Laban, Baha. 2007. "Reflections on the Rise and Decline of an Arab-American Organization." *Arab Studies Quarterly* 29 (3/4): 47–56.

Abu-Laban, Baha, and Michael W. Suleiman. 1989. *Arab Americans: Continuity and Change*. Belmont, MA: Association of Arab American University Graduates.

Aburish, Said K. 2004. *Nasser: The Last Arab*. New York: Macmillan.

Ackerman, Spencer. 2011a. "FBI Teaches Agents: 'Mainstream' Muslims Are 'Violent, Radical.'" *Wired*, September 14. Accessed at http://www.wired.com on July 8, 2015.

———. 2011b. "FBI Calls In the Army to Fix Its Counterterrorism Training." *Wired*, November 3. Accessed at http://www.wired.com on July 8, 2015.

ACLU (American Civil Liberties Union). 2009. *Blocking Faith, Freezing Charity: Chilling Muslim Charitable Giving in the "War On Terrorism" Financing*. New York: ACLU. Accessed at http://www.aclu.org on July 8, 2015.

———. 2012. *Eye on the FBI Alert: Mosque Outreach for Intelligence Gathering*. New York: ACLU. Accessed at https://www.aclu.org on July 8, 2015.

———. 2013. *Unleashed and Unaccountable: The FBI's Unchecked Abuse of Authority*. New York: ACLU. Accessed at https://www.aclu.org on July 8, 2015.

ADC (American-Arab Anti-Discrimination Committee). 1980a. "Organizing Drives with Jim Abourezk—to Launch the ADC." *ADC Reports* 1. Washington, DC: ADC.

——. 1980b. "ADC on the Move." *ADC Reports* 2. Washington, DC: ADC.

——. 1981. "The Other Anti-Semitism: The Arab as Scapegoat." *ADC Issues* 3. Washington, DC: ADC.

——. 1984a. "Decision 84: A Blueprint for Arab Americans." *ADC Reports* 21. Washington, DC: ADC.

——. 1984b. "Arab Americans in the Political Mainstream." *ADC Reports* 24. Washington, DC: ADC.

——. 1987. "Rainbow Shines of Arab Americans." *ADC Times* 8: 8. Washington, DC: ADC.

——. 1996. "ADC, CAIR Protest Arrest of Two Veiled Muslim Women." *ADC Times* 17: 7. Washington, DC: ADC.

——. 2001. *ADC 18th National Convention: Impacting US-Arab Relations: The Role of Arab Americans.* Washington, DC: ADC.

——. 2009. *NSEERS: The Consequences of America's Efforts to Secure Its Borders.* Washington, DC: ADC. Accessed at http://www.adc.org on July 8, 2015.

——. 2014. "2014 ADC Convention Program." *ADC.org.* Accessed at http://convention.adc.org on March 31, 2015.

——. 2015. "About Us." *ADC.org.* Accessed at http://adc.org on March 31, 2015.

Ahlers, Mike. 2010. "US Announces New Airport Security Measures." *CNN*, April 2. Accessed at http://www.cnn.com on July 8, 2015.

Aidi, Hisham. 2014. *Rebel Music: Race, Empire, and the New Muslim Youth Culture.* New York: Vintage.

Albrecht, Charlotte Karem. 2015. "Narrating Arab American History: The Peddling Thesis." *Arab Studies Quarterly* 37 (1): 100–117.

Alexander, Michele. 2012. *The New Jim Crow: Mass Incarceration in the Age of Colorblindness*, rev. ed. New York: New Press.

Ali, Wajahat, Eli Clifton, Matthew Duss, Lee Fang, Scott Keyes, and Faiz Shakir. 2011. *Fear, Inc.: The Roots of the Islamophobia Network in America.* Washington, DC: Center for American Progress. Accessed at https://www.americanprogress.org on July 8, 2015.

Alsultany, Evelyn. 2012. *Arabs and Muslims in the Media: Race and Representation after 9/11.* New York: New York University Press.

Andrews, Kenneth T., and Bob Edwards. 2004. "Advocacy Organizations in the U.S. Political Process." *Annual Review of Sociology* 30: 479–506.

Ansell, Amy E. 2006. "Casting a Blind Eye: The Ironic Consequences of Color-Blindness in South Africa and the United States." *Critical Sociology* 32: 2–3.

Apuzzo, Matt, and Adam Goldman. 2011a. "With CIA Help, NYPD Moves Covertly in Muslim Areas." *Associated Press*, August 23. Accessed at http://ap.org on July 8, 2015.

——. 2011b. "NYPD Keeps Files on Muslims Who Change Their Names." *Associated Press*, October 26. Accessed at http://ap.org on July 8, 2015.

——. 2011c. "Documents Show NY Police Watched Devout Muslims." *Associated Press*, September 6. Accessed at http://ap.org on July 8, 2015.

Asbridge, Thomas. 2011. *The Crusades.* New York: HarperCollins.

Associated Press. 2015. "Snyder Creates Middle-Eastern American Affairs Commission." *Detroit Free Press*, February 19. Accessed at http://www.freep.com on July 9, 2015.

Aswad, Barbara C. 2003. "Arab Americans." In *Race and Ethnicity: An Anthropological Focus on the United States and the World*, edited by Raymond Scupin. Upper Saddle River, NJ: Prentice Hall.

Axel, Brian Keith. 2001. *The Nation's Tortured Body: Violence, Representation, and the Formation of a Sikh "Diaspora"* Durham, NC: Duke University Press.

Bail, Christopher A. 2012. "The Fringe Effect: Civil Society Organizations and the Evolution of Media Discourse about Islam since the September 11th Attacks." *American Sociological Review* 77 (6): 855–879.

———. 2015. *Terrified: How Anti-Muslim Fringe Organizations Became Mainstream.* Princeton, NJ: Princeton University Press.

Bagby, Ihsan. 2012. *The American Mosque 2011: Basic Characteristics of the American Mosque Attitudes of Mosque Leaders*. Washington, DC: Council on American-Islamic Relations (CAIR). Accessed at https://www.cair.com on July 8, 2015.

Bakalian, Anny, and Mehdi Bozorgmehr. 2009. *Backlash 9/11: Middle Eastern and Muslim Americans Respond*. Berkeley, CA: University of California Press.

Ballantyne, Tony. 2006. *Between Colonialism and Diaspora: Sikh Cultural Formations in an Imperial World*. Durham, NC: Duke University Press.

Bankoff, Caroline. 2012. "Eric Holder Calls Sikh Temple Shooting a Hate Crime at Memorial." *New York Magazine*, August 10. Accessed at http://nymag.com on July 9, 2015.

Bawardi, Hani J. 2014. *The Making of Arab Americans: From Syrian Nationalism to U.S. Citizenship*. Austin: University of Texas Press.

BBC News. 2010. "Tennessee Mosque Fire 'Was Arson,' Investigators Say." *BBC News*, September 4. Accessed at http://www.bbc.co.uk on July 9, 2015.

———. 2015. "San Bernardino Shootings Investigated as Terrorism—FBI." *BBC News*, December 4. Accessed at http://www.bbc.com on April 5, 2016.

Bean, Alan. 2013. "Moral Monday Movement Unleashes 'Linguistic Trauma.'" *Friends of Justice* (blog), December 10. Arlington, TX: Friends of Justice. Accessed at https://friendsofjustice.wordpress.com on July 7, 2015.

Belkin, Lisa. 1991. "For Many Arab-Americans, FBI Scrutiny Renews Fears." *New York Times*, January 12. Accessed at http://www.nytimes.com on July 9, 2015.

Berry, Jeffrey M., and Clyde Wilcox. 2009. *The Interest Group Society*. 5th ed. New York: Pearson.

Beydoun, Khaled A. 2014. "Between Muslim and White: The Legal Construction of Arab-American Identity." *New York University Annual Survey of American Law* 69: 29.

Bilici, Mucahit. 2012. *Finding Mecca in America: How Islam Is Becoming an American Religion*. Chicago, IL: Chicago University Press.

Bloomberg, Michael. 2010 "Mayor Bloomberg Discusses the Landmarks Preservation Commission." New York City Office of the Mayor, August 3. Accessed at http://www.nyc.gov on July 9, 2015.

Bonilla-Silva, Eduardo. 2004. "From Bi-Racial to Tri-Racial: Towards a New System of Racial Stratification in the USA." *Ethnic and Racial Studies* 27 (6): 931–950.

———. 2014. *Racism Without Racists: Color-Blind Racism and the Persistence of Racial Inequality in America*. 4th ed. Lanham, MD: Rowman and Littlefield.

Brennan, John. 2010. "Remarks by the Assistant to the President for Homeland Security and Counterterrorism John Brennan at CSIS." White House Office of the Press Secretary, May 26. Accessed at https://www.whitehouse.gov on July 8, 2015.

Brooke, James. 1995. "Attacks on US Muslims Surge Even as Their Faith Takes Hold." *New York Times*, August 28. Accessed at http://www.nytimes.com on July 8, 2015.

Bush, George W. 2001a. "Address to a Joint Session of Congress and the American People." *White House Archives*, September 20. Accessed at http://georgewbush-whitehouse.archives.gov on July 8, 2015.

———. 2001b. "Remarks by the President at the Islamic Center of Washington, DC." *White House Archives*, September 17. Accessed at http://georgewbush-whitehouse.archives.gov on July 8, 2015.

Cahn, David. 2008. "The 1907 Bellingham Riots in Historical Context." Seattle Civil Rights and Labor History Project, University of Washington. Accessed at https://depts.washington.edu on July 8, 2015.

Cainkar, Louise. 2009. *Homeland Insecurity: The Arab American and Muslim American Experience After 9/11*. New York: Russell Sage Foundation.

CAIR (Council on American-Islamic Relations). 2010. "New TSA Rules Amount to Profiling." Washington, DC: CAIR. Accessed at https://www.cair.com on July 8, 2015.

———. 2012. "Top Internet Misinformation and Conspiracy Theories About CAIR." Washington, DC: CAIR. Accessed at https://www.cair.com on July 8, 2015.

———. 2013. *Legislating Fear: Islamophobia and Its Impact in the United States*. Washington, DC: CAIR.

———. 2015. "82 Groups Ask DOJ to Address Illegality of 'Muslim-Free Zone' Businesses." Washington, DC: CAIR. Accessed at https://www.cair.com on July 8, 2015.

Carr, Leslie G. 1997. *"Color-Blind" Racism*. Thousand Oaks, CA: Sage.

Census Bureau. *See* United States Department of Commerce, Census Bureau.

Center for Human Rights and Global Justice. 2011. *Targeted and Entrapped: Manufacturing the "Homegrown Threat" in the United States*. New York: New York University School of Law. Accessed at http://chrgj.org on July 8, 2015.

Chu, Arthur. 2015. "It's Not about Mental Illness: The Big Lie that Always Follows Mass Shootings by White Males." *Salon*, June 18. Accessed at https://www.salon.com on April 5, 2015.

Cole, David. 2003. "9/11 and the LA 8." *Nation*, October 9. Accessed at http://www.thenation.com on July 9, 2015.

Cole, Juan. 2013. "White Terrorist is 'Gunman,' 'Alleged Shooter,' No Mention of Wingnut 'New World Order' Beef." *Informed Comment* (blog), November 3. Accessed at http://www.juancole.com on July 9, 2015.

Collins, Patricia Hill. 2000. *Black Feminist Thought: Knowledge, Consciousness, and the Politics of Empowerment*. 2nd ed. New York: Routledge.

Clemetson, Lynette. 2004. "Homeland Security Given Data on Arab-Americans." *New York Times*, July 30. Accessed at http://www.nytimes.com on July 9, 2015.

CNN (Cable News Network). 2010. "Pilot Deliberately Crashed into Texas Building, Official Says." *CNN*, February 10. Accessed at http://www.cnn.com on July 8, 2015.

CNN Opinion Research. 2010. "For Release: Wednesday August 11 at Noon." *Poll*, August 11. Accessed at http://i2.cdn.turner.com on July 9, 2015.

Currier, Cora, and Murtaza Hussain. 2016. "Letter Details FBI Plan for Secretive Anti-Radicalization Committees." *Intercept*, April 28. Accessed at https://theintercept.com on April 29, 2016.

Dempsey, James X., and David Cole. 1999. *Terrorism and the Constitution: Sacrificing Civil Liberties in the Name of National Security*. New York: New Press.

Detrow, Scott. 2016. "Trump Calls to Ban Immigration from Countries with 'Proven History of Terrorism.'" *NPR*, June 13. Accessed at http://www.npr.org on June 14, 2016.

Diamond, Jeremy. 2016. "Ted Cruz: Police Need to 'Patrol and Secure' Muslim Neighborhoods." *CNN*, March 22. Accessed at http://www.cnn.com on April 18, 2016.

Diouf, Sylviane. 1998. *Servants of Allah: African Muslims Enslaved in the Americas*. New York: New York University Press.

Edwards, Holly. 2000. *Noble Dreams, Wicked Pleasures: Orientalism in America, 1870–1930*. Princeton, NJ: Princeton University Press.

EEOC. *See* United States Equal Employment Opportunity Commission.

Elaasar, Aladdin. 2004. *Silent Victims: The Plight of Arab and Muslim Americans in Post-9/11 America*. Bloomington, IN: AuthorHouse.

Elliott, Andrea. 2011. "The Man Behind the Anti-Shariah Movement." *New York Times*, July 30. Accessed at http://www.nytimes.com on July 8, 2015.

Elliott, Justin. 2010. "How the 'Ground Zero Mosque' Fear Mongering Began." *Salon*, August 16. Accessed at http://www.salon.com on July 8, 2015.

Espiritu, Yen Le. 1992. *Asian American Panethnicity: Bridging Institutions and Identities*. Philadelphia, PA: Temple University Press.

Espiritu, Yen Le, and David Lopez. 1990. "Panethnicity in the United States: A Theoretical Framework." *Ethnic and Racial Studies* 13 (2): 198–224.

Espiritu, Yen Le, and Michael Omi. 2000. "'Who Are You Calling Asian?': Shifting Identity Claims, Racial Classifications, and the Census." In *The State of Asian Pacific America: Transforming Race Relations*, edited by Paul M. Ong. Los Angeles: Leadership Education for Asian Pacifics, Asian Pacific American Public Policy Institute and University of California, Los Angeles Asian American Studies Center.

FBI. *See* United States Department of Justice, Federal Bureau of Investigation.

Feagin, Joe. 2014. *Racist America: Roots, Current Realities, and Future Reparations*. 3rd ed. New York: Taylor and Francis.

Fedarko, Kevin, Scott Macleod, Lara Marlowe, and Douglas Waller. 1996. "Terror on Flight 800: Who Wishes Us Ill?" *Time*, July 29.

Friedersdorf, Conor. 2013. "This Yemeni Man Loves America, Hates al-Qaeda, and Says Drone Strikes Make Them Stronger." *Atlantic*, April 24. Accessed at http://www.theatlantic.com/ on July 9, 2015.

Gale Group. 1980. *Encyclopedia of Associations*. 15th ed. Detroit, MI: Gale/Cengage Learning.

———. 2004. *Associations Unlimited*. Detroit, MI: Gale/Cengage Learning.

Gallup. 2009. *Muslim Americans: A National Portrait*. Washington, DC: Gallup. Accessed at http://www.gallup.com on July 8, 2015.

Garner, Steve, and Saher Selod. 2014. "The Racialization of Muslims: Empirical Studies of Islamophobia." *Critical Sociology* 41 (1): 9–19.

GhaneaBassiri, Kambiz. 2010. *A History of Islam in America: From the New World to the New World Order*. New York: Cambridge University Press.

Gibbs, Robert. 2010. "On the Plane Crash in Austin." Washington, DC: White House, February 18. Accessed at https://www.whitehouse.gov on July 8, 2015.

Goldman, Adam, and Matt Apuzzo. 2012. "NYPD: Muslim Spying Led to No Leads, Terror Cases." *Associated Press*, August 21. Accessed at http://ap.org on July 8, 2015.

Goodman, J. David. 2013. "Council Reverses Bloomberg Veto of Policing Bills." *New York Times*, August 22. Accessed at http://www.nytimes.com on July 8, 2015.

Goodstein, Laurie. 2010. "Across Nation, Mosque Projects Meet Opposition." *New York Times*, August 8. Accessed at http://www.nytimes.com on July 8, 2015.

Gotanda, Neil. 1991. "A Critique of 'Our Constitution Is Color-Blind.'" *Stanford Law Review* 44 (1): 1–68.

Gottschalk, Peter, and Gabriel Greenberg. 2007. *Islamophobia: Making Muslims the Enemy*. Lanham, MD: Rowman and Littlefield.

Greenberg, Jon. 2015. "War of Words: The Fight over 'Radical Islamic Terrorism.'" *Politifact*, December 11. Accessed at http://www.politifact.com on April 5, 2016.

Greenwald, Glenn. 2013. "NSA Collecting Phone Records of Millions of Verizon Customers Daily." *Guardian*, June 6. Accessed at http://www.theguardian.com on July 8, 2015.

Grosfoguel, Ramón, and Eric Mielants. 2006. "The Long-Durée Entanglement between Islamophobia and Racism in the Modern/Colonial Capitalist/Patriarchal World-System: An Introduction." *Human Architecture: Journal of the Sociology Self-Knowledge* 5 (1).

Gualtieri, Sarah. 2004. "Strange Fruit? Syrian Immigrants, Extralegal Violence and Racial Formation in the Jim Crow South." *Arab Studies Quarterly* 26 (3): 63–85.

———. 2009. *Between Arab and White: Race and Ethnicity in the Early Syrian American Diaspora*. Berkeley: University of California Press.

Haddad, Yvonne Yazbeck. 2004. *Not Quite American? The Shaping of Arab and Muslim Identity in the United States*. Waco, TX: Baylor University Press.

Haddad, Yvonne Yazbeck, John Obert Voll, John L. Esposito, Kathleen Moore, and David Sawan. 1991. *The Contemporary Islamic Revival: A Critical Survey and Bibliography*. Westport, CT: Greenwood Press.

Hagopian, Elaine. 1975. "Minority Rights in a Nation-State: The Nixon Administration's Campaign against Arab Americans." *Journal of Palestine Studies* 5 (1/2): 97–114.

Han, Hahrie. 2014. *How Organizations Develop Activists: Civic Associations and Leadership in the 21st Century*. New York: Oxford University Press.

Hannan, Larry. 2010. "Police Ask Jacksonville Community to Help Catch Mosque Bomber." *Florida Times-Union*, May 12. Accessed at http://jacksonville.com on July 8, 2015.

Hanson, Victor Davis. 2001. *Carnage and Culture: Landmark Battles in the Rise of Western Power*. New York: Anchor Books.

Hattaway Communications. 2012. *Message Manual: Talking to America about American Muslims*. Washington, DC: Hattaway Communications. Accessed at www.wkkf.org on July 8, 2015.

Hawley, Chris. 2012. "NYPD Monitored Muslim Students All Over Northeast." *Associated Press*, February 18. Accessed at http://ap.org on July 8, 2015.

Henderson, Peter. 2010. "Attorney General Eric Holder Defends Anti-Terrorism Stings." *Reuters*, December 11. Accessed at http://www.reuters.com on July 8, 2015.

Hing, Julianne. 2014. "Facing Race Spotlight: Palestinian-American Activist Linda Sarsour." *Colorlines: News for Action*. Accessed at http://www.colorlines.com on July 8, 2015.

Hitti, Philip Khuri. 1924. *The Syrians in America*. Piscataway, NJ: Gorgias Press.

Hollinger, David. 2006. *Postethnic America: Beyond Multiculturalism*. 10th ed. New York: Basic Books.

Hochschild, Jennifer L. 2005. "Looking Ahead: Racial Trends in the United States." *Daedalus* 134 (1): 70–81.

Howell, Sally, and Andrew Shryock. 2003. "Cracking Down on Diaspora: Arab Detroit and America's 'War on Terror.'" *Anthropological Quarterly* 76 (3): 443–462.

Hsu, Spencer S. 2010. "Napolitano Says Suicide Plane Crash Wasn't Related to Domestic Terrorism." *Washington Post*, March 9. Accessed at http://www.washingtonpost.com on July 5, 2015.

Human Rights Watch. 2014. *Illusion of Justice: Human Rights Abuses in US Terrorism Prosecutions*. New York: Human Rights Watch. Accessed at https://www.hrw.org on July 8, 2015.

Huntington, Samuel A. 1993. "The Clash of Civilizations?" *Foreign Affairs* 72: 22–49.

Ibish, Hussein, ed. 2003. *Report on Hate Crimes and Discrimination against Arab Americans: The Post-September 11 Backlash*. Washington, DC: American-Arab Anti-Discrimination Committee Research Institute.

ICIRR (Illinois Coalition for Immigrant and Refugee Rights). 2008. "New Americans Vote: 2008 Results." Chicago, IL: ICIRR. Accessed at http://icirr.org on April 24, 2010.

———. 2010. "New Member Application." Chicago, IL: ICIRR. Accessed at http://icirr.org on April 24, 2010.

Iyer, Deepa. 2015. *We Too Sing America: South Asian, Arab, Muslim, and Sikh Immigrants Shape our Multiracial Future*. New York: The New Press.

Jackson, Sherman A. 2005. *Islam and the Blackamerican: Looking Toward the Third Resurrection*. New York: Oxford University Press.

Johnston, Katie. 2013. "Report Finds No Racial Profiling at Logan." *Boston Globe*, September 17. Accessed at https://www.bostonglobe.com on July 8, 2015.

Joseph, Suad, ed. 1999. *Intimate Selving in Arab Families: Gender, Self, and Identity.* Syracuse, NY: Syracuse University Press.

Kahf, Mohja. 1999. *Western Representations of the Muslim Woman: From Termagant to Odalisque.* Austin: University of Texas Press.

Kang, Jerry. 2005. "Watching the Watchers: Enemy Combatants in the Internment's Shadow." *Law and Contemporary Problems* 68 (255): 255–283.

Kaplan, David E. 2005. "Nuclear Monitoring of Muslims Done Without Search Warrants." *US News and World Report,* December 22.

Kaplan, Jeffrey. 2006. "Islamophobia in America? September 11 and Islamophobia Hate Crime." *Terrorism and Political Violence* 18: 1–33.

Kaplan, Sarah. 2015. "'Terrorist, Go Back to Your Country,' Attacker Yelled in Assault of Sikh Man." *Washington Post,* September 10. Accessed at https://www.washingtonpost.com on October 15, 2015.

Kayyali, Randa A. 2006. *The Arab Americans.* Westport, CT: Greenwood Press.

———. 2013. "US Census Classifications and Arab Americans: Contestations and Definitions of Identity Markers." *Journal of Ethnic and Migration Studies* 39 (8): 1299–1318.

Kim, Claire Jean. 2000. *Bitter Fruit: The Politics of Black-Korean Conflict in New York City.* New Haven, CT: Yale University Press.

Kim, Hana. 2015. "Hindu Temple in Bothell and Nearby School Vandalized with Hateful Words." *Q13Fox.com,* February 16. Accessed at http://q13fox.com on July 8, 2015.

Kim, Nadia. 2007. "Critical Thoughts on Asian American Assimilation in the Whitening Literature." *Social Forces* 86 (2).

Kim, Victoria. 2012. "Federal Judge Throws Out Lawsuit Over Spying on OC [Orange County] Muslims." *Los Angeles Times,* August 15. Accessed at http://articles.latimes.com on July 8, 2015.

King, Peter. 2011. "The Terrorist Threat is Real." *USA Today,* March 10. Accessed at http://usatoday30.usatoday.com on July 8, 2015.

Knowlton, Brian. 1996. "Investigators Focus Closely on Terrorism As Cause of Explosion: Chemicals Found on Jet Victims, US Reports." *New York Times,* July 24. Accessed at http://www.nytimes.com on July 8, 2015.

Kravets, David. 2014. "How Obama Officials Cried 'Terrorism' to Cover Up a Paperwork Error." *Wired,* February 11. Accessed at https://www.wired.com on July 8, 2015.

Kumar, Deepa. 2012. *Islamophobia and the Politics of Empire.* New York: Haymarket Books.

Kurien, Prema. 2001. "Religion, Ethnicity and Politics: Hindu and Muslim Indian Immigrants in the United States." *Ethnic and Racial Studies* 24 (2): 263–293.

———. 2003. "To Be or Not To Be South Asian: Contemporary Indian American Politics." *Journal of Asian American Studies* 6 (3): 261–288.

Kurzman, Charles. 2011. *The Missing Martyrs: Why There Are So Few Muslim Terrorists.* New York: Oxford University Press.

———. 2013. *Muslim American Terrorism in 2013.* Durham, NC: Triangle Center on Terrorism and Homeland Security. Accessed at http://sites.duke.edu on July 8, 2015.

———. 2015. *Terrorism Cases Involving Muslim Americans, 2014.* Durham, NC: Triangle Center on Terrorism and Homeland Security. Accessed at http://sites.duke.edu on July 8, 2015.

Leonard, Karen. 1997. *The South Asian Americans.* Westport, CT: Greenwood Press.

———. 2003. *Muslims in the United States: The State of Research.* New York: Russell Sage Foundation.

———. 2006. "South Asian Religions in the United States: New Contexts and Configurations." In *New Cosmopolitanisms: South Asians in the US*, edited by Gita Rajan and Shailja Sharma, 91–114. Stanford, CA: Stanford University Press.

Levine, Ellen S. 1995. *A Fence Away from Freedom: Japanese Americans and World War II.* New York: G.P. Putnam's Sons.

Lichtblau, Eric. 2016. "FBI Steps Up Use of Stings in ISIS Cases." *New York Times*, June 8. Accessed at http://www.nytimes.com on June 10, 2016.

Lichtblau, Eric, and James Risen. 2005. "Eavesdropping Effort Began Soon After Sept. 11 Attacks." *New York Times*, December 18. Accessed at http://www.nytimes.com on July 8, 2015.

Little, Douglas. 2002. *American Orientalism: The United States and the Middle East since 1945.* Chapel Hill: University of North Carolina Press.

López, Ian Haney. 2006. *White By Law: The Legal Construction of Race.* 10th anniversary ed. New York: New York University Press.

Lysiak, Matthew. 2015. "Charleston Massacre: Mental Illness Common Thread for Mass Shootings." *Newsweek*, June 19. Accessed at http://www.newsweek.com on April 5, 2016.

Maghbouleh, Neda. 2017. *The Limits of Whiteness: Iranian Americans and the Everyday Politics of Race.* Stanford, CA: Stanford University Press.

Mahdavi, Sara. 2006. "Held Hostage: Identity Citizenship of Iranian Americans." *Texas Journal on Civil Liberties and Civil Rights* 11(2): 211–244.

Maira, Sunaina. 2004. "Youth Culture, Citizenship, and Globalization: South Asian Muslim Youth in the United States after September 11th." *Comparative Studies of South Asia, Africa and the Middle East* 24 (1): 221–235.

———. 2016. *The 9/11 Generation: Youth, Rights, and Solidarity in the War on Terror.* New York: New York University Press.

Maitland, Leslie. 1980. "High Officials Are Termed Subjects of a Bribery Investigation by the FBI." *New York Times*, February 3. Accessed at http://timesmachine.nytimes.com on July 8, 2015.

Malos, Stan. 2010. "Post-9/11 Backlash in the Workplace: Employer Liability for Discrimination against Arab- and Muslim-Americans Based on Religion or National Origin." *Employee Responsibilities and Rights Journal* 22 (4): 297–310.

Mamdani, Mahmood. 2004. *Good Muslim, Bad Muslim.* New York: Harmony.

Marvasti, Amir, and Karyn D. McKinney. 2004. *Middle Eastern Lives in America.* New York: Rowman and Littlefield.

Marquez, Benjamin. 2001. "Choosing Issues, Choosing Sides: Constructing Identities in Mexican-American Social Movement Organizations." *Ethnic and Racial Studies* 24 (2): 218–235.

Maryland Office of the Governor. 2007. "Governor's Commission on Middle Eastern American Affairs." Accessed at http://www.middleeastern.maryland.gov on April 24, 2010.

McAdam, Doug, Sidney Tarrow, and Charles Tilly. 2001. *Dynamics of Contention*. New York: Cambridge University Press.

McAlister, Melani. 2001. *Epic Encounters: Culture, Media, and US Interests in the Middle East, 1945–2000*. Berkeley: University of California Press.

McCloud, Aminah Beverly. 2003. "Islam in America: The Mosaic." In *Religion and Immigration: Christian, Jewish, and Muslim Experiences in the United States*, edited by Yvonne Yazbeck Haddad, Jane I. Smith and John L. Esposito, 159–174. Walnut Creek, CA: AltaMira Press.

———. 2014. *African American Islam*. Rev. ed. New York: Routledge.

Media Matters. 2013. "Fox Host Brian Kilmeade Asks Why Racial Profiling Isn't Used To Prevent Terrorism" (video). *Media Matters for America*, April 22. Accessed at http://mediamatters.org on July 8, 2015.

Meer, Nasar. 2013. "Racialization and Religion: Race, Culture, and Difference in the Study of Antisemitism and Islamophobia." *Ethnic and Racial Studies* 36 (3): 385–398.

Mehdi, Mohammad T. 1996. "Arabs and Muslims in American Society." In *The Politics of Minority Coalitions: Race, Ethnicity, and Shared Uncertainties*, edited by Wilbur C. Rich, 249–256. Westport, CT: Praeger.

Michel, Lou, and Dan Herbeck. 2001. *American Terrorist: Timothy McVeigh and the Oklahoma City Bombing*. New York: Harper.

Michigan Office of the Governor. 2015. "Gov. Rick Snyder Issues Executive Order Establishing the Middle-Eastern American Affairs Commission." Accessed at http://www.michigan.gov on July 9, 2015.

Minkoff, Debra C. 1991. "Organized Social Action: American Women's and Minority Group Organizational Responses to Inequality, 1955–1985." PhD diss., Harvard University.

Minkoff, Debra, Silke Aisenbrey, and Jon Agnone. 2008. "Organizational Diversity in the US Advocacy Sector." *Social Problems* 55 (4): 525–548.

Moore, Kathleen M. 1995. *Al-Mughtaribūn: American Law and the Transformation of Muslim Life in the United States*. Albany: State University of New York Press.

———. 2007. "Muslims in the United States: Pluralism under Exceptional Circumstances." *Annals of the American Academy of Political and Social Science* 612 (1): 116–132.

Moore, Peter. 2016. "Divide on Muslim Neighborhood Patrols but Majority Now Back Muslim Travel Ban." *YouGov*, March 28. Accessed at https://today.yougov.com on April 18, 2016.

Morris, Aldon D. 1986. *The Origins of the Civil Rights Movement: Black Communities Organizing for Change*. New York: Simon and Schuster.

MPAC (Muslim Public Affairs Council). 2012. *Post-9/11 Terrorism Incident Database*. Washington, DC: MPAC. Accessed at http://www.mpac.org on July 8, 2015.

———. 2015. "MPAC History." Washington, DC: MPAC. Accessed at http://www.mpac. org on July 8, 2015.

Naber, Nadine. 2000. "Ambiguous Insiders: An Investigation of Arab American Invisibility." *Ethnic and Racial Studies* 23 (1): 37–61.

———. 2012. *Arab America: Gender, Cultural Politics, and Activism*. New York: New York University Press.

Nacos, Brigitte Lebens, and Oscar Torres-Reyna. 2007. *Fueling Our Fears: Stereotyping, Media Coverage, and Public Opinion of Muslim Americans*. New York: Rowman and Littlefield.

Naff, Alixa. 1993. *Becoming American: The Early Arab Immigrant Experience*. Carbondale: Southern Illinois University Press.

Nagel, Joane. 1995. "American Indian Ethnic Renewal: Politics and the Resurgence of Identity." *American Sociological Review* 60 (6): 947–965.

National Counterterrorism Center. *See* United States Office of the Director of National Intelligence.

Nimer, Mohamed. 2002. "Muslims in American Public Life." In *Muslims in the West: From Sojourners to Citizens*, edited by Yvonne Yazbeck Haddad, 169–186. New York: Oxford University Press.

Nixon, Ron. 2016. "Minnesota TSA Manager Says He Was Told to Target Somali-Americans." *New York Times*, April 28. Accessed at http://www.nytimes.com on April 29, 2016.

Noah, Timothy. 2007. "Tom Tancredo's Final Solution." *Slate*, August 3. Accessed at http://www.slate.com on July 8, 2015.

NPR (National Public Radio). 2006. "'Axis of Evil' Comedy, on Tour." *All Things Considered*, July 28. Accessed at http://www.npr.org on July 8, 2015.

Obama, Barack. 2013. "Remarks by the President in a Press Conference." Washington, DC: White House, August 9. Accessed at https://www.whitehouse.gov/ on July 8, 2015.

Okamoto, Dina G. 2014. *Redefining Race: Asian American Panethnicity and Shifting Ethnic Boundaries*. New York: Russell Sage Foundation.

Omi, Michael, and Howard Winant. 2015. *Racial Formation in the United States*. 3rd ed. New York: Routledge.

O'Reilly, Bill. 2016. "It's Not Racist to Support a Wall on the Border." *FoxNews Insider*, April 6. Accessed May 31, 2016 at http://insider.foxnews.com.

Oxford English Dictionary. 2015. "Middle East." In *OED Online*. Oxford University Press. Accessed online on July 8, 2015.

Orlando, Alex, and Erin Sullivan. 2013. "Victim in Pasco Hate Crime Had a Gun, Decided Not to Use It." *Tampa Bay Times*, January 5. Accessed at http://www.tampabay.com on July 8, 2015.

Perliger, Arie. 2013. *Challengers from the Sidelines: Understanding America's Violent Far Right*. West Point, NY: Combating Terrorism Center at West Point, United States Military Academy. Accessed at https://www.ctc.usma.edu on July 8, 2015.

Perlstein, Rick. 2008. *Nixonland: The Rise of a President and the Fracturing of America.* New York: Scribner.

Pew Research Center. 2009. "Muslims Widely Seen as Facing Discrimination." *Results from the 2009 Annual Religion and Public Life Survey.* Washington, DC: Pew Research Center. Accessed at http://www.pewforum.org on July 8, 2015.

———. 2011. *Muslim Americans: No Signs of Growth in Alienation or Support for Extremism.* Washington, DC: Pew Research Center. Accessed at http://www.people-press.org on July 8, 2015.

———. 2012a. "Controversies Over Mosques and Islamic Centers Across the US." Washington, DC: Pew Forum on Religion and Public Life. Accessed at http://features.pewforum.org on July 8, 2015.

———. 2012b. "Little Voter Discomfort with Romney's Mormon Religion." Washington, DC: Pew Research Center. Accessed at http://www.pewforum.org on July 8, 2015.

Philanthropic Research Inc. Various Years. *Guidestar.* Accessed at http://www.guidestar.org/.

Phillips, Kate. 2008. "Palin: Obama Is 'Palling Around With Terrorists.'" *New York Times*, October 4. Accessed at http://thecaucus.blogs.nytimes.com on July 8, 2015.

Priest, Dana, and William M. Arkin. 2010. *Top Secret America: A Washington Post Investigation.* Accessed at http://projects.washingtonpost.com on July 8, 2015.

Putnam, Robert D. 2000. *Bowling Alone: The Collapse and Revival of American Community.* New York: Simon and Schuster.

Qureshi, Emran, and Michael Anthony Sells. 2013. *The New Crusades: Constructing the Muslim Enemy.* New York: Columbia University Press.

Rahmani, Sina. 2007. "Wrestling with the Revolution: The Iron Sheik and the American Cultural Response to the 1979 Iranian Revolution." *Iranian Studies* 40 (1): 87–108.

Rana, Junaid. 2011. *Terrifying Muslims: Race and Labor in the South Asian Diaspora.* Durham, NC: Duke University Press.

Rau, Alia Beard. 2010. "14 Organizations, 10 Individuals File Suit Over Arizona's Immigration Law." *Arizona Republic*, May 18. Accessed at http://www.azcentral.com on July 8, 2015.

Read, Jen'nan. 2008. "Discrimination and Identity Formation in a Post-9/11 Era: A Comparison of Muslim and Christian Arab Americans." In *Race and Arab Americans Before and After 9/11*, edited by Amaney Jamal and Nadine Naber. Syracuse, NY: Syracuse University Press.

RWG (Rights Working Group). 2010. "About RWG." Washington, DC: RWG. Accessed at http://rightsworkinggroup.org on April 24, 2010.

———. 2012. *The NSEERS Effect: A Decade of Racial Profiling, Fear, and Secrecy.* State College, PA: Penn State Law. Accessed at http://www.rightsworkinggroup.org on July 8, 2015.

Risen, James, and Eric Lichtblau. 2005. "Bush Lets US Spy On Callers Without Courts." *New York Times*, December 16. Accessed at http://www.nytimes.com on July 8, 2015.

Roediger, David R. 2005. *Working Toward Whiteness: How America's Immigrants became White: The Strange Journey from Ellis Island to the Suburbs*. New York: Basic Books.

Roberts, Dorothy. 2012. *Fatal Invention: How Science, Politics, and Big Business Re-Create Race in the Twenty-First Century*. New York: New Press.

Rosenberg, Eli. 2015. "Subway Pusher Erika Menendez Gets 24 Years for 2012 Shove That Killed a Man." *New York Daily News*, May 21. Accessed at http://www.nydaily-news.com on October 15, 2015.

Roy, Olivier. 1994. *The Failure of Political Islam*. Cambridge, MA: Harvard University Press.

Ruane, Michael E., Paul Duggan, and Clarence Williams. 2009. "At a Monument of Sorrow, a Burst of Deadly Violence." *Washington Post*, June 10. Accessed at https://www.washingtonpost.com on July 8, 2015.

Russell, David O. 2013. *American Hustle*. Culver City, CA: Columbia Pictures.

SAALT (South Asian Americans Leading Together). 2008. *A National Action Agenda: Policy Recommendations to Empower South Asian Communities in the United States*. Takoma Park, MD: SAALT. Accessed at http://www.saalt.org on May 15, 2010.

———. 2010a. *From Macacas to Turban Toppers: The Rise in Xenophobic and Racist Rhetoric in American Political Discourse*. Takoma Park, MD: SAALT. Accessed at http://saalt.org on July 8, 2015.

———. 2010b. "Chicago Townhall May 2010: Community Members Gather to Discuss Immigrant Rights in the South Asian Community." *SAALT*. Accessed from http://www.saalt.org on July 15, 2010.

———. 2014. *Under Suspicion, Under Attack: Xenophobic Political Rhetoric and Hate Violence against South Asian, Muslim, Sikh, Hindu, Middle Eastern, and Arab Communities in the United States*. Accessed at http://saalt.org on July 8, 2015.

Said, Edward. 1978. *Orientalism*. New York: Random House.

———. 2001. "The Clash of Ignorance." *Nation*, October 4. Accessed at http://www.thenation.com on July 8, 2015.

Saito, Natsu Taylor. 2001. "Symbolism Under Siege: Japanese American Redress and the 'Racing' of Arab Americans as 'Terrorists.'" *Asian Law Journal* 8 (1): 11–17, 24–26.

Saliba, Therese. 1999. "Resisting Invisibility: Arab Americans in Academia and Activism." In *Arabs in America: Building a New Future*, edited by Michael Suleiman. Philadelphia, PA: Temple University Press.

Samhan, Helen Hatab. 1999. "Not Quite White: Race Classification and the Arab-American Experience." In *Arabs in America: Building a New Future*, edited by Michael Suleiman. Philadelphia, PA: Temple University Press.

Sanchez, Ray, Evan Pérez, and Shimon Prokupecz. 2015. "Source: Man Fatally Shot by Officers in Boston Was Under Terror Investigation." *CNN*, June 2. Accessed at http://www.cnn.com on July 9, 2015.

Santora, Marc. 2012. "Woman Is Charged With Murder as a Hate Crime in a Fatal Subway Push." *New York Times*, December 30. Accessed at http://www.nytimes.com on July 8, 2015.

Sargent, Greg. 2010. "GOP Senate Candidates Drag Obama's Mosque Speech Into Their Races." *Washington Post*, August 16. Accessed at http://voices.washingtonpost.com on July 8, 2015.

Scahill, Jeremy. 2015. "The Drone Papers." *Intercept*, October 15. Accessed at https://theintercept.com on October 15, 2015.

Scahill, Jeremy, and Ryan Devereaux. 2014. "The Watch Commander." *Intercept*, August 5. Accessed at https://theintercept.com on October 15, 2015.

Schmidt, Michael S., and Eric Lichtblau. 2012. "Racial Profiling Rife at Airport, US Officers Say." *New York Times*, August 11. Accessed at http://www.nytimes.com on July 8, 2015.

Selzer, William, and Margo Anderson. 2001. "The Dark Side of Numbers: The Role of Population Data Systems in Human Rights Abuses." *Social Research* 68 (2): 481–513.

———. 2007. "Census Confidentiality under the Second War Powers Act." *Annual Meeting of the Population Association of America*, March 12. Accessed at http://www.uwm.edu/ on July 8, 2015.

Skocpol, Theda. 1999. "Advocates Without Members: The Recent Transformation of American Civic Life." In *Civic Engagement in American Democracy*, edited by Theda Skocpol and Morris P. Fiorina. Washington, DC: Brookings Institution Press.

Sethi, Arjun Singh. 2015. "Obama Says He Supports Ahmed Mohamed, But His Policies Don't." *Washington Post*, September 18. Accessed at https://www.washingtonpost.com on October 15, 2015.

Serrano, Richard A., Brian Bennett, and Soumya Karlamangla. 2015. "FBI Probes Islamic State, Terror Links to San Bernardino Massacre." *Los Angeles Times*, December 4. Accessed at http://www.latimes.com on April 5, 2016.

Shah, Mowahid. 1986. *The FBI and the Civil Rights of Arab Americans*. Washington, DC: American-Arab Anti-Discrimination Committee (ADC).

Shaheen, Jack G. 1980. "Abscam: Arabiaphobia in America." *ADC Issues*. Washington, DC: American-Arab Anti-Discrimination Committee (ADC).

———. 2003. "Reel Bad Arabs: How Hollywood Vilifies a People." *Annals of the American Academy of Political and Social Science* 588 (1): 171–193.

Shamsi, Hina. 2016. "Landmark Settlement in Challenge to NYPD Surveillance of New York Muslims: What You Need to Know." *ACLU.org*, January 7. Accessed at http://aclu.org on September 17, 2016.

Sherman, Bill. 2014. "Rep. John Bennett Stands Behind 'Threat of Islam' Statements" (video). *Tulsa World*. Accessed at http://www.tulsaworld.com on July 8, 2015.

Shryock, Andrew. 2008. "The Moral Analogies of Race." In *Race and Arab Americans before and after 9/11*, edited by Amaney A. Jamal and Nadine C. Naber, 81–113. Syracuse, NY: Syracuse University Press.

Singh, Jaideep. 2008. "Diasporic Community-Building Enterprises: Race, Religious Identity, and Sikh American Grassroots Political Organizing Before 9/11." PhD diss., University of California, Berkeley.

Skrentny, John D. 2006. "Law and the American State." *Annual Review of Sociology* 32: 213–244.

Smith, Andrea. 2006. "Heteropatriarchy and the Three Pillars of White Supremacy: Rethinking Women of Color Organizing." In *Color of Violence: The Incite! Anthology*, edited by Incite! Women of Color Against Violence, 66–67. Boston: South End Press.

Somander, Tanya. 2010. "Fox Host Brian Kilmeade Says 'All Terrorists Are Muslim' In Defense of O'Reilly's 'Muslims Killed Us' Remark." *ThinkProgress*, October 15. Accessed at http://thinkprogress.org on July 8, 2015.

Southern Poverty Law Center. 2009. *Terror from the Right: 75 Plots, Conspiracies, and Racist Rampages since Oklahoma City*. Montgomery, AL: Southern Poverty Law Center, Intelligence Project. Accessed at http://www.splcenter.org on July 8, 2015.

Spivak, Gayatri. 1987. *In Other Worlds: Essays in Cultural Politics*. New York: Methuen.

Suleiman, Michael. 1999. *Arabs in America: Building a New Future*. Philadelphia, PA: Temple University Press.

Sullivan, Eileen. 2011. "NYPD Spied on City's Muslim Anti-Terror Partners." *Associated Press*, October 6. Accessed at http://ap.org on July 8, 2015.

Takaki, Ronald. 1998. *Strangers from a Different Shore: A History of Asian Americans*. Rev. ed. New York: Little, Brown, and Company.

Tehranian, John. 2007. "Compulsory Whiteness: Towards a Middle-Eastern Legal Scholarship." *Indiana Law Journal* 82 (1): 11–17.

———. 2008. *Whitewashed: America's Invisible Middle Eastern Minority*. New York: New York University Press.

Tilly, Charles. 2006. *Regimes and Repertoires*. Chicago, IL: University of Chicago Press.

ThinkProgress. 2007. "Obama Smeared As Former 'Madrassa' Student, Possible Covert Muslim Extremist." *ThinkProgress.org*. Accessed at http://thinkprogress.org.

Thompson, Ginger. 2009. "Extremist Report Draws Criticism; Prompts Apology." *New York Times*, April 16. Accessed at http://thecaucus.blogs.nytimes.com on July 8, 2015.

Trump, Donald J. 2015. "Donald J. Trump Statement on Preventing Muslim Immigration." Press Release. Accessed at https://www.donaldjtrump.com on April 5, 2016.

US INS. *See* United States Department of Justice, Immigration and Naturalization Service.

US DHS. *See* United States Department of Homeland Security.

United States Department of Commerce, Census Bureau. 2003. *The Arab Population: 2000, Census 2000 Brief*. Washington, DC: United States Census Bureau.

———. 2011a. *Overview of Race and Hispanic Origin: 2010, 2010 Census Briefs*. Washington, DC: United States Census Bureau.

———. 2011b. *The White Population: 2010, 2010 Census Briefs*. Washington, DC: United States Census Bureau.

———. 2014a. "B04006: People Reporting Ancestry." *American Community Survey (ACS)*. Washington, DC: United States Census Bureau, American Community Survey Office. Accessed at factfinder.census.gov on February 2, 2016.

———. 2014b. "S0201: Selected Population Profile in the United States." *American Community Survey (ACS)*. Washington, DC: United States Census Bureau, American Community Survey Office. Accessed at factfinder.census.gov on February 2, 2016.

United States Department of Homeland Security (DHS). 2002–2014. *Yearbook of Immigration Statistics.* Washington, DC: Department of Homeland Security.

———. 2009. *Rightwing Extremism: Current Economic and Political Climate Fueling Resurgence in Radicalization and Recruitment.* Washington, DC: Department of Homeland Security.

United States Department of Justice. 2002. *Civil Rights Forum* 15:1. Washington, DC: Department of Justice, Civil Rights Division. Accessed at http://www.justice.gov on November 15, 2009.

———. 2007. "On Common Ground: Law Enforcement Training Video on Sikhism" (video recording). Washington, DC: Department of Justice, Community Relations Service. Accessed at http://www.justice.gov on July 8, 2015.

———. 2014. *Guidance for Federal Law Enforcement Agencies Regarding the Use of Race, Ethnicity, Gender, National Origin, Religion, Sexual Orientation, or Gender Identity.* Washington, DC: Department of Justice. Accessed at http://www.justice.gov on July 8, 2015.

United States Department of Justice, Federal Bureau of Investigation (FBI). 2005. *Terrorism 2002–2005.* Washington, DC: Federal Bureau of Investigation. Accessed at https://www.fbi.gov on July 8, 2015.

———. 2013. *Hate Crime Statistics.* Washington, DC: Federal Bureau of Investigation, Criminal Justice Information Services Division. Accessed at https://www.fbi.gov on July 8, 2015.

United States Department of Justice, Immigration and Naturalization Service (INS). 1969–1978. *Annual Report.* Washington, DC: Department of Homeland Security.

———. 1979–1988. *Statistical Yearbook.* Washington, DC: Department of Homeland Security.

United States Executive Office of the President. 2011. *Strategic Implementation Plan for Empowering Local Partners to Prevent Violent Extremism in the United States.* Washington, DC: White House. Accessed at https://www.whitehouse.gov on July 8, 2015.

United States Equal Employment Opportunity Commission (EEOC). 2002. *Questions and Answers about the Workplace Rights of Muslims, Arabs, South Asians, and Sikhs under the Equal Employment Opportunity Laws.* Washington, DC: EEOC. Accessed at http://www.eeoc.gov on July 8, 2015.

United States Office of the Director of National Intelligence, National Counterterrorism Center. 2014. "Historic Timeline." *National Counterterrorism Center.* Accessed at http://www.nctc.gov on July 8, 2015.

United States Senate. 1976. "Senate Select Committee to Study Governmental Operations with Respect to Intelligence Activities, 1975–76." Washington, DC: United States Senate, Select Committee on Intelligence. Accessed at http://www.intelligence.senate.gov on July 9, 2015.

Volpp, Leti. 2002. "The Citizen and the Terrorist." *University of California Los Angeles Law Review* 49: 1575.

Walsh, Jim. 2003. "Killer of Sikh after 9-11 Called Ill." *Tucson Citizen*, September 3. Accessed at http://tucsoncitizen.com on July 8, 2015.

Werbner, Pnina. 2005. "Islamophobia: Incitement to Religious Hatred—Legislating for a New Fear?" *Anthropology Today* 21 (1): 5–9.

Weinstein, Henry. 2007. "Final Two LA 8 Defendants Cleared: After 20 Years, US Drops Efforts to Deport Men Accused of Ties to Palestinian Terrorists." *Los Angeles Times*, November 1. Accessed at http://articles.latimes.com on July 9, 2015.

Whidden, Michael J. 2001. "Unequal Justice: Arabs in America and United States Anti-terrorism Legislation." *Fordham Law Review* 69: 2825–2829.

White House. 2010. *National Security Strategy*. Washington, DC: White House. Accessed at https://www.whitehouse.gov on July 8, 2015.

Wilgoren, Jodi. 2001. "Swept Up in a Dragnet, Hundreds Sit in Custody and Ask, 'Why?'" *New York Times*, November 25. Accessed at http://www.nytimes.com on July 8, 2015.

Winant, Howard. 1995. "Race: Theory, Culture, and Politics in the United States Today." In *Cultural Politics and Social Movements*, edited by Marcy Darnovsky, Barbara Epstein, and Richard Flacks, 174–188. Philadelphia, PA: Temple University Press.

Wright, John R. 1995. *Interest Groups and Congress: Lobbying, Contributions, and Influence*. London: Longman.

Yoder, Chris. 2013. "UC to Include Southwest Asian, North African Category on Next Year's Undergraduate Application." *Daily Californian*, May 27. Accessed at http://www.dailycal.org on July 8, 2015.

INDEX

abolition advocacy, 69

Abourezk, James, 126, 153, 158–59, 226n21

ABSCAM, 87, 127, 153

ad-hoc coalitions, 191–92

advisory committees, 169

advocacy organizations: advocacy strategies, 151–52, 187; and anti-racism, 19–20; Arab Americans, 123–30; and centrifugal/centripetal forces, 64; and civil rights, 118–19; and colorblindness ideology, 81; and complexity of Islamophobia, 143; and confronting Islamophobia, 117–18; and the future of civil rights, 207; and Islamophobia in American culture, 91; Muslim American advocacy organizations, 130–37; and the racial dilemma, 26–28; and racial formation, 68–72; and research methods, 31–33; South Asian, 138–42. *See also* civil rights organizations

affirmative action, 74–75, 144–46, 152–53, 182–83, 194, 200

Afghans, 36, 42–44, 54, *58*, 59, *60*, *61*, 106, 115, 121

African Americans: advocacy organizations, 165–66; and definitions of the Middle East, 42; Islamic organizations, 182; and Islamophobia in American politics, 95; and Middle Eastern American communities, 55; and Muslim American advocacy organizations, 132–35; and transactional coalitions, 187. *See also* Black identity

airport security, 67–68

Alcatraz Island occupation, 77

Algerians, 6, 46

"Alien Terrorists and Undesirables: A Contingency Plan," 99

All Dulles Area Muslim Society (AD-AMS), 205

al-Qaeda, 21, 26, 112

AMEMSA (Arabs, Middle Easterners, Muslims, and South Asians), 8

American-Arab Anti-Discrimination Committee (ADC), *154*, *156*; and Abourezk/Zogby split, 158–59, 226n21; background, 123, 126–30; and Census reform, 203–4; and complexity of Islamophobia, 143; and confronting Islamophobia, 118; and definitions of terrorism, 111; and durability of Islamophobia, 199, 201; existential crisis, 134; and international affairs, 141; and interviews, *211–13*; and Islamophobia in American culture, 90; and ongoing advocacy strategies, 193; origin of, 121–22, *122*; and post-9/11 counterterrorism policy, 136; and the post–civil rights era, 153–56, 158–60; and racial pressures after 9/11, 167–69, 171; and racial shifts after 1990, 161–66; and research methods, 32; and transactional coalitions, 187, 190–91

American-Arab Relations Committee, 120–21

American Civil Liberties Union (ACLU), 103

American Communities Survey (ACS), 60

ideology, 145–47, 157; coming to terms with race, 14–22; and durability of Islamophobic racism, 22; fluidity of, 15; and the future of civil rights, 208; "Middle Eastern" racial category, 2–5, 5–7, 7–10, 217n5; and Muslim Americans, 219n13; race-based activism, 192–94, 199, 204; race consciousness, 27; race conscious strategies, 34; race-neutral strategies, 25–26, 149, 167; racial diversity, 187–88; racial formation process, 9, 15–16, 84, 114–16, 118, 180, 183–84, 198, 201; racially defined groups, 24–25; racial nature of Islamophobia, 17; racial profiling, 18, 21, 26–27, 34, 104–8, 171, 201; racial segregation, 18; *racial state*, 68; and research methods, 31–33; stereotypes, 13; and transactional coalitions, 186–92. *See also* racial dilemma; racial paradox

racial dilemma: and civil rights advocacy, 143; coming to terms with race, 14–22; and confronting Islamophobia, 23–28, 117–18; and definitions of the Middle East, 38; and durability of Islamophobia, 198–201; and the future of civil rights, 206; and hate crimes, 1; and "looking Muslim," 2–10; and Middle Eastern American coalitions, 148–49; and the post–civil rights era, 152–53, 158–59, 161; and racial pressures after 9/11, 167, 184; and racism in the US, 85; and racist elements of Islamophobia, 116; and research methods, 28–33; and South Asian American advocacy organizations, 141; and structural racism, 10–14

racial paradox: and advocacy organizations, 68–72; and centrifugal/centripetal forces, 62–65; and colorblindness ideology, 78–82; and definitions of the Middle East, 38–43; described, 33–38; and durability of Islamophobia, 198,

201; and linked histories of migrant groups, 43–50; and Middle Eastern American coalitions, 148; and Middle Eastern American communities, 51–62; and panethnic unity, 142; race-based problems and solutions, 72–73; racial barriers, 50; racial formation process, 65–78; racial profiling, 67–68; racial project concept, 65; and racist elements of Islamophobia, 85, 114–17

racism: and centrifugal/centripetal forces, 64; and colorblindness ideology, 152; defining, 66–67; and durability of Islamophobia, 22, 200; institutional, 67; Islamophobia as, 114–17; and migration policies, 44; and Orientalism, 33, 40–42, 66, 74, 84, 86; and the racial dilemma, 26; and racial formation process, 66–67; racial nature of Islamophobia, 17–18, 116; and structural racism, 10–14; and transactional coalitions, 188; and US immigration policies, 44, 46–50

radicalism, 11–12, 21, 80
Rainbow Coalition, 155, 159, 201
Reagan, Ronald, 49, 98–99, 152
Reconstruction, 73
"Red Power," 77
reforms, 144
religious identity: and racial categories, 3, 15–19; religious discrimination and persecution, 19, 24, 201; religious freedom, 23–24; religious groups, 42; religious markers, 40. *See also specific religions*
Republican Party, 113
research grants, 218n46
research methods, 28–33
reverse discrimination, 144, 194
Rights Working Group (RWG), 171–75
right-wing extremism, 112–13
riot, 47
Roberts, John, 79

ABOUT THE AUTHOR

Erik Love is Assistant Professor of Sociology and former Chair of Middle East Studies at Dickinson College in Pennsylvania.